CW00368994

The Good Beach Guide

A guide to over 170 of Britain's best beaches

Dr ANNE SCOTT

Pollution Control Officer at the
Marine Conservation Society

EBURY PRESS ❁ LONDON

The author would like to thank the following people for providing
information and help in producing this book: district and local councils,
The National Trust, Tourist Authorities, The Townswomen's Guild,
coastal wardens and members of the Marine Conservation Society.

Published by Ebury Press
Division of The National Magazine Company Ltd
Colquhoun House, 27–37 Broadwick Street
London W1V 1FR

First impression 1988
Reprinted twice 1988
Revised and updated 1989

Text copyright © 1989 by The Marine Conservation Society

Illustrations copyright © 1988 by The National Magazine Company Ltd

All rights reserved. No part of this publication may
be reproduced, stored in a retrieval system, or
transmitted in any form or by any means, electronic,
mechanical, photocopying, recording, or otherwise,
without the prior permission of the copyright owner.

British Library Cataloguing in Publication Data
Scott, Anne
   The good beach guide. – Rev. ed
   1. Great Britain. Beaches
   I. Title II. Marine Conservation Society
   551.4'57'0941

   ISBN 0 85223 724 3

Edited by Gillian Haslam
Designed by Gwyn Lewis
Illustrations by Kate Simunek
Maps by ML Design

Computerset by MFK Typesetting Ltd, Hitchin, Herts
Printed and bound in Great Britain at The Bath Press, Avon

Contents

Foreword
by David Bellamy

A day trip or holiday at the seaside is a traditional summertime activity for many British families and visitors to our country. Weather permitting, a paddle or swim in the sea can be an additional treat and add to the fun.

Sadly, however, a visit to the seaside nowadays is not always the pleasure it should be. Instead of golden sands and a clear blue sea, you may well be confronted with the beach and waters spoilt by oil, rubbish and even raw sewage. All too often the sea is used as an outlet for the waste products of our society which means that many of our beaches fall far below the standard established by the EC for safe bathing.

This revised edition of The Good Beach Guide has been sponsored by Heinz, through their Guardians of the Countryside programme, and thoroughly researched by the Marine Conservation Society to give you a concise and up-to-date selection of 170 excellent beaches. This new edition includes details of some 20 additional beaches to the previous highly successful guide and drops any areas which have fallen behind the required standard. Now you can easily choose some of the best pollution-free beaches in Britain to make the most of swimming, sunbathing or exploring a beautiful and unspoiled coastline with its wealth of flora and fauna.

In recent months, there has been increasing public concern over the pollution of our seas and the harm caused to many aspects of marine life. By buying this book you will be supporting the very important work of the Marine Conservation Society in protecting the marine world for us all to enjoy.

The Marine Conservation Society is a rapidly expanding national conservation organisation formed to protect Britain's seashore and coastal waters by campaigning and lobbying on issues which threaten the seas. It also undertakes research and education to help develop a better understanding and awareness of the marine environment.

Already the Society can be proud of major achievements. It forced a ban on competitive spearfishing which threatened to decimate fish stocks in inshore areas. It successfully fought to have marine nature reserves included in the Wildlife and Countryside Act and has already seen the first statutory reserve declared – Lundy Island. It has actively promoted the creation of voluntary marine conservation areas, the most recent the Seven Sisters in Sussex. The Society has achieved a major victory in the fight against pollution by getting the Government to ban the use of anti-fouling paint containing the poisonous chemical TBT. Joining forces with the Coastal Anti-Pollution League, it has forced the authorities to make massive increases in the amount of money spent on cleaning up our bathing waters.

The Society is currently tackling the pollution problems of the North Sea, the quality of our beaches, the threats to sharks, the trade in corals and shells and the impact of fish farming on our coastal waters and their wildlife.

Membership is £8.00 a year (see page 191) and you will receive the quarterly magazine 'Marine Conservation' updating you on all the campaigns and issues affecting the sea, and how you can help.

Help make the proper protection of our seas, their resources and their wildlife a reality. Join the Society now.

Heinz Guardians of the Countryside is a major British conservation programme sponsored by Heinz in association with World Wildlife Fund–UK. Its objective is to help protect those wildlife species and habitats in greatest danger, thus safeguarding them for future generations.

Marine conservation initiatives via the MCS under the programme have included the funding of coastal wardening at several sites during the summer season; sponsorship of a marine conservation officer to co-ordinate a variety of national campaigns such as research into the habits of dolphins and basking sharks; and publication of the Marine Conservation Society's Coastal Directory.

Through the programme, protection of a number of important marine sites has been achieved, including the Helford River and sites in Devon, Dorset and Northumberland as well as the purchase of Cape Cornwall (including Priest's Cove) for the National Trust.

Introduction

Everyone's expectations of a day at the seaside are different. Some people look for quiet and solitude, an escape from the hustle and bustle of their everyday life. Others look for just the opposite – amusements and bright lights, ice cream and rock, sun-bathing by day and dancing by night.

Britain has more than 7,000 miles (11,000km) of coastline, with literally thousands of beaches, varying from long, sweeping sandy bays gently lapped by sparkling clear water, to tiny rocky coves. There are banks of groyne-ribbed shingle, flat golden sands pounded by Atlantic rollers, and secluded coves ringed by cliffs with rocky outcrops and pools waiting to be explored. In addition, there are the resort beaches, traditional promenades with their Victorian piers, pavilions, bandstands, funfairs and amusements. And every beach is someone's favourite!

'Why is my favourite beach not included in the guide?'

We have not attempted to describe every British beach; the beauty of many is the very fact that they remain undiscovered. The guide is a selection, a mere 170 of Britain's beaches, a mixture of popular holiday resorts, quieter secluded bays and some faraway places – hopefully a beach to suit every taste. Use the guide as a starting point for exploring the delights of our beautiful coastline. Part of the fun is searching out your own personal favourite.

If a beach is not featured, it does not necessarily mean that it suffers from problems or that it isn't good. However, some very good beaches *are* missing from the guide because water quality monitoring by the water authorities or River Purification Boards found that they did not meet the minimum EC standard for clean bathing water. Over a third of the beaches monitored during 1988 failed to meet this standard and in some areas over half of the beaches did not comply. Details of all the monitored beaches are given at the start of each regional section.

Any beach where there have been reports of significant pollution of the shore, whether industrial or domestic, are also excluded. We have not included beaches where there is major industrial development on the shore, beaches which are shadowed by power stations (nuclear or conventional), construction yards, refineries, or gas and oil terminals. If a beach is used for military purposes, there are times when it is a danger area with restricted access and therefore cannot be considered as a good beach.

In choosing good beaches we also felt that they had to be reasonably accessible; having to scramble down wet cliffs is probably not the ideal way to start a relaxing day on the beach. Beaches should also have reasonable parking facilities for beach users. Parking on narrow roads and verges should be avoided; it is not only very damaging, but also causes problems for the local people, rescue services and other visitors. Although there are lots of little secluded beaches, particularly in Scotland and Wales, most are only accessible to the walker who is prepared to explore the remoter areas of Britain.

The Blue Flag Award

The Blue Flag Award is part of the programme of awards for good beaches run by the Foundation for Environmental Education in Europe. It is conducted in the UK by the Tidy Britain Group. The Blue Flag is awarded to beaches which have a high standard of water quality, are cleaned daily during the bathing season and have good facilities, toilets, lifesaving equipment, first aid etc. On these beaches there is strict control of domestic animals, and driving or racing on the beach are prohibited. Provision is also made for environmental education, public information and safety.

Seventeen British beaches received the Blue Flag Award in 1988. However, only 15 of these beaches are included in the guide because the remaining two failed to meet the EC standard for clean bathing water in 1988. This failure highlights the fluctuating nature of the pollution of our shores, and the constant need for action to clean up our beaches and seas. If, on a visit to any of the beaches in the guide, you find pollution problems or changes in facilities, please write to the Society (see page 191) and let us know.

The Clean Beach Award

The Clean Beach awards mentioned in the text were won by beaches both for the general level of amenities provided for the public and for the efforts made by the local authorities towards promoting beach safety and the provision and use of litter bins. The awards are made by the Tidy Britain Group to encourage high standards of beach maintenance.

Visiting beaches

There is intense pressure at many beauty spots where the number of people visiting the beach and surrounding area leads to damage, particularly when cars are parked close to the beach. Sand dunes are particularly vulnerable, their protective covering of marram grass is easily damaged and, once lost, the wind blows the sand away, destroying the dunes. Only by taking care of what is often a fragile environment will we be able to continue to enjoy the unspoilt beauty of our coastline. So please remember to follow the seashore code whenever you are down at the beach and:

TAKE NOTHING BUT PICTURES.

WASTE NOTHING BUT TIME.

LEAVE NOTHING BUT FOOTPRINTS.

Marine Pollution

The death last year of thousands of common seals, massive blooms of algae, and the deaths and breeding failure in sea-bird colonies on the Orkney and Shetland islands, have highlighted the problems of our seas as never before. The causes have been the subject of fierce debate but few would deny that pollution is a major threat to the health of our seas and wildlife, and that something must be done to clean them up.

Pollution occurs when we introduce any substances into the sea which are harmful to wildlife, which threaten human health or reduce marine activities and amenities. An enormous range of such substances enters our seas – deliberately, accidentally, or through sheer negligence – often creating pollution problems far from their source.

Golden sands littered with rubbish, raw sewage at the water's edge, oil on the rocks and lumps of tar on your flip-flops. These are the highly visible signs for the holiday-maker. But there are other pollutants which remain unseen: for example, poisonous chemicals, pesticides, and radioactivity. Such pollutants may be invisible but their effects are not, and they can be equally or more damaging. The sea has no fences and therefore the effect of a pollutant never occurs in isolation, it spreads through the environment, combining with other pollutants to create a highly poisonous cocktail.

Types of Marine Pollution

Waste can be classed under three main types: domestic, industrial and agricultural. *Domestic waste* includes sewage, silt, oil, lead, tar and de-icing chemicals which are used on the roads. *Industrial waste* includes, for example, radioactive waste, toxic chemicals, thermal discharges, refuse and oil from ships, as well as degradable organic waste from the paper, pulp and food processing industries. *Agricultural waste* – fertilizers, herbicides and organic matter – is all potentially dangerous. Other pollutants that must also be considered are discarded pyrotechnics (e.g. ships' flares and distress rockets), as well as drugs, and chemicals leaked from the hulls of ships.

For years the sea has been used as a cheap and easy waste disposal system on a vast scale. Nine million tonnes of sewage sludge (the by-product of sewage treatment works), 42 million tonnes of dredged spoil – the silt removed from harbours and estuaries to keep them clear for shipping – and over 2 million tonnes of industrial waste, including coal waste and fly ash, are dumped off the UK shore each year. The wastes also contain high levels of chemical contamination with the result that the North Sea, for example, receives over 10 tonnes of mercury, 12 tonnes of cadmium, 1250 tonnes of lead and 200 tonnes of copper each year.

Sources of Pollution

The source of a pollutant may be easy to identify – an outfall pipe or a dump ship deliberately discharging waste into the sea. Waste also enters the sea via rivers, from ships, in land run-off, and from the atmosphere. Some of the sources are easy to locate, others are less easy to define and hence control. An estimated 5 million tonnes of oil enter the sea each year, but only 4% comes from major tanker accidents. The majority is released during routine shipping and oil refining operations. In many cases individual pollution incidents are neither obvious nor devastating to the local area. However, their cumulative effect means that all the trade routes and ocean currents abound with tar balls, many of which will eventually end up on beaches.

The sources of pesticides and other agricultural chemicals which find there way into streams, rivers and eventually the sea, are difficult to locate accurately. These chemicals, particularly the organochlorines like aldrin and dieldrin, are extremely stable and persistent. They accumulate in the sea and have been found in virtually all marine mammals and in humans.

The Effects of Pollution

In some cases, the effects of pollution are easy to identify and link to specific causes. Plastics discarded overboard entangle wildlife causing death by drowning or strangulation. It has been estimated that 2 million sea birds and 100,000 marine mammals are killed each year due to marine debris, either by eating it or becoming entangled in it. The death of a marine animal may not be as easily attributed to marine litter if the animal has eaten the refuse and died either because of some poisonous chemical in the waste or starvation due to a permanently full stomach. On the shoreline, where much refuse ends up, it remains a hazard for wildlife and the holiday-maker.

The consequences of oil pollution are not only the obvious oiled sea bird or oil-spotted sands; there are also toxic effects. Water-soluble chemicals in oil are poisonous to animals and plants. The dumping of solid wastes also causes direct physical damage to marine life, smothering animals and plants, but as with many pollution problems there are combined effects. For example, dredged spoil is highly contaminated with chemicals. Dumping wastes offshore not only does physical damage to the environment but the chemicals are released and may poison wildlife, or affect their growth and reproduction.

Thousands of chemicals like mercury (used in the paper and pulp industry), lead from petrol, titanium dioxide (a whitener in the paint industry), polychlorinated biphenols (found in electrical components), pesticides like organochlorines (e.g. DDT) are released into the sea and have been found in all marine life. They have been linked to fish diseases, the disappearance of species, and breeding failure.

In very low concentrations the chemicals may have minimal effect but the danger increases as they become concentrated up the food chain. A single shrimp may have a tolerable amount of a chemical in its body but when a fish eats lots of shrimps it absorbs all the chemicals from each shrimp and the result can be lethal. For example, around Minamata Bay in Japan, 46 people died and 2,000 people suffered from crippling mental and physical deformities. The tragedy was the result of eating shellfish from the bay which had accumulated methyl mercury released into the waters from a local factory.

Sewage is a particular problem that has direct effects on beaches and bathers. Over 300 million gallons of sewage are disposed of in our coastal waters each day, most is untreated or receives only primary treatment. It is frequently discharged close to the shore and the raw sewage, often including toilet paper, fat balls and other nuisance solids, is washed back on to the beach with each incoming tide. This is not only very unsightly but also harmful to health. The sewage contains bacteria and viruses that can cause a number of infections so that an upset stomach or bad throat suffered on holiday might have been caused by swimming in polluted water or eating shellfish that had accumulated the bacteria as they filtered the sea water to feed.

The discharge of sewage also has effects on marine life. The decomposition of the sewage requires oxygen, and the reduction in oxygen that occurs as the sewage is broken down can lead to a decline in the number and variety of plants and animals. This can also result from the high nutrient input from sewage, when plankton and vegetation bloom at the expense of less tolerant species. As the algal colonies die, they break up and create foam which is frequently washed ashore.

There has been much debate about the final fate and the effect of the many pollutants that find their way to our seas. Much, however, remains unknown. Are the problems we are seeing now the result of pollution? Are the algal blooms caused by the high nutrient inputs from sewage and agriculture? Where did the seal virus originate? The need for more information about the pollution problems of the sea and better understanding will help us answer these questions and protect the sea.

Pollution Control

There are several international and national agreements which aim to control pollution. The problem with many of these agreements is their successful implementation. For example, the International Agreement on the Prevention of Marine Pollution from Land (the Paris Commission, 1974) lists a series of chemicals that must only be discharged in 'trace amounts'. It is the interpretation of this definition that has caused problems in its implementation. The International Convention for the Prevention of Pollution from Ships (MARPOL 73/78) and its five annexes were originally drawn up in 1973. But they only come into force when enough countries, representing 50% of the world's shipping tonnage, sign each part of the agreement. Until then it could be effectively ignored even by those that had signed. The convention and Annexes 1 and 2 were agreed and became law in 1978. It was not until the end of 1987, ten years later, that the United States signed Annexe 5, concerning dumping of refuse from ships. This took the tonnage over the 50% mark making the annex law, 12 months later on December 31 1988.

As of the 1st of January 1989 it is illegal to dispose of any plastic from ships at sea. Added to this, other forms of garbage, biodegradable food waste etc, can only be discharged at sea under strictly controlled conditions. The refuse now has to be deposited at special reception facilities which should have been set up at ports and harbours. It is hoped this will improve the colossal problem of marine litter. Unfortunately the law only applies to the countries who have signed the annexe (approximately 75% of the world fleet). How the regulations are to be enforced remains to be seen. Annexes 3 and 4 of the convention are not yet ratified by sufficient countries.

The European Community has also introduced legislation to control pollution. But there have also been problems with the implementation of these regulations. The Directive on Discharges into the Aquatic Environment which attempted to stop dumping, was never introduced because of a UK veto. The Bathing Waters Quality Directive was introduced in 1976 when, after three years and much persuasion, Britain designated its 'bathing beaches'. It designated only 27. France designated 1,498, Italy 3,308 and even Luxemburg, with no coastline, came up with more bathing sites than Britain – 34. Resorts such as Brighton and Blackpool (without a doubt one of the largest bathing resorts in Europe) did not feature within the 27, indicating a lack of commitment to the spirit of the Directive. It was not until 1987, after much criticism, that the Government yielded to pressure and the number was increased to 391.

In the past, pollution control has very much been the implementation of regulations to solve problems as they have been proved to be damaging the environment. Regulations were quickly introduced to ban the use of anti-fouling paints containing tributyl tin once it was proved that the chemical was accumulating in fish and shellfish.

If we are to solve the problems of our seas we must adopt a precautionary approach. This acknowledges that we do not know the effects of all substances that are discharged and that we should therefore err on the side of precaution and not discharge these materials, even if there is no scientific evidence that they actually cause damage. Widely accepted throughout Europe, this is only just beginning to be given consideration in the UK. The acceptance of this approach by the second North Sea Ministerial Conference in 1987 was a major step forward in pollution control throughout Europe.

Governments are beginning to realise that the sea is not infinite and we cannot continue to use it as a huge dustbin. International agreements are being reached, often due to the pressure from people like you and me. Industry, bowing to public opinion and legal enforcement, is slowly cleaning up its act. However, there is a long way still to go, and if we are to enter the 21st century with cleaner seas, it is up to everyone who goes down to the shore to keep an eye out for any pollution and to report it to the water authority, environmental health department, local council, MP and the Marine Conservation Society. People and companies that pollute the sea and shore are criminals, offending by intent or neglect. **Don't let anyone get away with it – the more we remain silent, the worse it will become.**

Marine and Coastal Life

S. GUBBAY

Marine Site Protection Officer at Marine Conservation Society

Hot summer days, ideal for relaxing on the beach with an ice cream in your hand, don't seem to be that frequent in Britain! Despite this, there is plenty of entertainment to be found on the beach, perhaps only a short walk from where you might have been sunbathing. Most of our coastline has something to offer when it comes to marine life so that even the most empty-looking shore can become a place full of surprises and interest once you have been given a few clues on where to look.

At the Edge of the Sea

The best time for exploring a beach is when the tide is out. It is especially interesting to walk down to the water's edge at low tide where you can get a glimpse of the plants and animals which live permanently submerged by the sea.

At the edge of rocky shores you may be able to see the tops of kelp plants bobbing on the surface of the water. These are large brown seaweeds which form underwater forests just beyond the level of the lowest tide down to a depth of 50 feet (15m). Just like an oak tree in a forest on land, kelp plants provide shelter and are a source of food for other animals. They also provide a firm surface on which a variety of seaweeds and animals will attach themselves. The leafy parts of the kelp plant are known as fronds and a close look at these will usually reveal an encrusting layer of delicate, grey-coloured 'sea mats'. These are colonies of very small animals which are an important source of food, particularly for the many snails which wander over the surface of the kelp. The multi-coloured top shells also take advantage of this food so these too can be found in large numbers on the kelp. Another species which can be seen on the fronds is the attractive blue-rayed limpet. It may only be ½ inch (1cm) long but it is quite distinctive because of the iridescent blue stripes along the length of its shell.

Kelps do not have true roots like land plants. Instead they attach themselves to the rock surfaces by means of a 'holdfast'. This provides an ideal shelter for small animals which can live amongst its branches. A closer look will reveal brittle-stars, sponges, and even small shrimp-like animals.

Underneath the kelp plants, where less light penetrates, red sea-weeds are common. Many have delicate branches and resemble land plants but often the most common, although least obvious, are the encrusting red seaweeds. These species form a thin covering over rock surfaces giving them a pink appearance. They can be widespread, particularly where there are many sea urchins, as the urchins are efficient at grazing away most other species of seaweed.

The common sea urchin is one of the most distinctive animals you might find under the kelp and amongst the red seaweeds. It can be as large as 6 inches (15cm) in diameter which makes it one of the world's largest urchins. The spiky surface is very obvious and some of the spikes have small pincers at the ends to act as additional discourage-ment for predators. Because of their efficient grazing powers, sea urchins have a considerable influence on the type of kelp forest that develops, so it is particularly important not to collect them.

The water's edge is also a good place to look for fish. One species that comes close inshore to lay its eggs during the summer months is the lumpsucker. This is a large, round-bodied fish with rows of lumps along its side. The male, which has a distinctive bright orange belly during the breeding season, guards the eggs until they hatch, even if they were laid near low water. If you are lucky you might find one on the lower shore. Another fish you are likely to find is the butterfish. It has an eel-like body, up to 8 inches (20cm) long, with distinctive dark spots along the body. These fish depend on camouflage for protection so usually lie very still on the surface of a rock.

The Shore Between the Tides

Further up the beach is the area uncovered by every tide. Animals and plants that live here have to survive extreme conditions. They have to contend with the full force of storm waves breaking on the beach, and the danger of drying out on hot sunny days whilst the tide is out. To cope with this, many of the animals of the intertidal zone are likely to be hiding or tightly closed whilst the tide is out. The best places to find them are the damp areas between rocks, under overhangs and beneath stones and boulders. The shore crab in particular likes to hide in these places, but you might also find starfish, small shrimp-like animals, and snails. Remember these animals are in shaded places to stop them drying out so, after having a look, return them to the same area so they can survive until the tide comes in. Overhangs are the place to look for sponges but don't expect to find them the size of a bath-sponge! They are usually spread like a mat over the rock surface although you can see the pores through which they circulate seawater to feed. One conspicuous animal you are likely to find on a rocky shore is the Beadlet Anemone. It comes in a variety of colours ranging from red to green and yellowy-brown. Its surface is covered with a slimy film to prevent drying out during low tide. The anemone feeds by extending its tentacles which are covered with stinging cells, and catching small animals as they float past.

The animals on the open rock are better able to withstand drying out. Limpets, for example, clamp themselves down tightly against the rock face whilst the tide is out; whereas barnacles, which are permanently attached to the rock, close the valves at the top of their shells. When they are covered with water these valves slide apart and the barnacle, which looks like a shrimp lying on its back, sticks its legs out of the top to catch food. Amongst the barnacles you will probably find Dog Whelks. These are smaller versions of the Edible Whelk and measure up to 1 inch (2.5cm) in height. Dog Whelks feed on barnacles and mussels by boring a hole through their shells and sucking out the contents. Their diet is thought to influence shell colour, so Dog Whelks feeding on barnacles tend to have a light coloured shell, and those feeding mainly on mussels can have a shell with dark bands. Clusters of pale yellow egg cases of the Dog Whelk are easy to find if you look beneath overhangs or damp crevices.

Rock Pools

In some rocky intertidal areas pools of sea water remain after the tide has dropped. These rock pools are some of the most interesting places to look for marine life. They not only contain typical rock pool species but also offshore animals that have been stranded until the next tide.

The variety of life in a rock pool depends on its size. Deep, large pools can be a suitable habitat for some of the kelps but perhaps the seaweed most frequently seen in rock pools is the Coralweed. This small, tufty, red seaweed has a chalky skeleton and grows around the edge of the rock pool along with encrusting red seaweeds which make the rock surface appear pink. Rock pools are well known haunts of shrimps but you can also find small fish like the blenny and goby, along with starfish, mussels and sea anemones.

Sandy Beaches

The sandy shores we head for when looking for a good beach can be very hostile areas for marine life. Areas of coarse sand dry out quickly and do not contain much organic material for food. As the sand grains get finer, the sandy shores become more hospitable to marine life. These conditions limit the variety of animals which live on sandy beaches and those that do usually bury themselves into the sand whilst the tide is out. Despite this it is possible to find the hiding places of the animals by the clues they leave behind.

The Sand Mason Worm is a frequent inhabitant of many sandy beaches and can be found near the low water mark. It lives in a tube which it builds from coarse sand and fragments of shells. This projects above the beach surface as a ragged edged tube. On some beaches large areas of the lower shore are covered by these tubes with perhaps more than 25 in a square metre. The Lug Worm also leaves a clue of its whereabouts on the surface of the sand. These worms live in burrows and leave a conspicuous cast on the surface around the hole. A more obvious worm which can be found on sandy beaches where there are outcrops of rock is the Honeycomb Worm found on southern and western coasts of Britain. Each worm forms a tube of coarse sand on the rock surface which can build up as 'reefs' many metres across.

One of the larger animals which lives buried in the sand is the Sea Potato or Heart Urchin. This hairy, sandy coloured ball is a sea urchin but unlike the Common Sea Urchin of rocky areas it has a distinctive head and tail end. The Sea Potato tunnels its way through the sand feeding on small particles of organic matter. At the same time it maintains a channel to the surface through which water is drawn for respiration. The Masked Crab has a somewhat similar lifestyle. It also lives buried in sand and uses its two long antennae to form a tube to the surface, bringing down sea water from which it can extract oxygen.

Some of the more muddy beaches are colonised by 'beds' of Sea Grasses. These are flowering plants just like those found on land, which are able to survive when totally submerged by the tide. They produce small flowers during spring and summer, and it is also possible to find the seeds attached. Sea grass beds provide shelter for a variety of juvenile fish and Cuttlefish eggs, and small Stalked Jellyfish can be found attached to the leaves. These areas can be damaged by trampling so do try to walk around the edges of any Sea Grass beds.

The Strand Line

The strand line is a popular haunt for beachcombers because something new is brought in with every high tide. It is a particularly interesting area to explore after stormy weather because seaweeds and animals found in deeper waters are washed ashore. One of the more common types of animals found in this area are jellyfish. Often swarms are washed up on the beach, and here, without the support of the seawater, they lose all shape and look like a lump of jelly. Some jellyfish can still sting when dead so don't touch them with bare hands. These, along with other dead animals, are soon cleaned away by gulls, crabs and even small snails, leaving only the empty shells and egg cases on the shore.

The Sand Hopper is an animal commonly found near the strand line. It lives in burrows or under seaweeds and emerges at night to feed on any debris which has been brought in with the tide. It gets its name from its habit of springing away when disturbed.

Nature Conservation on the Coast

The coast around the British Isles is under continual pressure from urban, industrial and recreational uses. The sea and shore are also sources of food and minerals, and are often used for waste disposal. These competing demands have made it necessary to ensure that areas which have special features are not lost or damaged. This can only be achieved by proper management of the coastal zone. There is a network of protected and designated areas to help achieve this.

There are 38 stretches of undeveloped coastline of high scenic quality in England and Wales, totalling 785 miles (1263km), which have been designated as Heritage Coasts by the Countryside Commission. The Scottish Development Department have defined 22 Preferred Conservation Zones: coastline considered to be of environmental, scenic or ecological importance. Often these areas are also designated as Areas of Outstanding Natural Beauty in England, Wales and Northern Ireland or National Scenic Areas in Scotland. These various designations do not give specific protection but there are management plans drawn up which are referred to when local developments are being considered.

In addition, numerous Sites of Special Scientific Interest have been identified because of their flora, fauna, geology or physiography. They are not managed reserves but any development by the private landowner should be reported to the Nature Conservancy Council and potentially damaging operations can be restricted. There is also a wide range of reserves with coastal sections which are managed to protect their environment. For example National Nature Reserves, County Conservation Trust, Royal Society for the Protection of Birds, and local authority reserves.

However, all these designated conservation sites are for the management and protection of features above the tide line. The area below high water mark is owned by the Crown and managed by the Crown Estates Commission. Until recently even the most outstanding sites for marine life had no legal protection.

One method being used to afford some protection to the marine environment is the establishment of Voluntary Marine Conservation Areas. These are areas where some form of consultative/management group has been set up to bring together organisations and individuals involved with the sea, whether for work or recreation. Their aim is to promote harmonious use of the area, whilst preventing deterioration of the quality of the marine environment and the life it supports. There are nine of these Voluntary Marine Conservation Areas; five in England – Helford River, Roseland, Wembury, Purbeck and the Seven Sisters; two in Wales – Bardsey Island, Skomer Island; one in Scotland – St. Abb's Head; and one in Northern Ireland – Strangford Lough.

Since 1981 it has been possible to set up legally protected Marine Nature Reserves. The first one was declared in November 1986, around the island of Lundy which lies off the coast of Devon, an area which is particularly rich and varied in its marine life. At least six more Marine Nature Reserves are planned around the country. These are likely to be at special places along our coast but we still have a responsibility to be thoughtful when we explore the beach wherever we are. The Marine Conservation Society's 'Seashore Code' is a useful guide to help you enjoy exploring the coast while keeping it intact for those who follow you.

The Seashore Code

Enjoy the coastline and wildlife without harming it

This code, compiled by the Marine Conservation Society, with sponsorship via Heinz Guardians of the Countryside, shows how you can best enjoy the coast and its wildlife.

Care for sea creatures

Seashore creatures are marine animals. They have to avoid drying up when the tide is out. Some have shells for protection, but many need to hide under rocks or in the sand. That's why exploring the seashore is so much fun – there are lots of surprises.

BUT do remember:
- put animals back where you found them
- try not to keep them out of the water for too long
- never take the animals home
- turn back the rocks you have moved
- leave seaweed in place – there is plenty of loose seaweed on the strand line

or else you will kill the sea creatures.

Watch out for dangerous animals

Some of the animals you find on the beach can sting or hurt you if disturbed.

To be safe
- try not to touch jellyfish
- avoid picking up crabs with your fingers

Empty sea shells are the best sea shells

Shells come in all shapes, sizes and colours. Many contain living

animals so check to make sure a shell is empty before taking it home with you.
- Don't buy shells – most were still the homes of live animals when collected.

Time and tide

Low tide is the best time for rockpooling, but the tide can turn very quickly, cutting you off from the shore.
- tide times are given on the local pier or jetty, or in newsagents
- a red flag means don't swim – there are dangerous currents
- avoid going on long walks or exploring on your own.

Keep your car off the beach

Beaches, and particularly sand dunes, are easily damaged by cars.
- keep access to footpaths clear
- park in designated car parks.

The cliff code

Cliffs are slowly but surely being worn away – this makes them very dangerous.
- keep to the marked footpaths
- at the top, stay away from the edge – it often crumbles
- don't sit directly under a cliff – rock falls *do* happen.

Avoid disturbing seabirds

You can see seabirds at their best when they are at ease.
To do this
- it is best to watch them through binoculars
- keep some distance from them, especially if they are nesting
- make sure dogs are kept well clear of birds
- never, never, throw things over the cliff edge.

Don't drop litter – it can kill

Litter on the beach is unsightly and can also be dangerous; many sea creatures die through entanglement every year.
- please take all your litter home, burying it is no solution
- try and keep dogs from fouling the beach
- report canisters or drums that may be washed up on the beach.

Coastal Walks

ROB PALMER

Past Coastal Pollution Officer at Marine Conservation Society

Walking's without a doubt, the best way to see the beaches of Britain. You may just want to stroll along the beach exploring the rock pools or you may prefer a good walk, perhaps spending a week completing one of the long distance footpaths. Some of our finest coastline is just a little further from the car park than most of us stray on the average day at the seaside.

Above the water is familiar glory. Consider the western coast of Scotland, with its rocky cliffs, seals and otters, islands and mists. Then there are the sandy flats of East Anglia, the geese and the sand pipers, reed banks and frosts. Contrast these with the long dunes of Northumberland, the castles and harbours; the fishing ports of Nairn and Fife, and the sandy smugglers' coves of Wales and the West Country.

Just below the water is a different and mysterious world that is only really revealed when one is diving or snorkelling. Tantalising hints are cast up at low tide of the fascinating magic beneath. Pools hold small creatures, crabs, fish, anemones, separated temporarily from their natural world by a surrounding army of rock. That same rock is the anchorage for aquatic plants: seaweeds, whose slippery recumbent surface at low tide is in astonishing contrast to their forest-like nature when the tide is high.

So let's assume that it's not an average day, that we don't all have a Mountain Leader's Certificate and have no particular wish to get one, but we do want to get away from the candy floss and winkles, the kiss-me-quick hats and the deck chairs.

Most of Britain's coastline is wild, kept so deliberately by the National Trust, landowners, or conservation management bodies, such as the RSPB and County Trusts. The popular holiday beaches make up far less of it than you would probably imagine. You can walk for miles without seeing a soul, if you choose the time and place, and yet still be within a few miles of 'civilisation' should you so desire.

Once off the beaten track, however experienced a walker you may be, it makes sense to be prepared.

What equipment will help you get the most out of a coastal walk?

Firstly, you must realise that you may be a long way from shelter and that the ground may be rough going. Good walking boots are necessary if you are going to stray up rocky slopes, or wander across muddy streams. Waterproofs are essential, bearing in mind the unpredictable British climate and the exposed nature of most coastal walks – breezy and bracing!

A map and compass will certainly be needed; a 1:25,000, or 1:50,000 Ordnance Survey map is best (the former will give more detail). Also include some food and drink to keep you going and perhaps a small first aid kit. A towel will probably come in handy and a pair of binoculars will bring seals, birds and ships that much closer. An identification book is extremely useful – a pocket size guide is ideal for the general details of what to see and where. The best ones cover not only marine life but also birds, plants and animals as well. A small rucksack to carry everything will leave your hands free.

Now you are ready, you have to decide where to go!

It is worth planning your walk in advance. A trip to the local Tourist Information Office, National Trust Office or the information centre of any nature reserve will give you details of local walks and information on how to get the best out of a particular walk. Very often such organisations offer guided walks along particular stretches of the coast and the chance to accompany an expert should not be missed.

Several of the long distance footpaths and recreational routes are coastal or have coastal sections (details at end of this section). Many footpaths and bridleways have been joined to make long distance routes that are generally well signposted and easy to follow. The official long distance paths are marked by acorn signs, recreational routes usually use yellow for footpaths, blue for bridleways and red for byways. A complete holiday can be spent following one of these paths or an enjoyable day can be had using a circular section of the route.

In areas where paths are not indicated on the ground you will need to consult a map to plan a route for yourself. In country parks and National Trust properties walkers largely have freedom to wander away from set paths. National Parks, Areas of Outstanding Natural

Beauty and Heritage Coasts are in private ownership and access is only permitted in defined areas. If a path marked on an Ordnance Survey map is obstructed, a walker may remove as much of the obstruction as necessary to get through or walk around the blockage to continue along the pathway. At all times remember to follow the country and seashore codes.

There are obvious hazards to avoid. Don't go near the edge of cliffs, and look carefully to see how far up the shore the tide comes. Check the times of local tides before you start, and make sure you know of any places where you might be cut off by the rising tide. Remember rocks on the shore can have a covering of algae that make them very slippery – take care if you walk on rocky shores. Keep you camera well out of harm's way when not in use – salt water eats cameras!

Beyond the promenade and sideshows a coastal walk can be as much or as little as you wish. A good walk could take in a castle, cliffs, sand flats teaming with waders, rock pools and perhaps divert to a coastal pub for lunch. One of my favourite walks is from the family home in Alnmouth up to Dunstanburgh Castle, taking in a sandy beach, rock pools, and beautiful cliff scenery. For lunch there is a choice of beer in several good fishing village pubs and oak smoked kippers from Craster. From there, a grassy stroll beside the rocky shore takes you to the dramatic ruin on Dunstanburgh headland, with views of the Farne Islands with all the views reversed on the way back – it beats deck chairs and slot machines any day of the week.

Long distance footpaths

South-West Peninsula Coast Path
Divided into four sections, altogether 515 miles (829km) of path follow the coastline all the way from Minehead to Poole Harbour.

1. Somerset and North Devon
82 miles (132km) from Minehead through the Exmoor National Park to the Cornish border.

2. Cornwall
268 miles (431km) follow the South-West Peninsula to Plymouth.

3. South Devon
93 miles (150km) combine both easy and rugged walking and include the popular holiday area of Tor Bay.

4. Dorset
72 miles (116km) include some spectacular cliff scenery and the famous Chesil beach.

South Downs Way
80 miles (129km) in length, the whole of this path is open to both horseriders and cyclists in addition to walkers. The footpath from Eastbourne follows the coast (cycles and horses take an inland route) over Beachy Head and the Seven Sisters with spectacular sea views. The path runs parallel to the coast inland north of Brighton.

Peddars Way and Norfolk Coast Path
93 miles (150km). From the Suffolk border the Peddars Way runs north-west along the Norfolk ridge to the coast at Holme-next-the-Sea where it joins the Norfolk Coast Path to Cromer.

Cleveland Way
93 miles (150km). The moorland section of this path runs north from Helmsley to Redcar. From Redcar it is an easier coastal walk south along the Yorkshire coast to Filey.

Pembrokeshire Coast Path
180 miles (290km) mostly in the National Park, it is full of contrasts with rocky cliffs and sandy bays, from Cardigan in the north to Tenby in the south.

Recreational paths

Isle of Wight Coastal Path
60 miles (97km) circuit the island and there are links with several inland trails that make shorter circular routes.

Wayfarer's Walk
70 miles (113km). From Emsworth in Hampshire along the Solent Coast before turning north and leading eventually to Newbury in Berkshire.

Saxon Shore Way
143 miles (230km). East from Gravesend the path follows the Kent coast to Rye in Sussex.

The Ulster Way
A series of paths totalling 450 miles (725km) which have been linked to circle the Province; much of the route is coastal.

Key to the Entries

Water Quality

Approximately 460 beaches around the country have been monitored by the water authorities, River Purification Boards and Department of the Environment for Northern Ireland. The full results indicating those beaches which meet, and those beaches which failed to meet, the minimum EC standard for clean bathing waters in 1988 are given at the start of each regional section. (In most cases the water has been tested for total coliform bacteria, faecal coliform bacteria, solids, colour, transparency, mineral oil and phenols.)

The water quality entry for each featured beach indicates if it was monitored and details are given of any sewage discharged into the sea from the beach. The number of outfalls, the distance offshore that they discharge, the size of the population that they serve and the type of treatment the sewage receives before discharge are all indicated. In the worst case, the sewage goes straight from the toilet or sink to the sea. Initial treatment takes the form of screening or maceration. This means that it is passed through a type of sieve to remove the non-biodegradable solids and is then mashed to speed the breakdown of the organic material after sea disposal. Further treatment takes a number of different forms:

Primary treatment Sewage is passed through settlement tanks, large solids settle out and are disposed of as a sludge either by dumping on land or at sea.

Secondary treatment After primary settlement, the sewage passes to an activated sludge plant where it is mixed to increase the oxygen content and hence increase bacterial activity which breaks it down. The effluent then passes slowly through a final treatment pond, where the bacterial numbers fall before the treated effluent is discharged.

Alternatively, after initial settlement the sewage is trickled through a gravel bed before disposal through a pond. There is bacterial growth on the large surface area of the gravel and this ensures the breakdown of the sewage.

Other treatments A number of different chemical treatments can be used to disinfect and sterilize sewage effluent before discharge. Hydrogen peroxide, chlorine and ozone can be used in this way. An alternative to disinfection is flocculation. A lime-based chemical slurry is combined with the sewage in a single-stage upward-flow treatment tank. This makes the suspended solids combine with the slurry to form a sludge that can be removed from the tank. If the waters off a beach are shallow a tidal tank may be used. The sewage, treated or untreated, is stored in a tank and is only released as the tide is going out. The aim is to achieve maximum dilution and prevent the sewage washing back on to the beach.

Litter

Wherever possible we have tried to include details of any significant litter problems reported and any cleaning undertaken on a regular basis.

Dogs

We have tried to indicate where dogs are not permitted on beaches. In most cases local by-laws have been introduced to restrict the access of dogs to the beach, with provisions for their control on the surrounding land – promenades, paths, gardens etc. In some areas, removal of canine faeces laws have also been applied, with the owners required to clean up any mess their pet makes. At some beaches 'poop scoops' are available.

Bathing safety

Reported conditions that make bathing dangerous are indicated, but always remember to take great care wherever you enter the water. Always follow the Do's and Don'ts for safer swimming.

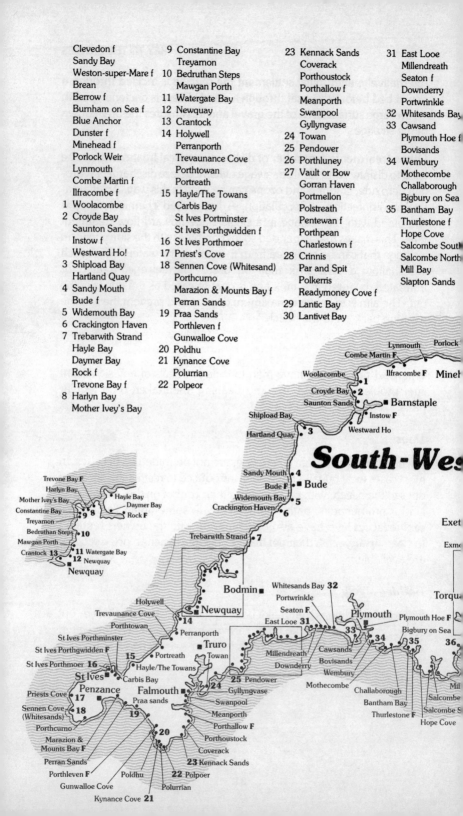

Clevedon f
Sandy Bay
Weston-super-Mare f
Brean
Berrow f
Burnham on Sea f
Blue Anchor
Dunster f
Minehead f
Porlock Weir
Lynmouth
Combe Martin f
Ilfracombe f
1 Woolacombe
2 Croyde Bay
Saunton Sands
Instow f
Westward Ho!
3 Shipload Bay
Hartland Quay
4 Sandy Mouth
Bude f
5 Widemouth Bay
6 Crackington Haven
7 Trebarwith Strand
Hayle Bay
Daymer Bay
Rock f
Trevone Bay f
8 Harlyn Bay
Mother Ivey's Bay

9 Constantine Bay
Treyarnon
10 Bedruthan Steps
Mawgan Porth
11 Watergate Bay
12 Newquay
13 Crantock
14 Holywell
Perranporth
Trevaunance Cove
Porthtowan
Portreath
15 Hayle/The Towans
Carbis Bay
St Ives Portminster
St Ives Porthgwidden f
16 St Ives Porthmoer
17 Priest's Cove
18 Sennen Cove (Whitesand)
Porthcurno
Marazion & Mounts Bay f
Perran Sands
19 Praa Sands
Porthleven f
Gunwalloe Cove
20 Poldhu
21 Kynance Cove
Polurrian
22 Polpeor

23 Kennack Sands
Coverack
Porthoustock
Porthallow f
Meanporth
Swanpool
Gyllyngvase
24 Towan
25 Pendower
26 Porthluney
27 Vault or Bow
Gorran Haven
Portmellon
Polstreath
Pentewan f
Porthpean
Charlestown f
28 Crinnis
Par and Spit
Polkerris
Readymoney Cove f
29 Lantic Bay
30 Lantivet Bay

31 East Looe
Millendreath
Seaton f
Downderry
Portwrinkle
32 Whitesands Bay
33 Cawsand
Plymouth Hoe f
Bovisands
34 Wembury
Mothecombe
Challaborough
Bigbury on Sea
35 Bantham Bay
Thurlestone f
Hope Cove
Salcombe South
Salcombe North
Mill Bay
Slapton Sands

f = failed to meet EC standard for clean bathing water in 1988.
Numbered beaches are included in the following chapter.

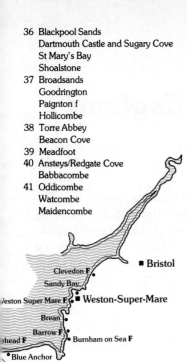

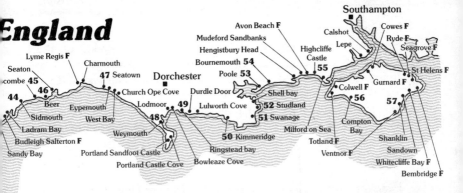

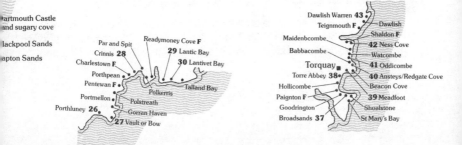

South-West England

There are hundreds of miles of glorious coastline along the South-West Peninsula. Long sweeping bays and small secluded coves are separated by rugged headlands. There are spectacular rocky cliffs to contrast with smooth turfed slopes where wild flowers abound. Some of Britain's loveliest unspoilt scenery is to be found along this coast. But the area is not completely free of problems. Various forms of pollution affect the beaches; untreated sewage discharged close inshore is washed back onto the sands at several places. A number of beaches are affected by industrial pollution. The china clay industry has covered some sands with a film of white dust and the Cornish tin mining industry discharges waste either directly into the sea or into rivers flowing to the sea, for instance the beautiful beaches on the eastern side of St Ives Bay are affected by a 'red' river. The river, containing suspended mining waste, flows across the sand, turns the waves pink and the waste is washed back on to the shore.

Large numbers of tourists flocking to the beaches during the summer can cause problems. Long queues of traffic develop on the narrow lanes and the picturesque Cornish fishing villages become congested. The beaches become crowded and this can lead to damage, for example the erosion of dunes is a particular problem. Careless visitors leaving rubbish will ruin an otherwise lovely beach. To avoid some of these problems a visit in spring or autumn is recommended and in winter you can have miles of golden sands to yourself.

Beaches monitored by the water authorities and found not to meet the minimum EC standard for clean bathing water in 1988:

Clevedon, Weston-super-Mare (Grand Pier and Uphill Slipway), Berrow, Burnham-on-Sea, Dunster, Minehead, Combe Martin, Ilfracombe, Instow, Bude, Rock, Trevone Bay, St Ives Porthgwidden, Marazion and Mounts

Bay, Porthleven, Porthallow, Pentewan, Charlestown, Readymoney Cove, Seaton, Plymouth Hoe, Thurlestone, Salcombe South, Paignton, Shaldon, Teignmouth, Exmouth, Budleigh Salterton, Lyme Regis, Christchurch Avon Beach, Milford-on-Sea, Calshot, Totland, Colwell Bay, Gurnard, Cowes, Ryde, Bembridge, Ventnor, St Helens, Whitecliffe Bay and Seagrove.

Beaches receiving the European Blue Flag in 1988:

Porthmoer – St Ives, Crinnis (Carolyn Bay), Blackpool Sands, Broadsands, Paignton, Torre Abbey Sands, Meadfoot, Ansteys Cove, Oddicombe, Exmouth, Sidmouth, Weymouth, Poole and Bournemouth.
NB – Bathing water quality at Exmouth and Paignton did not meet the minimum EC standard in 1988 and they have therefore not been featured in the guide.

Beaches receiving Clean Beach Awards from the Tidy Britain Group in 1988:

Weston-super-Mare, Porth Beach – Newquay, Portreath, Hayle Gwithian Towans (St Ives Bay), Sennen Cove, Praa Sands, Porthpen, Dawlish Warren, and Teignmouth.

1 Woolacombe Sand, Woolacombe, Devon   OS Ref: SS4500

Two rugged headlands, Morte Point and Baggy Point, bound this long, straight, west-facing beach. 2 miles (3.3km) of lovely flat sands extend south from the rocky shore at Woolacombe to the sandstone cliffs of Baggy Point at Putsborough. The 380 yard (350m) wide sands are backed by extensive dunes behind which the shrub-covered slopes of Woolacombe Down rise. The beach is popular with surfers because of the crashing waves that wash the shore and with families wanting to relax on the beach. After building sand castles and exploring the rock pools, you can escape from the crowds by taking a stroll on the headlands at either end of the bay. On the northern side of Woolacombe is a pocket-sized beach, in complete contrast to the long sweeping sands to the south. The small sandy Barricane beach nestles within the rocky shore stretching to Morte Point and is overlooked by the hotels and guesthouses of Woolacombe.

Water quality Beach monitored by the water authority and found to meet the EC standard for clean bathing water in 1988. One outfall serving 5,000 people discharges fully treated sewage 110 yards (100m) below low water, north of the beach.

Bathing safety It is dangerous to swim near the rocks or at low tide due to undertow currents. Lifeguards patrol the beach from Whitsun to the second week in September.

Access A turning off the approach road to Woolacombe from the B3231 leads to car parks behind the beach. There are paths through the dunes to the sands.

Parking There are several car parks behind the dunes which provide over 1,000 spaces.

Toilets There are toilets in the car park behind the dunes and at the Putsborough end of the beach.

Food Cafés and shops at the Woolacombe end of the beach; shop at Putsborough car park.

Seaside activities Swimming, surfing, windsurfing, diving, sailing and fishing. Surfboards are available for hire. Hang gliding from Woolacombe Down.

Wildlife and walks The North Devon Coast Path leads in both directions from Morte Bay. To the south, the gorse-clad Baggy Point affords excellent views across the bay, as does the jagged slate headland of Morte Point. On a clear day you can see Lundy Island lying 15 miles (24km) away in the Bristol Channel. This island is a Marine Nature Reserve, renowned for the rich marine wildlife around its rocky shores. The steep cliffs that soar 130 yards (120m) above the sea are the haunt of numerous sea birds. Trips to the island to explore its superb shore in greater detail are available from Ilfracombe harbour.

2 Croyde Bay, Croyde, Devon   OS Ref: SS4439

A good flat scenic beach of soft sand. The mile (1½km) of sand is separated from the picturesque village of Croyde by sand dunes. The pale sandstone cliffs of Baggy Point stretch away at right angles from the northern end of the beach. The southern side of the beach is flanked by a grassy headland which is the seaward end of Saunton Down. The rocky shore below the cliffs at either side of the bay contains rock pools perfect for exploring. The beach is noted for the variety of shells that are washed up. It is popular with surfers, and a surfing centre in the village caters for their needs. There is some marine litter.

Water quality Beach monitored by the water authority and found to meet the EC standard for clean bathing water in 1988. One outfall serving 5,000 people discharges macerated raw sewage at low water mark on the southern side of Baggy Point.

Bathing safety Strong undertows make bathing unsafe particularly at low tide; the beach is patrolled by lifeguards from Whitsun to the second week in September.

Access Croyde Bay signposted from Croyde village. Road leads to car park from which beach is signposted. A path leads through dunes to the beach.

Parking Holiday park behind dunes has a car park with 100 spaces open to the public.

Toilets At beach entrance.

Food Shop, beach club and café on path through dunes.

Seaside activities Swimming, surfing, windsurfing, diving, sailing, fishing. There is a surf centre in the village from which boards may be hired.

Wet weather alternatives The Croyde Rock and Gem Museum.

Wildlife and walks Baggy Point provides excellent walks from this beach; there are numerous flowers to be seen and the steep cliffs are home to many types of sea bird. The point provides excellent views south across the extensive sands of Bideford Bay. The path skirts the headland leading north to Morte Bay and Woolacombe.

3 Shipload Bay, Hartland, Devon   OS Ref: SS2428

Far removed from the seaside resort or the quaint tourist attraction, this is a small unspoilt cove on the northern side of Hartland Point. The 330 foot (100m) cliffs rise sharply above the half moon of shingle and low tide sand. There are rocky reefs at either side of the beach below the grassy covered cliffs. The steps down to this sheltered beach are steep and quite difficult.

Water quality No sewage is discharged in the vicinity of this beach.

Bathing safety Safe bathing from the centre of the beach but beware of currents that may cause problems.

Access From Hartland take the road signposted to Hartland Point lighthouse. The bay lies just off the road a mile before the point; there are steps down the steep cliffs.

Parking There is a National Trust car park on the cliff top.

Toilets None.

Food None.

Seaside activities Swimming.

Wildlife and walks The North Devon Coast Path leads along the cliff path to Hartland Point. The strenuous walk is rewarded with excellent views along the rocky shore to the south and to Lundy Island on the far horizon. From the point, you look down onto the lighthouse standing on a lower promontory (the lighthouse is not open to the public).

4 Sandy Mouth, Bude, Cornwall OS Ref: SS2010

Typical of so much of the north coast of Cornwall, wide, flat, golden sands are shadowed by towering cliffs. Sandy Mouth is part of a beach which extends 4 miles (6km) north from Bude. A moderately steep path and steps lead down to the beach, where pebbles give way to extensive flat sands at low tide. The sand is dotted with rocky outcrops below the jagged cliffs which edge the beach. The rocks are encrusted with mussels and barnacles, a sure indicator that none of the beach remains exposed at high tide. Great care is required as the crumbling cliffs cannot be climbed, and there are areas of the beach where the unwary could be cut off. Many surfers take advantage of the roaring waves that predominate along this coastline, but surfing can be dangerous at high tide due to the rocks.

Water quality Bude at the southern end of this long beach is a designated Eurobeach; unfortunately it failed to meet the European standard for bathing water quality in 1988. One outfall serving 18,000 people discharges untreated sewage 20 yards (75m) below low water mark through a tidal tank. There is a scheme to improve water quality at Bude due to commence shortly. No sewage is discharged at Sandy Mouth but there has been nondegradeable sewage waste sighted at this beach.

Bathing safety Bathing is dangerous at low tide and surf bathing is dangerous at high tide. Lifeguards patrol the beach during the summer.

Access Signposted from the A39 north of Bude, a lane descends steeply to the car park on the cliff top. A path and steps lead down to the sand.

Parking A National Trust car park on the cliff top with space for 75 cars.

Toilets At the car park.

Food Snacks available at the car park.

Seaside activities Swimming, surfing and fishing.

Wildlife and walks The coast path north of the bay follows the cliffs for a mile and a quarter (2km) to Duckpool where a valley opens to the shore. There are nature trails through the woods which cover the valley slopes. The coast path continues north to the twin headlands of Lower and Higher Sharpnose Points. The two are separated by sheer crumbling cliffs which enclose tiny rocky coves, a wild and remote stretch of coast..

5 Widemouth Sand, Widemouth Bay, Cornwall OS Ref: SS2002

In contrast to a lot of beaches in North Cornwall, the flat sands at Widemouth Bay are backed by low cliffs and undulating grassy fields which stretch down to the beach from the whitewashed houses of Widemouth village. Flat rocks, which can be too hot to lie on, stretch away in either direction from this popular surfing beach. A grassy slope leads down to this safe, sandy beach. The easy access, which is so important if you do not wish to negotiate steep cliff paths, unfortunately often means that in summer the beach becomes very congested. The cliffs that rise on either side of the beach provide walks away from the busy sands.

Water quality Beach monitored by the water authority and found to meet the EC standard for clean bathing water in 1988. No sewage is discharged in the vicinity of the beach.

Litter There are reports of bottles and containers being washed up on the beach. The beach is cleaned by the local authority.

Bathing safety Surf bathing is dangerous at low tide, and beware of currents near the rocks at each side of the beach. Lifeguards patrol the beach during the summer.

Access Widemouth Bay is signposted from the A39 south of Bude. Sandy slopes and steps lead from the car parks on to the beach.

Parking There are two car parks behind the beach, at either end of the bay, with space for approximately 200 cars in each.

Toilets At the car parks.

Food A café at the southern car park and a beach shop at the northern car park.

Seaside activities Swimming, surfing, windsurfing and fishing. Surfboards are available for hire.

Wildlife and walks The coast path leads off the road south of the beach, climbing Penhalt cliff towards Dizzard Point. There are superb views looking back along the straight coastline stretching north of Bude.

6 Crackington Haven, Cornwall   OS Ref: SX1496

A steep-sided valley opens to the coast at Crackington Haven. At its mouth is a small 'V' shaped sandy beach, flanked on either side by sheer, dark cliffs. Those of Pencarrow Point on the north-eastern side of the beach rise 400 feet (120m) above the sands, which are edged with rocky outcrops. Surfers ride the waves that wash this beach, although anyone swimming or surfing should steer well clear of the rocks on either side of the bay. A perfect little beach for the family wishing to spend a day on a beach with a lovely setting; there are superb walks along the coast path for those that tire of the sand and surf. Unfortunately the village can be rather congested in summer. Dogs banned from the beach between Easter Sunday and 1st October.

Water quality Not monitored. No sewage is discharged in the vicinity of this beach.

Bathing safety Bathing is safe in the centre of the bay, but the rocks on the southern shore are very dangerous. Lifeguards patrol the beach in summer.

Access Signposted from the A39, steep lanes lead down to the village where there is a small car park; it is a short walk to the sands. A road runs parallel with the beach, and grass slopes and rocky outcrops edge the beach.

Parking There is a car park in the village. This fills very quickly in summer.

Toilets There are public toilets in the village.

Food There is a shop and café in the village.

Seaside activities Swimming, surfing and fishing.

Wildlife and walks The stretch of coast that lies both north and south of this bay must be one of the wildest and most magnificent in the country. The coast path follows the grass slope which rises south of the bay: the path leads to High Cliff – a stretch of extremely rugged shale cliffs that rise 731 feet (222m) above the waves. As its name suggests, this is one of the highest cliffs in England. Below is a sandy beach known as The Strangles because of the numerous boats that have found their final resting place on this shore. The rock-studded sands can be reached down an extremely steep and rough path, which is not to be recommended. Bathing from the beach is very dangerous. There are superb views all along the coast path from Crackington to Boscastle; the path can be reached from parking off the road south of Trevigne.

7 Trebarwith Strand, Treknow, Cornwall   OS Ref: SX0587

The lane through a deep wooded valley ends at what can appear to be a tiny rocky cove with cliffs framing an attractive view to Gull Rock. But as the tide recedes, an expanse of sand stretching north below steep cliffs is revealed. From the lane end smooth rocks must be crossed to reach the rock-studded sand. A most impressive beach but one on which great care must be taken as the rising tide can cut off the unwary visitor; signs at the entrance to the beach warn of the dangers.

Water quality No sewage is discharged in the vicinity of this beach. There are, however, concerns about the quality of the stream which flows across the sands.

Bathing safety Swimming can be dangerous at low water and close to rocks. Great care must be taken when surfing. The beach is patrolled by lifeguards during the summer months.

Access Trebarwith Strand is signposted from the B3236, Camelford to Tintagel road. The road ends at the shore, with smooth rocks leading down on to the sand.

Parking There are two car parks off the road with about 140 spaces; it is a 2 minute walk down to the beach.

Toilets At the entrance to the beach.

Food There is a café, hotel, restaurant and pub at the beach entrance.

Seaside activities Swimming and surfing. There is a surf school based on the strand.

Wildlife and walks From the coast path which follows the cliffs there are good views of the rocky cliffs, beach and the Gull Rock, (in appearance, a small version of the Ailsa Craig rock on the Clyde coast). North, the path leads to Tintagel with its clifftop castle, the legendary seat of King Arthur. In the village the Old Post Office and King Arthur's Hall can also be visited. Tintagel is a honey pot for for visitors and becomes very congested in summer.

8 Harlyn Bay, Harlyn, Cornwall   OS Ref: SW8776

A wide bite into the cliffs on the sheltered eastern side of Trevose Head contains the sandy arc of Harlyn Bay, ⅔ mile (1km) in length. A bank of soft sand overlaid with a scattering of pebbles gives way to gently shelving surf-washed sand. Backed by the dunes of Harlyn Warren which are themselves bounded by the dark grey and brown-flecked cliffs towards Cataclews Point. There is a small indent in the cliffs, forming Big Guns Cove. Access to the beach is from the south eastern corner at Harlyn Village, where a stream flows across the beach below St Cadoc's Point. The remains of an Iron Age cemetery were found below the sands behind the beach.

Water quality Beach monitored by the water authority and found to meet the EC standard for clean bathing water in 1988. One outfall serving 2,300 people discharges secondary treated sewage at low water mark east of Cataclews Point.

Litter Some sea borne litter is washed on to the shore. The beach is cleaned by the local authority.

Bathing safety Safe bathing. The beach is patrolled by lifeguards during the summer.

Access The road from the B3276 to Harlyn runs along the south-eastern corner of the beach. There is a footpath from the car park to the sand.

Parking There is a car park off the road directly behind the beach.

Toilets At the car park.

Food Refreshments available close to the beach.

Seaside activities Swimming, surfing and fishing.

Wildlife and walks The walk along the cliffs north east of the bay skirts Mother Ivey's Bay; a lifeboat house stands on the northern shore of this rocky cove. The footpath continues along the cliffs to the point of Trevose Head where a lighthouse stands sentinel. There are superb sea views towards Pentire Head in the north-east and south towards Newquay, with several small, rocky islands lying just east of the head.

9 Constantine Bay, Treyarnon, Cornwall OS Ref: SW8575

This wide, sweeping arc of gently shelving soft pale sands, backed by large marram-covered dunes and bounded on either side by low headlands with rocky outcrops stretching seawards, is a picture to behold. There is very limited parking and there are few facilities available at the beach.

Water quality Beach monitored by the water authority and found to meet the EC standard for clean bathing water in 1988. No sewage is discharged in the vicinity of this beach.

Bathing safety Bathing is dangerous near the rocks.

Access A road off the B3276 at St Merryn is signposted for Constantine Bay. The road ends behind the dunes.

Parking A small car park behind the dunes has spaces for only 30 cars.

Toilets At the car park.

Food None.

Seaside activities Swimming, surfing.

Wildlife and walks The dunes behind the beach are under restoration, with marram grass being planted to stabilise the sands. There are interesting rock pools to explore. The coast path skirts the bay but the low cliffs do not provide the spectacular views that can be found elsewhere on this coastline.

10 Bedruthan Steps, Trenace, Cornwall OS Ref: SW8469

The beach that lies below the towering grey cliffs is a visual marvel, best appreciated from the cliff-top. The steep slopes of the granite cliffs are reflected in the many islands and rock stacks that have been left isolated by the retreating cliff line. At low tide the rock stacks which punctuate the beach are separated by golden sands. At high tide the beach completely disappears and the rocks are pounded by the waves that have created this wonderful scenery. From Carnewas Island the sands stretch 1 1/4 miles (2km) north to Park Head. Steep steps lead down the cliff to the beach. Visitors should note that swimming from the beach is dangerous and that there are areas of the beach that are quickly cut off by the rising tide. Legend says that the rocks were used by a giant, Bedruthan, as stepping stones and this gives the beach its name.

Water quality No sewage is discharged in the vicinity of this beach.

Bathing safety Bathing is dangerous, particularly at low tide.

Access Signposted from B3276 north of Trenace, the road ends at the car park. A path leads to steep steps down the cliff.

Parking There is a National Trust car park on the cliff-top.

Toilets Public toilets at car park.

Food There is a National Trust shop and a café near the car park.

Seaside activities Swimming.

Wet weather alternatives There is a National Trust Information Centre close to the beach.

Wildlife and walks The Cornwall North Coast Path provides good walking north and south of the beach, with fine views along this beautiful rocky coastline.

11 Watergate Bay, Newquay, Cornwall   OS Ref: SW8365

Watergate Bay, like so many of the beaches around Newquay, is a surfer's paradise. 2 miles (3km) of unspoilt sands lie below vertical crumbling cliffs, stretching from Trevelgue Head north to Griffin's Point. A narrow valley cuts through the high cliffs providing access to these flat golden sands, which disappear at high tide.

Water quality Beach monitored by the water authority and found to meet EC standard for clean bathing water in 1988. No sewage is discharged in the vicinity of the beach.

Litter A lot of rubbish is left by beach users during the summer; this is cleared by the lifeguards daily.

Bathing safety Bathing is safe with care. Lifeguards patrol the beach during the summer.

Access The B3276 north of Newquay descends steeply into a narrow valley south of Tregurrian. A short path leads to the beach.

Parking Car park off B3276 south of Tregurrian.

Toilets Toilet at the car park.

Food Shop at beach entrance.

Seaside activities Swimming, surfing and fishing. Surfboards are available for hire.

Wildlife and walks There are excellent walks along the cliffs above this beach with some spectacular views along the coastline. To the north, Griffin's Point overlooks the sandy Beacon Cove.

12 Newquay, Cornwall   OS Ref: SW8262

Originally a fishing port with a busy harbour, Newquay is now one of the foremost holiday centres in Cornwall with all the facilities of a good holiday resort. Newquay boasts several lovely, safe, sandy beaches that are famous for their booming surf. The excellent surf conditions have made Newquay the surfing capital of Britain, and the World Championships are regularly held here. On the eastern side of Towan Head lies Newquay Bay with its four sandy beaches which merge at low tide to give a long sweep of sand below the steep encircling cliffs. Adjacent to the harbour is the sheltered Towan Beach. A promenade at the base of the cliffs is reached by steps from the town above. This beach is bounded to the east by an island, linked to the cliffs by a bridge. Beyond the island, on the south-eastern side of the bay, are the Great Western and Tolcarne Beaches; both are popular for surfing and are separated by Tolcarne Point. Lusty Glaze beach is beyond Barrowfield, an area of open grassland. The final beach which faces Newquay is Porth beach. As its name suggests, this beach has long, narrow sands and is located at the mouth of a valley. Cliffs rise on either side of the sands but in contrast to the other beaches there is level access and soft sands which remain exposed at high tide. Porth beach was awarded a clean beach award in 1988. Dogs are banned from Porth beach between Easter and 1st October.

Water quality Towan and Fistral beaches monitored by the water authority and found to meet EC standard for clean bathing water in 1988. One outfall serving 100,000 people discharges macerated sewage 80 yards (75m) below low water mark off Towan Head.

Litter Beaches are cleared daily during the summer.

Bathing safety Safe bathing from all beaches, unless red flag is flying. The beach is patrolled by lifeguards during the summer.

Access Beaches are signposted from Newquay. Ramps and steps down the cliffs to the beaches.

Parking For Newquay Bay beaches there are car parks at Narrowcliff, Manor Road, Dane Road and Headland Road. For the Fistral beach there is a car park at the end of the Headland Road, adjacent to the Headland Hotel.

Toilets There are toilets at the North and South piers of the harbour, at Fore Street (with disabled facilities), and at Narrowcliff and Trebarwith Crescent.

Food There is a full range of cafés, shops and restaurants.

Seaside activities Swimming, surfing, windsurfing, sailing, diving and fishing. There are sea angling trips available from the harbour. Trenance Gardens pitch and putt, a golf driving range, and a boating lake.

Wet weather alternatives Sports centre, aquarium, Huers Hut, Trenance Cottages Museum and Tunnels through Time. Trenance Leisure Park has indoor and outdoor pools, indoor bowling club, and Zoo.

Wildlife and walks There are some pleasant walks only a short distance from Newquay. Taking the coast path north of the town, the path climbs on to a headland which overlooks the Whipsderry, a small cove walled by high cliffs. On the headland, there are two Bronze Age burial mounds and the remains of a fortress. Continuing along the coast there are excellent views back across Newquay Bay and Watergate Bay. There are also walks south onto Towan Head where you are rewarded with excellent views north along the coast. The coast path continues along Fistral Beach to Pentire Head East which overlooks Crantock Beach.

13 Crantock, Cornwall   OS Ref: SW7761

An excellent sandy beach nestles between the twin headlands of Pentire Point East and Pentire Point West. The beach is backed by high dunes and Rushy Green, an area of undulating grassland behind the dunes. The tidal channel of the River Gannel bounds the northern side of the beach, below Pentire Point East. There is a deep inlet in the low cliffs on the south side of the bay, Vugga Cove, which can only be reached at low tide. There are also a number of caves; the one closest inshore can be explored at low tide. There are many signs of man's activities around the bay; two slipways are cut into the rocks of Vugga Cove, a poem is carved on a rock in the cave and there is evidence along the Gannel of its past use as a natural harbour.

Water quality Beach monitored by the water authority and found to meet the EC standard for clean bathing water in 1988. There is no sewage discharged in the vicinity of this beach.

Bathing safety Bathing is dangerous at low tide and near the Gannel. Flags indicate where and when it is safe to swim. The beach is patrolled by lifeguards between mid-May and mid-September.

Access Crantock is signposted from the A3075 south of Newquay. A lane from Crantock leads to a car park behind the dunes. There is a path through the dunes to the beach. The beach can also be reached from West Pentire; a path leads from the village to steps down the cliffs. The Gannel can be crossed from Newquay by either ferry or tidal bridge at Fern Pit or Trethellan.

Parking There is a car park behind the dunes and another in West Pentire.

Toilets There are toilets at both car parks.

Food There are cafés, shops and pubs in Crantock and West Pentire.

Seaside activities Swimming, surfing and fishing.

Wildlife and walks There is a network of paths south of the beach providing pleasant circular walks. The footpath which follows the cliffs on the southern side of the beach passes Piper's Hole, a deep crevice in the cliffs where fulmars may be seen nesting. The path continues to the end of the headland where there is a collapsed cave and beautiful views to be enjoyed. Tucked below the headland is a tiny unspoilt cove, Porth Joke. The walker can either continue around the next headland, Kelsey Head, toward Holywell beach or make the return journey across Cubert Common.

14 Holywell Bay, Holywell, Cornwall   OS Ref: SW7559

Holywell Bay gets its name from a well in the area said to contain waters with healing powers. ⅔ mile (1km) of lovely sands sweep south from the low cliffs of Kelsey Head to Penhale Point. The beach is backed by dunes that rise to 200 feet (60m). At the southern end a stream flows through the dunes and across the sands. A narrow cave entrance in the cliffs, at the northern end of the bay, can be explored at low tide.

Water quality Beach monitored by the water authority and found to meet the EC standard for clean bathing water in 1988. No sewage is discharged in the vicinity of this beach.

Bathing safety Bathing is only safe between the orange and red flags. Surfing is dangerous at low tide. Lifeguards patrol the beach during the summer months.

Access Holywell is signposted from the A3075 south of Newquay. A path leads from Holywell village along the side of the stream to the beach.

Parking There is a car park in Holywell village.

Toilets There are toilets in Holywell.

Food There are shops and pubs in Holywell.

Seaside activities Swimming and surfing.

Wet weather alternatives Holywell Bay Leisure Park on the approach road to the village.

Wildlife and walks There is a path north along the beach, it follows the cliffs on to Kelsey Head, where the scant remains of a castle can be seen. From the headland there are excellent views back across the beach, north to the adjacent Pentire Point West and also over 'The Chick', a small rocky island offshore. Seals may often be seen around the island. To the south of the bay the path leads to Penhale Sands, an extensive area of sand hills stretching to Perranporth 3½ miles (5.5km) away. Unfortunately the path is sometimes closed because parts of the dunes are used by the Ministry of Defence as a range. A red flag indicates when access is restricted.

15 Hayle, St Ives, Cornwall OS Ref: SW5639

St Ives Bay has a magnificent necklace of golden beaches, backed on its southern edge by high dunes and some rocky outcrops. The approach to the beach at Hayle is uninspiring; there has been a lot of development on the landward side of the dunes which is rather unattractive and an army of telegraph poles marches across the scene. However, once down on these lovely sands, all is forgotten — the 3 miles (5km) of rippled, pale golden sands remain untouched by the development behind. From the mouth of the River Hayle the sands, fringed by magnificent dunes and rocky outcrops, stretch north towards Godrevy Point where Godrevy lighthouse stands on an island just offshore. Dogs are banned from Easter to 1st October.

Water quality Beach monitored by the water authority and found to meet the EC standard for clean bathing water in 1988. No sewage is discharged in the vicinity of this beach, an outfall is to be constructed at Gwithian to discharge St Ives and Penzance sewage.

Litter The beach is cleaned regularly and was awarded a Clean Beach award by the Tidy Britain Group in 1988.

Bathing safety There are strong currents around the river mouth which make bathing dangerous.

Access The beach is signposted from the A30 through Hayle. The road leads up to the car parks behind the dunes and the sands are less than 5 minutes walk away.

Parking Car parks behind the dunes provide plenty of spaces.

Toilets At the car parks.

Food Beach shop and café at the car parks. A hotel provides snacks and meals.

Seaside activities Swimming and surfing. Surfboards are available for hire.

Wet weather alternatives In Hayle, Paradise Park and West Cornwall Leisure and Bowling Club.

Wildlife and walks Following the beach north brings you to the rocky shore towards Godrevy Point where the coast path leads along the cliffs to Navax Point. There are lovely views back across St Ives Bay and numerous sea birds can be seen nesting on the cliffs.

16 Porthmoer, St Ives, Cornwall OS Ref: SW5241

The delightful old buildings which are crowded together on the narrow streets around the harbour spill directly on to the beach at Porthmoer. A row of stone houses faces on to the sands but they in no way spoil this most attractive of beaches. Below St Ives Head, also known as the Island, 1 mile (1.6km) of soft

47

sand backed by low cliffs stretches west. Unlike the more sheltered beaches on the other side of the headland, Porthmoer is a surfer's beach, with the waves from the Atlantic rolling on to the shore. A promenade at the foot of the cliffs provides all the facilities needed for a day on this lovely beach which was awarded a Blue Flag in 1988. St Ives is famous for its quality of light and this has made it popular with artists, a fact reflected in the numerous art galleries and craft workshops to be found in the town. Dogs are banned from Easter until 1st October.

Water quality Beach monitored by the water authority and found to meet the EC standard for clean bathing water in 1988. No sewage is discharged in the vicinity of this beach. An outfall off Porthminster beach on the St Ives Bay side of the headland discharges sewage through a tidal tank.

Litter The beach is cleaned daily in the summer.

Bathing safety Care must be taken. The beach is patrolled by lifeguards in the summer. An area for use of surfboards is marked with buoys.

Access The beach is signposted within the town but it is best to use the large car park above the town and walk down to the beach. There are steps and a lane down on to the sands.

Parking The main car park for the town is signposted on the approach roads. There are car parks at either end of the beach, each has space for about 40 cars.

Toilets At the car parks.

Food Beach shop and café on the promenade.

Seaside activities Swimming and surfing. Deck chairs, surfboards and beach huts are available for hire. Boat trips around St Ives Bay are available from the harbour.

Wet weather alternatives Art galleries, craft workshops, Barbara Hepworth Museum, St Ives Museum, St Ives Leisure and Squash Club.

Wildlife and walks From the beach a coastal path leads west along the low rocky cliffs to a series of sandy and rocky coves.

17 Priest's Cove, St Just, Cornwall   OS Ref: SW3532

Cape Cornwall was recently presented to the National Trust by Heinz, as part of their Guardians of the Countryside programme with the World Wide Fund for Nature. The headland and surroundings remain unspoilt having escaped the commercialisation of Land's End. A tall chimney stands sentinel on the domed headland, a disused ventilation shaft for the mines far below. The rocky Priest's Cove shelters on the southern side of the Cape, its 200 feet (60m) of shingle ringed by low rugged cliffs. There are numerous quiet and unspoilt coves around the toe of Cornwall; rocky shores with a small fishing boat or two drawn up onto the pebbles. A good starting point to enjoy this rugged windswept coastline and explore the shore where marine life is plentiful.

Water quality No sewage is discharged in the vicinity of this beach.

Bathing safety Bathing can be unsafe due to the rocky nature of the shore and the large swell that develops.

Access A narrow lane from St Just leads to a car park behind the beach. There is a path and concrete ramp to the shore.

Parking Car park with 70 spaces behind the beach.

Toilets Toilets at the car park.

Food Occasionally an ice cream van in the car park.

Seaside activities Swimming and fishing.

Wet weather alternatives North of St Just at Trewellard is Geevor Mine and Mining Museum and at Pendeen a mineral and mining museum.

Wildlife and walks There is a pleasant walk onto the Cape with good views along the coast towards Land's End and out to the Brisons Rocks where seals can be seen. The coast path provides good walking both north and south along the rugged granite cliffs which are dotted with the remains of mines.

18 Whitesand Bay, Sennen Cove, Cornwall OS Ref: SW3626

On the rugged Land's End Peninsula the splendid sweep of Whitesand Bay is in sharp contrast to the many rocky coves that indent the cliffs. From the picturesque little harbour of Sennen Cove the beach stretches north 1 mile (1.6km) to Aire Point, with steep cliffs ringing the northern section. The southern end of this moderately shelving beach is good for swimming and surfing, being sheltered by offshore reefs. The northern end is open to the full force of the Atlantic and conditions can be wild and dangerous. The beach received a Tidy Britain Group Clean Beach award in 1988. Dogs are banned from the beach between Easter and 1st October.

Water quality Beach monitored by the water authority and found to meet the EC standard for clean bathing water in 1988. One outfall serving 1,500 people discharges untreated sewage at low water mark by the harbour.

Bathing safety Bathing and surfing are safe at the southern end of the bay. Lifeguards patrol the beach during the summer months.

Access Sennen Cove lies just off the A30 to Land's End and there is a path from the village to the beach.

Parking There is a car park in Sennen Cove and another on the approach road.

Toilets There are toilets in the village.

Food There are shops, cafés and a pub in the village.

Seaside activities Swimming, surfing and angling. Fishing trips are available from the harbour. Surfboards can be hired.

Wildlife and walks The granite cliffs south from Sennen Cove to Land's End are owned by the National Trust. The coast path follows the cliff top which can be wild and windswept. It is probably the best way to approach Land's End avoiding the severe summer congestion of the most westerly tip of Britain, which has been rather spoilt by uncontrolled development.

19 Praa Sands, Ashton, Helston, Cornwall   OS Ref: GR5827

This fine, attractive sweep of sand between rocky headlands is a popular beach for the family. Sheltered by Hoe Point cliffs to the west, the 1 mile (1.6km) sandy strip edged by high dunes stretches east to Lesceave Cliff and the granite Rinsey Headland. At low water 110 yards (100m) of gently sloping sand is exposed, with rockpools at either end containing an interesting variety of marine life. The beach received a Tidy Britain Group Clean Beach award in 1988. A holiday camp close by makes the beach busy.

Water quality Beach monitored by the water authority and found to meet the EC standard for clean bathing water in 1988. No sewage is discharged in the vicinity of this beach.

Bathing safety A rip current makes bathing at low tide very unsafe; the beach is patrolled by lifeguards during the summer season.

Access Praa Sands is signposted from the A394 between Helston and Penzance. From the car park that is a short walk down a sloping path to the beach. From the car park further up the hill there are steps and a steeper path to the beach.

Parking On the road down to the beach is a car park with 100 spaces. At the bottom of the hill, adjacent to the beach entrance is another small car park.

Toilets At the entrance to the beach.

Food Cafés/takeaways and a pub/restaurant at beach entrance.

Seaside activities Swimming, diving, surfing, windsurfing, sailing, raft racing and fishing.

Wildlife and walks The coast path from the eastern end of the beach leads away from the often crowded sands up Lesceave Cliff and on to Rinsey Head. Wheal Prosper, the engine house of an old copper mine, stands on the headland; the property and surrounding land is owned by the National Trust. The mine shaft has been capped and the building restored. A mile (1.6km) further east the ruin of another mine stands on Trewavas Head. To the west of Praa Sands the coast path rises over the cliffs at Hoe Point, passing Kenneggy Sands and Prussia Cove before reaching Cudden Point.

20 Poldhu Cove, Mullion, Cornwall   OS Ref: GR6620

A stream crosses this sheltered, sandy cove backed by dunes and bordered by steep, turf-covered slopes. At high tide there is a fair-sized beach, and the falling tide reveals wide, gently sloping sands, washed by clear green seas. This cove is easily accessible and is overlooked by a large hotel; it is therefore popular and can be busy. It can be a good starting point for reaching coves north and south which are quieter. The South Cornwall coastal path leads south to the Marconi Memorial ¾ mile (1.2km) away, and north to Church and Dollar Coves. Both are fine, sandy coves framed by low, rocky cliffs, but they are unsafe for swimming at low tide. On the rocks of Church Cove stands the 15th-century church of St Winwaloe.

Water quality Beach monitored by the water authority and found to meet the EC standard for clean bathing water in 1988. There is no sewage discharged to Poldhu Cove. One outfall serving 2,000 people discharges macerated sewage 500m below low water mark in Church Cove.

Bathing safety Signs warn that it is unsafe to swim for one hour either side of low tide. The beach is patrolled by lifeguards during the summer season.

Access A lane north-west of Mullion signposted to Poldhu leads to the car park behind the beach. There is a path to the sands.

Parking There is a car park with 100 spaces close to the beach.

Toilets There are toilets on the beach.

Food There is a beach shop/café.

Seaside activities Swimming, surfing, windsurfing, and fishing from the beach, but no hiring facilities for boards etc.

Wildlife and walks There are pools among the rocks that fringe the beach, with plenty of marine life to be examined.

21 Kynance Cove, The Lizard, Cornwall   OS Ref: GR6912

A classic Cornish cove which is extremely well known for its magnificent cliff scenery and is therefore popular with visitors. 200 feet (60m) cliffs shadow the golden sands which are revealed at low tide. Softer layers of rock between the black serpentine have been eroded to form some spectacular cliff formations, impressive isolated stacks, arches and caves. This includes 'The Devil's Bellows' stacks which tower as high as the cliffs and are surrounded by the sands of the cove at low tide. The beach completely disappears at high tide, so take great care to avoid being cut off by the rising tide.

Water quality No sewage is discharged in the vicinity of this beach.

Bathing safety Safe bathing away from the rocks.

Access A toll road from the A3083 north of The Lizard leads to a car park on the cliff top. It is a 5 minute walk to steps cut in to the cliff.

Parking There is a National Trust car park on the cliff top.

Toilets None.

Food None.

Seaside activities Swimming.

Wildlife and walks There is good walking on the coast path along the cliffs from which views of the sea birds nesting on the cliffs and stacks can be best appreciated. There are caves that can be explored at low tide.

22 Polpeor, the Lizard, Cornwall   OS Ref: SW7012

The Lizard Peninsula is beautiful and remote, with much of interest for the naturalist. Unfortunately, in the summer it is overwhelmed by visitors and the narrow roads become congested with traffic. If you want to appreciate the lovely coves around the headland, make your visit early or later in the season to avoid some of the crowds. Polpeor is a small rock and shingle cove at the southern most tip of the Lizard, framed by the cliffs of the Lizard Head and the Lizard Point, a rocky promontory that shelters the beach. The 110 yard (100m) wide beach disappears at high water. A former lifeboat house and slipway adjoin the beach on to which a few boats are still drawn. The turning of the local marble-like serpentine rock has become a small local industry with many of the items sold locally.

Water quality No sewage is discharged from this beach.

Bathing safety Safe bathing.

Access There is a path from the car park 500 yards (450m) from the beach.

Parking There are 2 car parks with 100+ spaces.

Toilets On the beach.

Food Cafés close to the beach.

Seaside activities Swimming and fishing.

Wet weather alternatives Museum of Cornish History in the village, light-house and lifeboat house open to the public.

Wildlife and walks Several rare plant species flourish in the mild climate of the Lizard Peninsula, particularly those of the maritime heathland which is a feature of the headland.

23 Kennack Sands, Kuggar, Cornwall   OS Ref: SW7316

Probably the best swimming beach on the Lizard. Two separate 550 yard (500m) beaches merge at low tide to form one wide, gently sloping sandy beach. The pale sands, on the sheltered eastern side of the Lizard Peninsula, are fringed by dunes. At either end of the bay the sand gives way to shingle, which is bounded landwards by cliffs. This is a popular family beach.

Water quality Beach monitored by the water authority and found to meet the EC standard for clean bathing water in 1988. No sewage is discharged in the vicinity of this beach.

Bathing safety Safe bathing.

Access A road from Kuggar village signposted for Kennack ends behind the beach; there is a short walk through dunes to the sands.

Parking There is a car park at the beach entrance with 250 spaces.

Toilets There is a toilet in the car park.

Food There are cafés at the entrance to the beach.

Seaside activities Swimming, surfing, diving, windsurfing and fishing. Surf boards are available for hire adjacent to the beach.

Wildlife and walks The Cornwall South Coast Path proceeds east from the beach along the cliff tops towards Black Head where you can enjoy good sea views.

24 Towan Beach, Portscatho, Cornwall   OS Ref: SW8733

A safe and sandy beach south of the fishing village of Portscatho. 550 yards (500m) of sand and pebbles are encircled by low shale cliffs on which wild flowers abound. The headland south-east of the beach guards the entrance to Carrick Roads.

Water quality No sewage is discharged in the vicinity of this beach.

Litter Fishing materials and plastics are regularly washed up on the beach although the beach is cleaned by the owners, the National Trust.

Bathing safety Safe bathing.

Access From Portscatho take the road to St Anthony's Head. The car park is off this road. There is a 330 yard (300m) level walk from the car park behind the beach to the sands.

Parking There is a car park behind the beach with 200 spaces.

Toilets There are toilets, including disabled facilities, 275 yards (250m) from beach.

Food None.

Seaside activities Swimming, windsurfing, diving and fishing.

Wildlife and walks The beach lies on the Cornwall South Coast Path, which can be followed in either direction. There is a 4 mile (6.4km) circular route starting at the beach; follow the path inland along the Foe Creek, turning east along the Percuil to Carricknath Point and beach. From there continue to the lighthouse on St Antony's Head, where there is a super panorama of Falmouth Bay and the Black Rock. The path returns to Towan beach along the cliff top.

25 Pendower Beach, Veryan, Cornwall   OS Ref: SW9038

A lovely, unspoilt beach with an attractive setting facing Gerrans Bay; there are good views from the beach towards the gorse-covered cliffs of Nare Head. There is a ⅔ mile (1km) strip of coarse sand fringed by dunes which have suffered from erosion. In order to repair the damage, access is restricted with areas fenced off. Further west the sand gives way to the rocky outcrops and sand of Carne Beach. There are rocky platforms below the steeply sloping cliffs towards Nare Head. A good family beach with easy access.

Water quality Beach monitored by water authority and found to meet the EC standard for clean bathing water in 1988. No sewage is discharged in the vicinity of the beach.

Bathing safety Safe bathing.

Access A turning off the A3078 leads to the car park behind the beach. There are board walks across the dunes suitable for wheelchairs.

Parking A National Trust car park behind the dunes has about 200 spaces.

Toilets There are toilets in the car park.

Food The Pendower House Hotel Café overlooks the beach.

Seaside activities Swimming, windsurfing, diving, sailing, canoeing, waterskiing and fishing. Surf skis are available for hire from the hotel.

Wet weather alternatives Veryan Sports Club.

Wildlife and walks There is abundant marine life to be found in the rock pools along the shore. The coast path follows the cliffs that rise to the south east of the beach. There are excellent views from Nare Head and from Carne Beacon. The panorama along the coast stretches from Zone Point in the west to Dodman Point in the east.

26 Porthluney, St Michael Caerhays, Cornwall   OS Ref: SW9741

Steep, tree-lined cliffs with rocky outcrops at their base shelter this lovely, sandy beach. A lush wooded valley opens to the arc of sand. An ornate Victorian gothic castle stands sentinel among the trees. The ease of access and safe swimming mean that the beach can become crowded in summer.

Water quality Beach monitored by the water authority and found to meet the EC standard for clean bathing water in 1988. No sewage is discharged in the vicinity of this beach.

Litter There is a very small amount of litter on this beach.

Bathing safety Safe bathing.

Access A lane south from St Michael Caerhays slopes steeply down to the beach; the road runs parallel with the beach. It is only a short walk to the sand.

Parking There is a car park off the road directly behind the beach.

Toilets There are toilets at the car park.

Food There is a beach kiosk/café.

Seaside activities Swimming, windsurfing and fishing.

Wildlife and walks The coast path extends in either direction from the beach, with views along the cliffs which ring Veryan Bay from Nare Head to Dodman Point. The wooded valley behind the beach forms the private grounds of the castle. These are only open to the public on a few occasions during the year in aid of charity.

27 Bow or Vault Beach, Gorran Haven, Cornwall   OS Ref: SX0141

Sheltered on the eastern side of Dodman Point is the superb Vault Beach, a sweep of sand and shingle below steep bracken and heather-clad cliffs. From Maenease Point the beach curves for ⅔ mile (1km) to the rock outcrop of Penveor Point. The cliffs rise beyond to the impressive 370 feet (110m) bulk of Dodman Point. The beach can only be reached along the coast path and by descending a steep path to the sand, a route probably unsuitable for small children.

Water quality One outfall servicing 2,000 people discharges untreated sewage at low water mark on the north side of Maenease Point.

Litter There is only a very small amount of litter on this beach.

Bathing safety Bathing is safe with care.

Access The coastal footpath must be followed south from Gorran Haven to reach a steep path down the cliffs.

Parking There is a car park off the road south of Gorran Haven.

Toilets None.

Food None.

Seaside activities Swimming.

Wildlife and walks The coast path along the cliff-top leads on to Dodman Point – there is evidence of an Iron Age fort with a ditch and bank. At the point, a granite cross stands as a memorial to all the ships that have been wrecked around the point. There are superb views along much of the Cornish coast.

28 Crinnis Beach, Carolyn Bay, Cornwall OS Ref: SX0652

Awarded a blue flag for its clean, safe sands in both 1987 and 1988. Carolyn Bay is rather untypical of Cornish beaches, with a large leisure complex providing the entertainment facilities that a holiday-maker may wish for. This is combined with clean, unspoilt sands. A mile and a quarter (2km) of steeply shelving, somewhat coarse, white sand is backed by dune scrubland, bordered by steep cliffs. The bay, with its gently lapping waters, is considered as three separate beaches, although there is very little geographical or physical distinction. Crinnis Beach, backed by the Cornish Leisure World complex, stretches from the rocks bounding the south of the bay east to the white river. The river, stained white from the china clay workings of St Austell, has carved steep sand banks as it meanders across the beach. Beyond the river are the smaller Shorthorn and Polgaver sections of beach, the latter being designated for use by naturists. Both Shorthorn and Polgaver can be reached using the miniature railway which runs along behind the sands.

Water quality Beach monitored by the water authorities and found to meet the EC standard for clean bathing water in 1988. No sewage is discharged from this beach.

Litter The beach is cleaned twice a day by the owners, Cornish Leisure World, who also provide continuous litter patrols during the summer.

Bathing safety Safe bathing except near stream. Lifeguards patrol the beach and an inshore rescue boat patrols the waters. There is a first aid post at the leisure centre.

Access Carolyn Bay is signposted from St Austell and the road leads to the car park behind the beach. A miniature railway gives access to the more distant sections of the beach.

Parking A large car park adjacent to the leisure complex has space for approximately 400 cars.

Toilets At the beach leisure complex.

Food Restaurants, cafés, and takeaways at the main beach complex. A beach café at Polgaver.

Seaside activities Swimming, windsurfing, fun pool, miniature railway and crazy golf. Boats, floats, deck chairs and windbreaks are available for hire. Windsurfing tuition is available.

Wet weather alternatives Roller skating arena, amusement arcade, and a giant screen video lounge are part of the leisure complex which also includes the Cornwall Coliseum. This stages a range of concerts and entertainments throughout the year.

Wildlife and walks There is a nature trail behind the Shorthorn section of the beach. In the less crowded seasons a wander along the strand line provides an interesting insight into the marine life offshore, with a variety of seaweed and shells washed ashore.

29 Lantic Bay, Polruan, Cornwall OS Ref: SX1451

A superb sandy cove framed by high turf and shrub-covered cliffs which can only be reached by a 10 minute walk from the nearest road. The shingle and sand beach shelves steeply. The undulating land approaches and the smooth profiled cliffs give the area an impression of gentleness in comparison to the jagged outlines of the cliffs to the east. This is a fine bathing beach owned by the National Trust, but much care is needed when swimming due to a strong undertow.

Water quality No sewage is discharged in the vicinity of this beach.

Litter Plastic bottles, caps and rope are regularly washed up on to the beach which is cleaned by the National Trust.

Bathing safety Strong undertow.

Access From the car park off the Polruan to Polperro road there is a 10 minute walk along the coast path towards Pencarrow Head to reach a very steep path down to the cove. This path can be dangerous when wet.

Parking There is a National Trust car park on the cliff-top road east of Polruan.

Toilets None.

Food None.

Seaside activities Swimming.

Wildlife and walks The 400 foot (120m) Pencarrow Head rises east of the beach and from its summit you can see from Devon to the Lizard on a clear day. The coastal path that skirts the headland leads to the adjoining Lantivet Bay. To the west of Lantic Bay the coastal path follows the cliffs to St Saviour's Point and Polruan at the mouth of the Fowey. Grey seals may often be seen in the bay.

30 Lantivet, Lansallos, Cornwall   OS Ref: SX1651

This lovely small sandy cove owned by the National Trust is completely unspoilt. This cove shadowed by high cliffs is reached by a 15 minute walk from Lansallos and this ensures that it remains relatively secluded even during high summer. The grass-topped cliffs slope gently to the rock-studded beach below. There are many rock pools full of interesting marine life, and seals are a common sight offshore.

Water quality No sewage is discharged in the vicinity of this beach.

Bathing safety Safe bathing.

Access From the A387 north of Polperro there is a side road to Lansallos. It is approximately 15 minutes' walk from the village to the steep path down the cliff to the cove.

Parking There is a National Trust car park at the top of the cliff.

Toilets None.

Food None.

Seaside activities Swimming and fishing.

Wildlife and walks The coastal path east of the beach leads to Pencarrow Head, a 400 foot (120m) high headland which provides magnificent views of the Cornish coast. West of the beach the path leads along the cliffs to Polperro some 4 miles (6.4km) away.

31 East Looe, Looe, Cornwall   OS Ref: SX2653

Looe is an attractive fishing port. Its narrow streets terrace up the slopes which overlook the river mouth and the harbour busy with fishing and pleasure craft. East and West Looe were once separate townships on either side of the river but are now joined by an arched bridge. Safe, sandy beaches stretch away in either direction from the river. On the northern shore the sands extend from the Banjo Pier to the point where cliffs rise north of the town. Backed by a sea-wall and promenade this 550 yard(500m) beach all but disappears at high tide. Dogs are banned from the beach during the summer. Looe is a popular angling and diving centre.

Water quality Beach monitored by the water authority and found to meet EC standard for clean bathing water in 1988. No sewage is discharged in the vicinity of this beach.

Bathing safety Safe bathing.

Access Steps from the promenade lead onto the beach.

Parking The narrow streets of Looe are closed to non-resident traffic. There is car parking on the outskirts of town.

Toilets There are toilets on the promenade.

Food There are cafés on the promenade.

Seaside activities Swimming, windsurfing, sailing, diving and fishing. Motor-boats are available for hire in the harbour. Bowls, putting and amusements on the promenade at West Looe.

Wet weather alternatives Cornish Museum, Old Guildhall Museum and Aquarium. Amusements.

Wildlife and walks Offshore lies Looe Island where numerous sea birds nest. They can be viewed more closely by taking a boat trip from Looe harbour. The cliff path east of Looe leads to Millendreath beach.

32 Whitesand Bay, Freathy, Cornwall   OS Ref. SX4052

A 3 mile (5km) sweep of sand backed by 250 feet (75m) cliffs stretches from Portwrinkle south-east to Rame Head. The rugged slate cliffs slope gently down to the beach where rocky outcrops dot the pale grey sands. Portwrinkle, at the eastern end of the bay, with its tiny harbour overlooks the rocky shore at the western end of the bay. Once a pilchard fishing village, it is now given over to the holiday industry with holiday development spreading over the cliff top. Further east the beach remains unspoilt by development. There are not many access points to this long stretch of beach. There are paths down the cliffs at Tregantle and Freathy. The former provides the easiest route down, but the beach lies below the Tregantle Fort which is used as a firing range. There have also been reports that this section of beach suffers considerably from marine litter washed onto the shore. At Freathy the path is steeper but the reward is a superb clean and quiet beach. There are excellent views along the bay to Rame Head, its seaward pointing finger ends in a knoll topped by a small chapel. On a calm day the water may look very inviting, but beware of strong rip currents.

Water quality Portwrinkle monitored by the water authority and found to meet the EC standard for clean bathing water in 1988. One outfall serving 700 people discharges untreated sewage 80 yards (75m) above low water mark at Portwrinkle.

Litter There is a problem in some parts of the bay, with marine litter being washed onto the beach. There is a considerable amount of plastic including bottles, old buckets and packaging.

Bathing safety Bathing is unsafe; the beach is valleyed which causes a tidal race and undertow. Two lifesaving clubs patrol the beach at weekends.

Access Whitesand is signposted from the B3247. There are paths down the cliffs at Portwrinkle, Tregonhawke, Tregantle and Freathy. The area around Tregantle Barracks is used by the army as a firing range and a red flag indicates when access is prohibited.

Parking There are cliff-top car parks at the access points; there are 150 spaces at Freathy.

Toilets There are public toilets on the beach at Freathy.

Food At Freathy there is one café on the cliff top and another at the base of the cliff.

Seaside activities Swimming, surfing and fishing.

Wildlife and walks Tregantle Cliffs and Rame Head are owned by the National Trust and provide good walks over the scrub headland with fine sea views.

33 Cawsand Bay, Cawsand, Cornwall   OS Ref: SX4451

Cawsand Bay is at the approaches to Plymouth Sound, the largest of the series of rias (drowned river valleys) along the south coast. The bay overlooks the Plymouth breakwater, built in the 19th century to provide a safe and sheltered anchorage. There is a continually changing scene of traffic, naval and civilian, plying in and out of the Sound. The bay curves 3 miles (5km) from Pickle-combe Point to Penlee Point. The two villages of Cawsand and Kingsand fringe the southern end of the bay. Their colourful houses overlook the sand and shingle beach which is sheltered by the Rame Head peninsula to the south. The beach is a series of moderately shelving sandy pockets between rocky outcrops. At either end of the beach the sand gives way to rocky foreshore backed by wooded slate cliffs.

Water quality No sewage is discharged in the vicinity of this beach.

Bathing safety Bathing is safe except when there are south-east winds.

Access A launching ramp leads from the village to the beach.

Parking There is a car park in the village with 100 spaces.

Toilets There are public toilets adjacent to the beach.

Food There is a beach shop, and there are hotels and cafés in the village.

Seaside activities Swimming, windsurfing, sailing, diving and fishing. There are boats available for hire.

Wet weather alternatives Cremyll and Rame Churches, Mount Edg-cumbe House in country park.

Wildlife and walks 2 miles (3km) north along the coast path lies the Mount Edgcumbe Country Park, 800 acres of wooded park land with superb views of Drake Island and Plymouth Sound. The park contains the original Tudor house and a deer park. South of the beach the coastal path follows the wooded slopes to Penlee Point and continues westwards along the cliffs to Rame Head.

34 Wembury, Devon OS Ref: SX5248

Wembury is a marine protected area set up to maintain its diverse marine wildlife. It is a particularly attractive and unspoilt bay. A valley opens to the back of the beach where the only development is a car park and a small shop and café. Flanked on either side by low cliffs, a narrow strip of sand curves round the bay. Low tide reveals a series of sandy pockets between rocky reefs which contain numerous pools. This area is of significant marine biological interest and, while beach users should take the opportunity to investigate the shore life, a great deal of consideration is required to ensure the area remains unspoilt. The disturbance or collection of marine life should be avoided, as should littering, or any other type of damage to the beach and its surroundings. The view from the beach is dominated by the Great Mew Stone just offshore. There is excellent snorkelling in the area.

Water quality Beach monitored by the water authority and found to meet the EC standard for clean bathing water in 1988. One outfall serving 3,000 people discharges primary treated sewage 110 yards (100m) below low water mark west of the bay.

Litter A small amount of marine litter, including plastic and metal containers, is washed up onto the beach.

Bathing safety Safe bathing but beware of rocks offshore.

Access Wembury is signposted from the A379. A lane from the village leads to the car park behind the beach, and a path approaches the beach about 33 yards (30m) away.

Parking National Trust car park behind the beach.

Toilets At the car park.

Food National Trust café and shop adjacent to beach.

Seaside activities Swimming, windsurfing, diving, sailing and fishing.

Wildlife and walks The South-West Peninsula Coast Path skirts the bay, but the path to Wembury Point is frequently closed when the firing range around the point is in use.

35 Bantham Bay, Bantham, Devon   OS Ref: SX6643

The picturesque village of Bantham with its whitewashed cottages stands on the banks of the Avon. To the south, a dune-covered promontory gives access to this lovely beach at the mouth of the river, with its large area of gently shelving fine sand. There are good views along the river and across the estuary to Bigbury-on-Sea and Burgh Island which lies just offshore. This is a popular but unspoilt beach, bounded to the north by the river. Bathers should be extremely cautious of dangerous currents around the river mouth. The sands are replaced by rocky shore at the southern end of the beach, where cliffs rise above the shore.

Water quality Beach monitored by the water authority and found to meet the EC standard for clean bathing water in 1988. No sewage is discharged in the vicinity of this beach.

Bathing safety Rip currents make bathing on some parts of this beach unsafe. (signs indicate where it is safest). The beach is patrolled by lifeguards during the summer months.

Access Very narrow lanes lead west from the A379 and A381, through Bantham village to the car park. There is a short walk across the dunes to the beach.

Parking There is a car park with about 600 spaces behind the dunes.

Toilets At car park.

Food None; the nearest refreshment facilities are in the village $^1/_2$ mile (800m) away.

Seaside activities Swimming and windsurfing.

Wildlife and walks There are walks through the dunes but great care is required not to damage the fragile marram covering. The Devon South Coast Path leads south from the beach along the cliffs towards Hope Cove. This sandy cove and harbour sheltering below the impressive bulk of Bolt Tail marks the start of a 6 mile (10km) stretch of spectacular rugged cliffs which offer excellent walking.

36 Blackpool Sands, Stoke Fleming, Devon   OS Ref: SY8747

Blackpool Sands is a complete contrast to its Lancashire cousin. The only development of this beach, an unspoilt cove at the northern end of Start Bay, comprises a car park, café and toilet block. A crescent of coarse pink sand and pebbles $^2/_3$ mile (1km) long is flanked by steep wooded cliffs. On the southern side of the cove below Matthew's Point, a valley opens to the shore, from which the stream, the Gara, flows, across the moderately shelving sands. This lovely beach with a most attractive setting was awarded a blue flag in 1988. Easy access and safe bathing make it very popular. Dogs are banned between May and September.

Water quality Beach monitored by the water authority and found to meet the EC standard for clean bathing water in 1988. No sewage is discharged in the vicinity of the beach.

Bathing safety Safe bathing but care is required because the beach shelves steeply.

Access The A379 south of Stoke Fleming leads to Blackpool Sands. A side road leads to the car park where there is a ramp to the beach.

Parking There is a car park with approximately 80 places adjacent to the beach.

Toilets There are public toilets at the car park.

Food Beach shop and café.

Seaside activities Swimming, windsurfing, sailing and fishing. Windsurf boards and canoes are available for hire. Windsurfing school.

Wildlife and walks North of the beach the South Devon Coast Path can be followed north, passing Leonard's Cove and Redlap Cove to the entrance to the Dart Estuary. South, the footpath leads to Forest and Pilchard Cove at the northern end of Start Bay which sweeps 5 miles (8km) south, fringed by shingle beaches.

37 Broadsands, Torbay, Devon   OS Ref: SY9057

On the southern side of Tor Bay, this wide arc of gently shelving red sand was awarded a Blue Flag in both 1987 and 1988. The beach is set among pleasant scenery: on the northern flank, green fields slope steeply down to the shore and to the south there are the gentle grass slopes of Elberry Down. A concrete promenade, with good facilities, backs the sands which disappear at high tide. The steam trains of the Dart Valley Railway can be seen on the viaduct which crosses the valley behind the beach. Dogs are banned from the beach between May and September.

Water quality Beach monitored by the water authorities and found to meet the EC standard for clean bathing water in 1988. No sewage is discharged in the vicinity of this beach.

Litter Easterly winds can bring a lot of litter on to the beach. It is cleaned daily from April to October by the local authority.

Bathing safety Safe bathing.

Access Broadsands beach is signposted from the A3022 between Paignton and Brixham. The road leads down to the car park behind the beach. There are ramps from the promenade to the sands.

Parking Car park with over 100 spaces behind the beach.

Toilets On the promenade.

Food Café and beach shop on the promenade.

Seaside activities Swimming, windsurfing, sailing and fishing. Boats are aviable for hire. Pitch and putt course on Elberry Down.

Wildlife and walks There is a pleasant walk over Elberry Down to Elberry Cove, with good views out across Torbay.

38 Torre Abbey Sands, Torquay, Devon   OS Ref: SY9263

Torbay is referred to as the English Riviera on account of the mild climate that the bay enjoys. The palm-filled gardens, the white hotels and the new marina all contribute to the riviera atmosphere which is particularly evident on Torre Abbey Sands. The beach gets its name from the abbey ruins which stand in gardens of the same name close by. The main A379 linking Torquay and Paignton runs directly alongside the sands separating the beach and gardens. A wide concrete promenade edging the sands is popular for sun bathing at high tide when the beach disappears. As the tide recedes, fine red sands typical of most of Torbay's beaches are revealed, stretching from the harbour/marina south to the rocky outcrops at Corbyn's Head. In Torbay, entertainments are provided throughout the summer and should keep anyone looking for sun, sea and fun happily occupied. Dogs are banned from May to September.

Water quality Beach monitored by the water authorities and found to meet the EC standard for clean bathing water in 1988. There are three stormwater overflow pipes at the harbour; sewage is discharged off Hope's Nose at the north end of the bay.

Litter The beach is cleaned regularly by the local authority. The beach was awarded a Blue Flag in 1988.

Bathing safety Safe bathing.

Access The A379 runs parallel with the beach. There are steps and a slipway from the promenade to the sands.

Parking Car parks are signposted close to the beach.

Toilets At either end of the beach and in Torre Abbey Gardens.

Food Ice cream and snacks are available at the beach; the hotel overlooking the beach has a restaurant and bar open to non-residents.

Seaside activities Swimming, windsurfing and sailing. In August there is a children's week: throughout the week, entertainment competitions and games are provided for the younger members of the family. During the summer there is also the Paignton regatta, the Torbay Carnival and regular firework displays.

Wet weather alternatives Torbay Leisure and Sports Centre, aquarium.

39 Meadfoot, Torquay, Devon   OS Ref: SY9463

This 1988 blue flag winning beach has an attractive natural setting below steep shrub-covered slopes on the southern side of Hope's Nose headland. 880 yards (800m) of moderately shelving fine sand and shingle is backed by a sea wall and road which makes access very easy. The wooded Ilsham valley opens to the northern end of the shore with the cliffs towards Hope's Nose rising beyond. From the cliff tops there are panoramic views across Tor Bay and the Thatcher Rock standing just offshore. Dogs are banned between May and September.

Water quality Beach monitored by the water authorities and found to meet the EC standard for clean bathing water in 1988. One outfall serving 101,000 people discharges untreated sewage at low water mark off Hope's Nose.

Litter The beach is cleaned daily during the season.

Bathing safety Safe bathing.

Access Marine Drive, which turns off the Torquay to Babbacombe road close to the harbour, leads to, and runs alongside, the beach. There are ramps on to the sands.

Parking There is some car parking along the road and a car park on the cliff top.

Toilets At the southern end of the beach.

Food Café and beach shop.

Seaside activities Swimming, windsurfing. Beach huts are available for hire.

Wet weather alternatives Torquay Sports and Leisure centre.

Wildlife and walks There are good cliff walks on Hope's Nose, with excellent sea views and sites for observing sea birds. The path continues north passing through the woods which fringe Anstey's Cove.

40 Anstey's Cove, Torquay, Devon   OS Ref: SY9465

A path winds down a steep wooded slope to a short walkway which leads round the rocky Devil's Point to a short promenade overlooking this most picturesque of coves. The small shingle beach nestles below towering lime-stone cliffs. On the western side of the cove, the shingle is flanked by large boulders strewn at the base of the cliff. Here rock samphire grows in profusion in the crevices and on the slopes above. Redgate Cove shares the same bay and the small sandy beach is reached by a footbridge. On either side of the bay the rugged cliffs extend seawards, falling sheer to the water, their mellow colour perfectly complementing the blue of the sea. The cove is a sun-trap and the soft shingle is often too hot to walk on. Dogs are banned between May and September in both Anstey's Cove and Redgate Cove.

Water quality Beach monitored by the water authority and found to meet EC standard for clean bathing water in 1988. One outfall serving 101,000 people discharges untreated sewage at low water mark off Hope's Nose.

Litter Cleaned daily from April to October. Awarded a Blue Flag in 1988.

Bathing safety Safe bathing.

Access The beach is signposted off the Torquay to Babbacombe road. A steep concrete path opposite the car park leads down to the beach.

Parking Car park at cliff top with 60 spaces.

Toilets On the promenade.

Food Refreshment kiosk.

Seaside activities Swimming, diving and fishing. Deck chairs and beach cabins for hire.

Wet weather alternatives Kent's Caverns, a network of show caves open to the public, are close to the beach.

Wildlife and walks On the cliff top there is a series of walks through the woods on the southern side of the bay. The paths provide pleasant walks onto Black Head and Hope's Nose.

41 Oddicombe Beach, Torquay, Devon   OS Ref: SX9366

One of a series of sheltered coves north of Torquay. Oddicombe was awarded a Blue Flag in 1987 and 1988 as part of the 'Foundation for Environmental Education in Europe' programme of awards for good beaches (cleanliness and facilities), conducted in Britain by the Tidy Britain Group. It is a busy beach but it remains relatively natural in comparison to the beaches that face Tor Bay itself. Oddicombe's 550 yards (500m) of pink shingle is ringed by steep cliffs. The dark green of their wooded slopes contrasts with exposed dark red sandstone outcrops and makes an attractive setting for the beach. A cliff railway descends to the beach giving easy access to the promenade at the cliff base where there is a café and beach shop. The beach is bounded to the north by the rocky Petit Tor Point and stretches to Half Tide Rock at the centre of the bay. This separates it from Babbacombe Beach – a short shingle beach stretching south to a stone pier below the cliffs, which is popular with fishermen. Oddicombe Beach loses the sun in the late afternoon because of the high cliffs. The beach is cleaned daily form April to October. Dogs are banned from May to September.

Water quality Beach monitored by the water authority and found to meet the EC standard for clean bathing water for 1988. No sewage is discharged in the vicinity of this beach.

Bathing safety The beach shelves steeply and care is required when bathing.

Access The beach is signposted from Torquay and Babbacombe. A steep lane meanders down the cliffs to the beach, and there is also a cliff railway to the beach.

Parking There is parking along the roads on the cliff top.

Toilets Public toilets on the promenade.

Food Café and beach shop on the promenade.

Seaside activities Swimming, sailing and fishing. Boats, pedalos, deck chairs and beach cabins are available for hire. Boat trips to Torquay and around Lyme Bay are available. There is a model village in Babbacombe.

Wildlife and walks There are walks across Babbacombe Down, open grassland on the cliff top. This is part of the Tor Bay Coast Path which extends from Maidencombe in the north to Elberry Cove in the south.

42 Ness Cove, Shaldon, Devon   OS Ref: SX9372

Steps down a well-lit smuggler's tunnel some 110 yards (100m) in length lead down to a small sandy cove; the tunnel may not be for the wary. Sheer cliffs wall the quarter of a mile (½km) of unbroken, gently sloping red sands and put the beach in shade by late afternoon. The sands disappear at high tide and there is no escape up the crumbling red cliffs. The beach is cleaned daily in the summer.

Water quality Beach monitored by the water authority and found to meet the EC standard for clean bathing water in 1988. No sewage is discharged in the vicinity of this beach but there are water quality problems at the mouth of the Teign estuary which may affect the beach at times.

Bathing safety Safe bathing from the beach.

Access The beach is signposted from the A379 just south of Shaldon. The road leads steeply down to the car park close to the entrance of the tunnel cut through the cliffs.

Parking Ness car park is a short distance from the tunnel entrance and has spaces for 370 cars.

Toilets There are toilets at the entrance to the tunnel and in the car park.

Food Snacks and ice cream are available at the entrance of the tunnel. Pubs, restaurants, cafés etc are to be found in Shaldon.

Seaside activities Swimming and windsurfing.

Wildlife and walks Close to the tunnel entrance is a wildlife collection and there is a botanic garden in Shaldon. The lawns and gardens of the Ness and the wooded headland above provide walks with excellent views from the beacon over Teignmouth and the Teign estuary.

43 Dawlish Warren, Devon   OS Ref: SX9778

From the Langstone rock a 220 yard (200m) wide sandy beach extends 4½ miles (2.8km) north-east and forms the seaward facing edge of a double sand spit at the mouth of the River Exe. The south-west end of the beach is backed by a promenade with shops, cafés, amusements and a grassy picnic area. This contrasts sharply with the main body of the beach. This forms part of the Dawlish Warren nature reserve which includes the dunes that lie behind the beach and the mudflats on the estuary side of the spit. This beach provides something of interest for everyone, from swimming, surfing and family fun, to beachcombing and birdwatching. Great care must be taken to ensure that the dunes and sand spit are not damaged. Dogs are banned between 1st May and 30th September.

Water quality Beach monitored by the water authority and found to meet the EC standard for clean bathing water in 1988. No sewage is discharged at Dawlish Warren but there are water quality problems at Exmouth on the other side of the Estuary.

Litter Waste paper and plastic left by tourists is a regular problem although the beach is cleaned regularly and received a Tidy Britain Group Clean Beach award in 1988.

Bathing safety Currents from the mouth of the Exe affect parts of the beach; signs indicate where it is safe to swim. The beach is patrolled by lifeguards from May to September.

Access Dawlish Warren is signposted form the A379 north of Dawlish and the beach is signposted from the village. There is a short walk from the car parks to the beach; steps and a ramp lead from the promenade.

Parking Four car parks close to the beach provide 1,500 spaces.

Toilets There are toilets behind the promenade and at the car park entrance.

Food Cafés, snack-bars and ice cream stalls behind the promenade.

Seaside activities Swimming and surfing. Windsurfing from the south-west end of the beach only.

Wet weather alternatives Amusement arcade. Dawlish has all the usual facilities of a seaside town.

Wildlife and walks Dawlish Warren nature reserve is a Site of Special Scientific Interest owned by Teignbridge District Council and Devon Trust for Nature Conservation. It covers 505 acres on the spit at the mouth of the Exe and includes a wide variety of habitats: sandy shore, mud-flats, salt-marsh and dunes. Together these provide diverse flora and fauna. Over 180 types of birds can be seen annually at the reserve, with thousands of waders, geese and ducks over-wintering on the mud-flats. There are 778 species of plant and fungi, including some rare species. The reserve is also a bird sanctuary, and a hide overlooks the mud-flats. Guided walks of the reserve begin at the visitors' centre, signposted from the north-east end of the promenade.

44 Sidmouth, Devon   OS Ref: SY1287

An elegant Regency seaside resort overlooking Lyme Bay which has escaped over-commercialisation. Sidmouth has two beaches: the town beach and Jacob's Ladder beach to the west. This steeply shelving beach, backed by a promenade, was awarded a blue flag in 1988. To the west are the West Chit Rocks and the Connaught Gardens, which give access to the 1 mile (2km) shingle and sand beach of Jacob's Ladder. Sidmouth has all the amenities one may require of a quiet resort and is an ideal place for relaxing on the beach or walking in the surrounding countryside, but not a spot for those seeking bright lights and amusements. Dogs are banned between 1st May and 30th September.

Water quality Beach monitored by the water authority and found to meet the EC standard for clean bathing water in 1988. One outfall serving 17,000 discharges screened and macerated sewage through a tidal tank 550 yards (500m) offshore.

Litter Generally a clean and litter-free beach, cleaned by local authority.

Bathing safety Safe bathing. The beach is patrolled at weekends by the Sidmouth Inshore Rescue Club.

Access Steps and slope from the promenade lead onto the town beach; a sloping ramp gives access to Jacob's Ladder.

Parking Ham, Manor and Bedford car parks close by in the town.

Toilets In the Connaught Gardens and Port Royal.

Food Cafés and kiosks at the town beach and a kiosk at the Jacob's Ladder.

Seaside activities Swimming, windsurfing, sailing and fishing. There are paddle floats, windsurfboards, and deck chairs available for hire. Putting course. Golf course.

Wet weather alternatives Sports centre, museum and theatre.

Wildlife and walks There are some good walks on the surrounding hills and cliffs; the prospect of Sidmouth, and the Heritage Coast from Peak Hill, Fire Beacon and Salcombe Hill are excellent.

45 Branscombe, Devon   OS Ref: SY2188

A quiet undeveloped 3 mile (4.8km) pebble beach stretching from Beer Head to Weston Mouth. A wide valley opens to the coast at Branscombe Mouth with grassland stretching down to the edge of the beach. The cliffs and crags to the east are chalk, whereas to the west there are steep red sandstone cliffs. At Weston Mouth, a stream flows down a steep grassy valley to the beach which is more secluded due to the restricted access (pedestrian only).

Water quality No sewage is discharged in the vicinity of this beach.

Litter A clean beach normally free of litter.

Bathing safety Safe bathing.

Access Branscombe is signposed off the A3052 between Sidmouth and Seaton. At Branscombe Mouth a short, level walk from the car park.

Parking There is a car park adjacent to Branscombe beach with 400 spaces; limited parking in Weston village.

Toilets Public conveniences.

Food Café on the beach.

Seaside activities Swimming, windsurfing, sailing, diving, jet-skiing and fishing. Boats available for hire. Snorkelling and fishing competitions.

Wet weather alternatives Roman camp, pottery, forge and bakery all open to the public.

Wildlife and walks East of Branscombe, walks along the Hooken Cliffs take you to Beer Head. In the other direction the South-West Way follows the cliffs to Weston, Sidmouth and beyond. The area is geologically very interesting with landslips, deep cut valleys and fossils. There is a varied and interesting flora and rock pools on the shore abound with marine life.

46 Beer, Devon OS Ref: SY2589

A delightful little coastal village where small-scale tourism and fishing exist in harmony. The 330 yard (300m) steeply shelving pebble beach is fringed by traditional bathing huts and cafeteria, with steep chalk cliffs rising behind. The road which ends at the beach becomes a slipway where the local fishing boats are drawn up. The pebbles can be rather hard on the feet and some local bathers wear sandshoes when swimming. During the summer season mats are laid along the beach to make walking easier. By climbing onto the breakwater at the eastern end of the beach, a view around the rocky headland to Seaton can be enjoyed.

Water quality Beach monitored by the water authority and found to meet the EC standard for clean bathing water in 1988. One outfall serving 4,000 people discharges untreated sewage off Beer Head.

Bathing safety Bathing with care due to a very steep shelf off the beach.

Access A road from the town gives way to a slipway which leads directly on to the beach.

Parking Cliff-top car park and large car park in the centre of the village.

Toilets Behind the beach, in the village and at cliff-top car park.

Food Three cafés adjacent to the beach.

Seaside activities Swimming, windsurfing, sailing and fishing. Motor boats are available for hire. Fishing trips leave from the beach.

Wet weather alternatives Beer model railway exhibition, Roman quarry caves. A variety of entertainments held in village hall throughout the summer.

Wildlife and walks West of Beer, the South-West Way Coastal Path follows the cliff tops to Beer Head, a short but rewarding walk with views back across the beach and village. The path continues along the cliffs towards Sidmouth. East of Beer at the mouth of the river Axe lies the resort of Seaton. East of the river Axe is the Seaton to Lyme Regis section of the path, stretching 6 miles (10km) along the craggy and wooded cliffs. A 15 minute walk from the river is Goat Island formed by the Brindon and Downlands landslip of 1839; 8 million tons of chalk slumped leaving a deep cleft between the newly formed island and the main cliff. There are no access points between the start of the landslip and Lyme 4 miles (6.4km) away.

47 Seatown, Bridport, Devon OS Ref: SY4292

This is an undeveloped and completely unspoilt beach in a most attractive setting. The green and lush Winniford valley opens to the coast at Seatown, where a lovely shingle beach shelves steeply to some sand at low tide. Steep sandstone cliffs rise on either side of the valley, the mellow coloured sandstone making a pleasing contrast to the green grassland above. The cliffs show the distinctive signs of the sea's continual attack, sheer exposed rock at their summit with rock slumped at their base. To the west lies Golden Cap, the highest point on the southern coast, where the cliffs rise 626 feet (190m) above the shore. The beach is very popular with fishermen.

Water quality Beach monitored by the water authority and found to meet the EC standard for clean bathing water in 1988. No sewage is discharged in the vicinity of the beach.

Bathing safety The beach shelves steeply and great care is required when bathing.

Access A narrow lane from Chideock on the A35 leads to the shore.

Parking Car park behind the beach.

Toilets None.

Food The pub overlooking the beach serves food.

Seaside activities Swimming and fishing.

Wildlife and walks On either side of the beach the rugged sandstone and shale cliffs rise and fall steeply where river valleys cut through to the sea. To the west of the beach the Dorset coast path climbs on to the Golden Cap, and from its flat table summit there are terrific views along the coastline and inland over the undulating patchwork of fields.

48 Weymouth, Dorset OS Ref: SY6779

The wide sweep of soft sand overlooked by the elegant Georgian houses of the esplanade makes this a very popular beach. To the north of the town, the beach is backed by the Lodmoor Country Park which extends round the bay to Overcombe and Bowleaze Cove. To the south lies Weymouth harbour which combines the old and the new; the modern berths used by cross-channel ferries and luxury yachts contrast with the picturesque 17th-century fishing harbour. This is set in the old town which provides a pleasantly different atmosphere to the busy sea-front. Through the lift bridge in the old town lies a marina for 1000 craft, beyond which lies the Radipole Lake. There are views from the beach of the Isle of Portland and Portland Harbour. Dogs are banned from the main beach areas. Dogs on a lead are permitted in a designated area near the Weymouth Pavilion Complex. Poop scoops are available free.

Water quality Beach monitored by the water authority and found to meet the EC standard for clean bathing water in 1988. No sewage is discharged in the vicinity of this beach. Screened and macerated sewage is discharged through an outfall 1378 yards (1300m) off Chesil Beach.

Litter Cleaned daily during the summer; was awarded a Blue Flag in 1988.

Bathing safety Very safe swimming from all of the beach, which is patrolled by lifeguards throughout the holiday season, April to October.

Access There are steps and ramps from the promenade to the sand. There is an hourly open-top bus service along the esplanade to Overcombe and Bowleaze Cove, and also to Portland.

Parking There are car parks at Swannery: 800 spaces, Lodmoor: 1000 spaces and Pavilion: 300 spaces.

Toilets Men/Women and disabled at three points along the beach.

Food Cafés all along the esplanade.

First aid St John's Ambulance post on the beach near the King's statue.

Seaside activities Swimming and boating from the beach, with rowing and motor boats available for hire. There are organised sailing and windsurfing regattas throughout the season. Sand sculpture, Punch and Judy, merry-go-rounds, swings, bumper boats and a free children's beach club provide traditional entertainment on the beach. The Weymouth country park at Lodmoor provides a number of seaside attractions including mini golf, model world and miniature railway, shire horse centre and leisure ranch.

Wet weather alternatives Pavilion Theatre and complex. Swimming pool, diving and shipwreck centre, Northe Forte museums, sea life centre, butterfly farm, Portland Bill lighthouse and open days at Portland navy base.

Wildlife and walks Radipole Lake and swannery is a nature reserve with a wide variety of habitats from freshwater lagoon to grassland and scrub. There are many walks through the reserve where numerous types of birds can be seen, including the bearded tit and cetti warbler. There are conducted tours from the RSPB visitors' centre. The Lodmoor Country Park also contains a nature reserve with walks providing views across Weymouth Bay. There are cliff-top walks on Portland with an excellent outlook across the bay.

49 Ringstead Bay, Dorset   OS Ref: SY760814F

Chalk cliffs and undercliffs produced by chalk landslips surround Ringstead Bay, and at their foot, a pebble beach with scattered rock pools curves 1¼ miles (2km) round the bay. Burning Cliff to the east of the beach is so named because oil shale ignited and smouldered for several years in the early 19th century. There are magnificent views from Whitenothe Undercliff Nature Reserve at the eastern side of the bay.

Water quality Beach monitored by the water authority and found to meet the EC standard for clean bathing water in 1988. No sewage is discharged in the vicinity of this beach.

Bathing safety Care is required when swimming as the beach shelves steeply.

Access Ringstead is signposted off the A353 east of Weymouth, from Upton village a toll road leads to a cliff-top car park.

Parking There are 2 car parks with approximately 400 spaces.

Toilets Public conveniences.

Food Small café and shop.

Seaside activities Swimming, windsurfing, sailing, diving and fishing.

Wildlife and walks The area is of interest for its geology, fossils and the vegetation and wildlife of the undercliffs, particularly invertebrates. The Whitenothe Undercliff Nature Reserve is run by the Dorset Trust for Nature Conservation. The Dorset Coast Path skirts the cliff top. To the east, Durdle Door and Lulworth Cove are reached and westwards the path leads past the medieval village site towards Bowleaze and Weymouth, 5 miles (8km) away.

50 Kimmeridge, Nr. Wareham, Dorset   OS Ref: SY9078

The beach has no sand and is formed of cobbles and stones sheltered below crumbling shale cliffs. It is a good spot for combining a coastal walk with explorations of the excellent rock pools. The bay is part of the Purbeck Marine Wildlife Reserve, and a wealth of marine life abounds on the shore and in the shallow waters. On the eastern headland of this square bay stands the Clavell Tower, which was built as a folly and for a time used as a coastguard look-out post. The tower now stands empty overlooking the bay. The opposite side of the bay marks the edge of the army firing range which covers the land between the bay and Lulworth Cove to the west. The shale cliffs around the bay are very unstable and beach users should not climb on the cliffs or sunbathe below them because of the danger of falling rocks.

Water quality Beach monitored by the water authority and found to meet the EC standard for clean bathing water in 1988. No sewage is discharged in the vicinity of this beach.

Litter A lot of plastic rubbish is frequently washed up on to the beach; cleaned occasionally.

Bathing safety Bathers must beware of submerged rocks that can make swimming dangerous. There are, however, no strong currents or dangerous tides. A coastguard's hut is manned by auxiliary coastguards at weekends and sometimes in rough weather during the summer.

Access A toll road from Kimmeridge village leads to the bay, and a track leads from the car park to the beach.

Parking There are two car parks on the cliff top with about 700 spaces.

Toilets There are two toilet blocks near the beach and a toilet for the disabled in Kimmeridge village, 1 mile (1.6km) from the beach.

Food Ice cream kiosk. There is a shop/restaurant in Kimmeridge.

Seaside activities Swimming, diving, surfing, windsurfing and fishing. There are two slipways for launching small boats from the beach.

Wildlife and walk There is an information centre at the eastern end of the bay run by the Dorset Trust for Nature Conservation who sponsor the Purbeck Marine Wildlife Reserve. The centre can provide information on the numerous animals and plants to be found around the bay. In addition, they produce a leaflet describing a nature trail which is laid out in the area. There are well marked walks across the firing range to the west. Information about opening days can be obtained by ringing Bindon Abbey 462721.

51 Swanage, Dorset   OS Ref: SZ0379

Swanage Beach was awarded a blue flag in 1987 for its high standard of cleanliness and facilities. The safe sheltered bay is flanked by magnificent chalk headlands on either side: Ballard Point in the north and Peveril Point to the south of the bay. The gently sloping sands form a good 1¼ mile (2km) family beach with a promenade providing all the facilities of a small seaside resort. The development has not spoilt the seafront. Swanage is an ideal spot for a holiday combining days on the beach with explorations of the superb Dorset coastline. The beach is very popular and there can be major traffic problems at the height of the summer. Dogs banned from beach between 1st May and 3rd September.

Water quality Beach monitored by the water authority and found to meet the EC standard for clean bathing water in 1988. One outfall serving 20,000 people discharges screened and macerated sewage 110 yards (100m) below low water mark off Peveril Point.

Litter A clean beach with only a small amount of litter left by visitors; the beach is cleaned daily. There are reports that marine litter can be a problem after an east wind.

Bathing safety Safe bathing. No lifeguard, but a beach inspector patrols the beach during the summer. There is a first aid post on the Promenade adjacent to the tourist information centre.

Access Steps and ramps from the promenade lead to the sand.

Parking There are car parks at Broad Road, De Moulham Road, Victoria Avenue and one in the town centre.

Toilets Public toilets with facilities for the disabled at several points along the promenade.

Food Numerous cafés, restaurants and take-aways within easy reach of the beach.

Seaside activities Swimming, windsurfing, diving, sailing and fishing. There are pedalos and motor boats for hire. Fishing and boat trips are available from the quay, where there is also a diving school.

Wet weather alternatives Tithe Barn Museum and Arts Centre, Railway Station Steam Museum, Harrow House Sports Centre, indoor bowling complex. The lifeboat house is open to visitors.

Wildlife and walks The Dorset Coast Path extends in both directions from Swanage Bay, passing through beautiful countryside along this section of coast. To the north of the beach Ballard Cliff rises onto Ballard Down, and the path follows the cliffs round to Handfast Point, which provides excellent views of Old Harry Rocks lying just offshore, and across Poole Bay. South of Peveril Point above Durlston Bay and Head is the Durlston Country Park. There is parking within the park and an information centre provides details of a series of walks in the area. The long distance coast path follows the cliffs beyond Anvil Point Lighthouse, passing the Dancing Ledge, Seacombe Cliff and continuing to St Aldhelm's Head and beyond. There are a series of shorter circular routes starting from the country park that explore both the coast and the beautiful scenery inland. A leaflet produced by the Dorset Heritage Coast Projects describes the various walks.

52 Studland, Dorset   OS Ref: SZ0483

A lovely clean beach that has been designated an Area of Outstanding Natural Beauty. 3 miles (5km) of excellent sandy beach is backed by unspoilt dunes. The beach sweeps south from the entrance to Poole harbour to the splendid chalk cliffs of Handfast Point, once connected to the Needles of the Isle of Wight, visible on the horizon. The beach can be divided into three areas, south beach, middle beach and the north, or Knoll beach. There is separate access to all three areas with facilities at each. Behind the Knoll beach there is a brackish lake and marsh area which forms the Studland Heath National Nature Reserve. A section of the beach is used by naturists.

Water quality Beach monitored by the water authority and found to meet the EC standard for clean bathing water in 1988. No sewage is discharged in the vicinity of this beach.

Litter A very clean beach, largely due to the efforts of the National Trust.

Bathing safety Safe bathing off the main beach; strong currents at the entrance to Poole harbour make bathing at the northern end of the beach unsafe. The beach is patrolled by National Trust Wardens from Easter to September.

Access Each section of the beach is signposted from Studland. It is a short walk from the car parks to the sand. There is a wheelchair ramp at Knoll beach.

Parking 4 car parks provide space for 2,500 cars.

Toilets 5 blocks. Toilets at middle and Knoll beach have disabled facilities, with provision for nursing mothers at Knoll beach.

Food Cafés and kiosks.

Seaside activities Swimming, surfing, windsurfing, diving, sailing, water-skiing and fishing. Windsurfboards are available for hire.

Wildlife and walks The Studland Heath National Nature Reserve containing the brackish lagoon, Little Sea, lies on the landward side of the beach. The reserve cannot be reached from the beach but must be entered from the road which bounds its western edge. There is a wide variety of wildlife including the rare smooth snake and adders. Walkers are advised to wear stout shoes and stick to the marked paths. A leaflet describing 7 local walks is available from National Trust information centre at Knoll beach. Some 1¼ miles (2km) inland lies the Agglestone. This 16 foot (5m) high triangle of ironstone was dropped by the devil, according to folklore. The Dorset Coast Path starts, or alternatively finishes, at the entrance to Poole Harbour. It follows the bay south and onto the Foreland. There are splendid views of the cliffs and the chalk pillars, Harry and Old Harry's Wife, isolated from the adjacent headland by the ever eroding waves. The path continues south towards Ballard Point where there are fine views of Swanage Bay.

53 Sandbanks, Poole, Dorset   OS Ref: SZ0487

This excellent beach won a Blue Flag in 1988. From North Haven Point at the end of the Sandbank spit, the fringe of golden sand stretches 3 miles (5km) north-east to merge with the beaches of Bournemouth. The pedestrian promenade is backed by the steep pine- and shrub-covered Canford Cliffs. Flaghead Chine, Cranford Chine and Branksome Chine cut through the cliffs to the beach. To the south-west the cliffs give way to the low lying Sandbanks peninsula at the mouth of Poole harbour. Here the beach is edged by dunes and overlooked by holiday development and the Sandbanks Pavilion and recreation area. The whole of Poole Harbour is a centre for sailing and water sports, and there is an everchanging boating scene at the harbour entrance. There are excellent views across the harbour and of Brownsea Island from Evenning Hill off the western shore road. Dogs are banned from the beach between 1st May and 30th September, except in two areas. Dogs must be kept on a lead on the promenade. A removal of canine faeces by-law is to be introduced in 1989.

Water quality Beach monitored by the water authority and found to meet the EC standard for clean bathing water in 1988. No sewage is discharged in the vicinity of this beach.

Litter A very clean beach.

Bathing safety Safe bathing except at extreme western end of the beach near the harbour entrance. Warning signs indicate where not to swim. Beach is patrolled by lifeguards at weekends and on bank holidays from May to September.

Access There is easy access along the length of the beach; paths lead down the cliffs to the promenade.

Parking There are 7 car parks along the length of the beach with 1,400 spaces. There is also parking available on adjacent streets.

Toilets There are male, female and disabled toilet facilities along the beach.

Food Cafés and kiosks close to the beach.

Seaside activities Swimming, windsurfing, sailing and fishing. There are windsurfboards and boats for hire. Poole harbour has several windsurfing and sailing schools. There is also a putting green, crazy golf and a variety of children's amusements.

Wet weather alternatives in Poole Sports centre, swimming pool, aquarium, Guildhall Museum, Archeological Museum, Royal National Lifeboat Museum, Maritime Museum, Arts Centre and Poole Pottery.

Wildlife and walks There is a car and pedestrian ferry from North Haven Point to Shell Bay where the extensive Studland Heath National Nature Reserve backs an excellent beach. There is also a pedestrian ferry to Brownsea Island. 200 acres of this 500 acre National Trust owned island form a nature reserve run by the Dorset Trust for Nature Conservation. There are many different types of habitat to be found on the island, including heathland, woodland, freshwater lakes, salt-marsh and the seashore. There is a nature trail and guided walks are available during the summer. Further information is available from the National Trust shop on the island's landing quay.

54 Bournemouth, Dorset   OS Ref: SZ4109

Bournemouth is often referred to as 'the garden city by the sea' because of its many parks, including the upper and lower Bourne Gardens. These wind their way through the town centre following the Bourne Valley, and emerge at the sea front. Bournemouth has an excellent family beach which was awarded a Blue Flag in 1988. Throughout the summer the wide promenade, which backs the miles of golden sands, is traffic-free. The steeply sloping shrub-covered cliffs that rise above the promenade are bisected by a series of deep wooded glades, known as chines. These valleys all have their own individual characters and divide the long sea front into distinctive sections. This is not merely a seaside town, but truly a holiday centre. You may just want to enjoy the sun, sea and sand, but you can also take advantage of the resort's numerous facilities. There are two piers, amusements, and a children's beach-club. There is a full programme of events throughout the summer including carnivals, regattas and competitions. Dogs are not permited between Fisherman's Walk and Durley Chine from 1st May to 30th September. Dogs must be kept on a lead on the promenade.

Water quality Beach monitored by the water authority and found to meet EC standard for clean bathing water in 1988. No sewage is discharged in the vicinity of this beach.

Litter Beach cleaned daily.

Bathing safety Red flags indicate when conditions are safe for swimming. Lifeguards, using inflatable safety boats, patrol the beach. The 'Beach Leisure Department' survey the beach by closed circuit television during the season.

Access The promenade is reached by zig-zag pathways down the cliff. There is a cliff-lift to the east and west of the pier.

Parking Several car parks close to the beach and in the town, plus spaces along the roads.

Toilets There are 15 public conveniences along the promenade.

Food There are numerous catering outlets along the promenade.

Seaside activities Swimming, surfing, windsurfing, sailing and fishing. Rowing boats and pedalo floats available for hire. Boat trips from the beach.

Wet weather alternatives Bournemouth International Conference Centre. Leisure centre 110 yards (100m) from the beach with indoor swimming pool. Russell-Cotes Art Museum. Transport Museum and the Shelley Museum. The Pier leisure centre and seafront amusements.

Wildlife and Walks Stretching east from Bournemouth is the mile long Hengistbury headland which separates Poole Bay and Christchurch Harbour on its landward side. Most of the headland remains undeveloped and has been designated as a site of Special Scientific Interest because of the wide variety of plant and animal life it supports. The headland is a nature reserve owned by Bournemouth Borough Council. It contains a wide variety of habitats including grassland, heath, woods, salt-marsh, freshwater marsh, dunes, rocky and shingle shore. There is a nature trail on the eastern slopes of the headland. The summit of Warren Hill on the landward end of the headland provides good views of Christchurch Bay, Poole Bay, the Solent and the Isle of Wight beyond. There is a south-facing 3 mile (5km) pebble beach below the imposing sandstone cliffs. In sharp contrast to this undeveloped beach is the sand spit stretching north from the headland to the entrance of Christchurch harbour, where the groyne-ribbed sands are backed by beach huts.

55 Highcliffe Castle, Highcliffe, Dorset OS Ref: SZ2093

From Highcliffe Castle (which resembles the ruins of an impressive cathedral rather than a castle), steps lead down the gently sloping shrub and tree-covered cliffs directly onto the sand. A lovely, long, soft sandy beach, with only a few patches of pebbles, extends from Mudeford Quay in the west to Milford-on-Sea in the east. It includes Avon beach, Friar's Cliff, Steamer Point, Highcliffe Castle and Highcliffe Nest beaches along its length. This is an unspoilt beach which is ideal for a day relaxing in the sunshine. Between 1st May and 30th September, dogs are not permitted on the beach. On the promenade, cliff paths and adjacent car park, dogs must be kept on a lead. Owners are asked to clean up after their dogs.

Water quality Beach monitored by the water authority and found to meet the EC standard for clean bathing water in 1988. No sewage is discharged in the vicinity of this beach. Avon beach towards the entrance to Christchurch harbour failed to meet the EC standard; there have been complaints about the quality of this beach.

Litter There have been complaints about litter and debris washed on to shore. Beaches cleaned in the summer.

Bathing safety Safe bathing but care is required because the beach shelves quite quickly. The beach is patrolled by lifeguards and a patrol boat daily from mid-July to early September. This stretch of coast has separate designated areas for swimming and windsurfing, which are signposted on the beach. There is a slight problem with weaver fish.

Access From the A337 through Highcliffe a side road leads to Highcliffe Castle. There are steps and a path down the cliff. The steps are quite gentle but access may be difficult for the elderly and the disabled, particularly the walk back up.

Parking Car park at Highcliffe Castle with 100 spaces, 110 yards (100m) walk to the beach. Car park at Steamer Point with 172 spaces, 330 yards

(300m) walk to the beach and car park at Highcliffe top with 600 spaces, 440 yards (400m) walk to the beach.

Toilets In Highcliffe Castle grounds.

Food Shop/café in the grounds of Highcliffe Castle. During the summer there is often someone selling ices along the beach from a 'cool box'.

Seaside activities Swimming and windsurfing; the latter is restricted to Highcliffe Nest, Steamer Point and Avon beach; swimming is confined to Highcliffe Castle and Friar's Cliff. Fishing.

Wildlife and walks There are woodland and nature walks on the cliffs at Steamer Point, where an information centre can provide details of the flora and fauna to be seen in the area.

56 Compton Bay, Isle of Wight   OS Ref: SZ3841

Two steep ravines, Shippards Chine and Compton Chine, cut through the chalk cliffs, giving access to the 770 yard (700m) wide sandy beach below. At high water a mere 20 feet (7m) remain exposed at the base of the 200 foot (60m) cliffs. From Compton Chine, shadowed by the 500 foot (150m) Compton Down, the beach extends south-east to Hanover Point. Here the sand is replaced by expanses of flat rocks, and the remains of a fossil forest can be seen at low tide. There are good views from the cliffs west to the chalk stacks which form the Needles.

Water quality Beach monitored by the water authority and found to meet the EC standard for clean bathing water in 1988. No sewage is discharged in the vicinity of this beach.

Litter Beach cleaned from Easter to end of September. A lot of debris is washed ashore during winter.

Bathing safety Bathing safe.

Access Car parks reached off the A3055 south of Totland. A short walk from the cliff-top car parks lead down the ravine paths to the beach.

Parking There are 3 car parks with 50, 120 and 70 spaces. Two are situated at the Compton Chine end of the beach, the other at Brook Chine.

Toilets There are toilets at the Brook Chine and Shippards Chine car parks.

Food Mobile refreshment van.

Seaside activities Swimming, surfing, windsurfing and fishing.

Wildlife and walks The cliffs and undercliffs adjoining the beach are part of a Site of Special Scientific Interest stretching from the Needles to St Catherine's Point. They support a particularly interesting flora and nearly half of the British population of the rare butterfly, Glanville Fritillary (Melitaea cinxia) which is only found on the south coast of the Isle of Wight. The coastal footpath that circumnavigates the island leads east along the cliff top to Freshwater Bay, Tennyson Down and the Needles. West of Hanover Point the path leads to Brook where a steep chine leads down to the extensive sands of Brightstone Bay, fringed by soft clay cliffs. Brook is the starting point for the Hamstead trail, a footpath which crosses the Island.

57 Sandown Bay, Isle of Wight   OS Ref SZ5984

The twin resorts of Sandown and Shanklin face Sandown Bay, the largest bay on the Isle of Wight. From Shanklin Chine, a deep wooded cleft cutting through the cliffs, a safe and sandy beach curves gently northwards to Sandown and the white cliffs of Culver Down beyond. Almost two miles (3km) of unbroken sands separate the piers of these busy holiday resorts made popular by the Victorians, and now traditional resorts for a family stay by the sea. Houses and hotels perch on the cliffs and downs which ring the bay, sloping down to the esplanades which edge the beach. There are pleasant walks at each end of the bay, and the old village of Shanklin itself can be explored.

Water quality Beach monitored by the water authority and found to meet the EC standard for clean bathing water in 1988. One outfall serving 50,000 people discharges secondary treated effluent.

Litter The beach is cleaned by the local authority.

Bathing safety Safe bathing.

Access Steps and ramps from the esplanade in both Sandown and Shanklin. There is a lift down the cliff to the esplanade in Shanklin.

Parking In Shanklin two car parks off the esplanade. In Sandown several car parks off the High Street.

Toilets At either end of the esplanade in both resorts.

Food Shops, cafés, pubs and restaurants along the esplanades.

Seaside activities Swimming, windsurfing, and fishing. Beach huts and deck chairs for hire.

Wet weather alternatives Pier and amusements, Sandown Leisure Complex, zoo and museum. In Brading, just outside Sandown, a wax museum, animal world and Roman villa.

Wildlife and walks The Shanklin Chine provides a pleasantly contrasting walk away from the sea front. A footpath south of Shanklin leads along the cliffs to Luccombe. Here another chine gives access to Luccombe Bay, with its small and undeveloped beach. North of Sandown the cliffs can be followed on to Curver Down. There are excellent sea views back across the bay and along the cliffs.

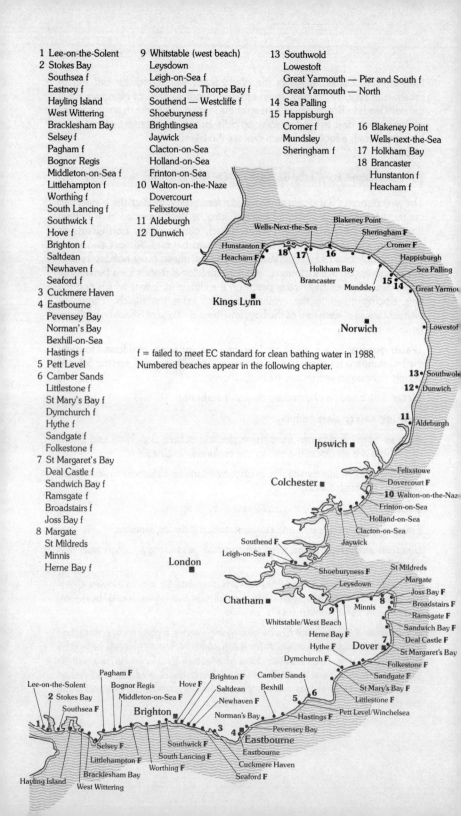

1 Lee-on-the-Solent
2 Stokes Bay
  Southsea f
  Eastney f
  Hayling Island
  West Wittering
  Bracklesham Bay
  Selsey f
  Pagham f
  Bognor Regis
  Middleton-on-Sea f
  Littlehampton f
  Worthing f
  South Lancing f
  Southwick f
  Hove f
  Brighton f
  Saltdean
  Newhaven f
  Seaford f
3 Cuckmere Haven
4 Eastbourne
  Pevensey Bay
  Norman's Bay
  Bexhill-on-Sea
  Hastings f
5 Pett Level
6 Camber Sands
  Littlestone f
  St Mary's Bay f
  Dymchurch f
  Hythe f
  Sandgate f
  Folkestone f
7 St Margaret's Bay
  Deal Castle f
  Sandwich Bay f
  Ramsgate f
  Broadstairs f
  Joss Bay f
8 Margate
  St Mildreds
  Minnis
  Herne Bay f

9 Whitstable (west beach)
  Leysdown
  Leigh-on-Sea f
  Southend — Thorpe Bay f
  Southend — Westcliffe f
  Shoeburyness f
  Brightlingsea
  Jaywick
  Clacton-on-Sea
  Holland-on-Sea
  Frinton-on-Sea
10 Walton-on-the-Naze
  Dovercourt
  Felixstowe
11 Aldeburgh
12 Dunwich

13 Southwold
  Lowestoft
  Great Yarmouth — Pier and South f
  Great Yarmouth — North
14 Sea Palling
15 Happisburgh
  Cromer f
  Mundsley
  Sheringham f

16 Blakeney Point
  Wells-next-the-Sea
17 Holkham Bay
18 Brancaster
  Hunstanton f
  Heacham f

f = failed to meet EC standard for clean bathing water in 1988.
Numbered beaches appear in the following chapter.

South-East England

The south-east of England is rich in sharp coastal contrasts. There are long shingle banks, sand dunes, salt marshes and the wide open skies of Norfolk. Low clay cliffs predominate in Suffolk, powerless to resist the forces of the invading sea. The creeks and mud flats of Essex and the Thames Estuary provide yet another different coastline, while the striking white cliffs of the south coást form an impressive backdrop to many busy holiday resorts and ferry terminals that are the gateway to Europe. Long empty sands and crowded promenades are all to be found.

The south-east has some of the most heavily developed coastal regions and with people and popularity come problems. The heavy traffic in the Channel creates a continual problem with marine litter and oil being washed up on to the beaches. Extensive stretches of the coastline suffer from pollution by sewage. Sludge dumping off the Thames Estuary, nuclear and industrial discharges are all causes for concern. The disturbance around Shakespeare Cliff that will result from construction of the Channel Tunnel will have a severe long term impact on marine and coastal life. On a coastline under pressure from every type of human activity, tourism, industry, and residential development, continual effort is needed to ensure that those areas left unspoilt will remain so for future generations.

Beaches monitored by the water authorities and found not to meet the minimum EC standard for clean bathing water in 1988:

Southsea, Eastney, Selsey, Pagham, Middleton-on-Sea, Littlehampton, Worthing, South Lancing, Southwick (Shoreham), Hove, Brighton, Newhaven, Seaford, Hastings, Littlestone-on-Sea, St. Mary's Bay, Dymchurch, Hythe, Sandgate, Folkestone, Deal Castle, Sandwich Bay, Ramsgate, Broadstairs, Joss Bay, Herne Bay, Shoeburyness, Westcliff, Southend, Thorpe Bay, Leigh-on-Sea, Dovercourt, Great Yarmouth (South and Pier), Cromer, Sheringham, Heacham, and Hunstanton.

Beaches receiving European Blue Flags in 1988:

Lee-on-the-Solent and Stokes Bay.

Beaches receiving Clean Beach Awards from the Tidy Britain Group in 1988:

Southsea, Bracklesham Bay, Selsey, Felpham, Bognor, Littlehampton, Hastings, Bexhill, Pett Level/Winchelsea, Camber Sands, Greatstone-on-Sea, Broadstairs, Ramsgate, Margate, Sheerness, Leysdown, Minster Leas, South Lowestoft, and Hunstanton.

1 Lee-on-the-Solent, Hampshire   OS Ref: SU5700

A long, gently curving ribbon of groyne-ribbed shingle with sand at low tide faces the Solent, with views of Southampton Water and the Isle of Wight. The residential development along Marine Parade overlooks this uncommercialised beach which was awarded a Blue Flag in 1988. Marine Parade West is separated from the beach by the Solent Gardens which slope down to a promenade on two levels edging the shingle. A promenade and flat lawns separate Marine Parade East from the beach. The steep shingle may not be the most comfortable for sunbathing on but it is popular with the more active beach user. There is a designated area for water skiing, and recommended launching area for windsurfers and jet skis. There is always something to watch offshore, whether it is the water sports or the continual shipping traffic plying the Solent. Dogs are banned from the central section of the beach. Dogs on the promenade must be kept on a lead and must not foul the footpaths or the adjoining grass verges.

Water quality Beach monitored by the water authority and found to meet the EC standard for clean bathing water in 1988. One outfall serving 200,000 people discharges primary treated sewage 1,100m below low water mark off Peel Common, north of the beach.

Litter The beach is cleaned regularly by the local authority. Heavy usage of the Solent leads to problems on the beaches, with marine debris and oil being washed ashore.

Bathing safety Safe bathing. Water skiers must use the area buoyed near the Daedalus slipway, jet skis should be launched from the beach adjacent to the slipway and windsurf boards should be launched from the Hill Head end of the beach.

Access Lee-on-the-Solent is signposted from the A32; the B3385 leads to Marine Parade running parallel with the shore. There is level access and ramps to the promenade from which there are steps and ramps to the shingle.

Parking 2 car parks with approximately 250 spaces are signposted off Marine Parade, 2 car parks with approximately 150 spaces are located at the Hill Head end of the beach.

Toilets At the Solent Gardens and the Daedalus slipway.

Food There are shops and cafés on Marine Parade opposite the Solent Gardens. There is a café and sheltered terrace garden off the promenade and a pub at Hill Head.

Seaside activities Swimming, water skiing, jet skiing, and windsurfing. Hill Head Sailboards is a RYA windsurfing centre.

Wet weather alternatives In Gosport there is a local museum, Fort Brockhurst and the submarine museum.

Wildlife and walks The Solent Way coastal footpath can be followed in either direction from the beach. To the north, it skirts the Titchfield Haven Nature Reserve and continues along the shore to the River Hamble, an extremely popular yachting centre. To the south it can be followed to Stokes Bay. A section of the grassland adjacent to the Daedalus slipway has been set aside as a conservation area; do not pick flowers or plants from this area.

2 Stokes Bay, Gosport, Hampshire   OS Ref: SZ5998

The arc of Stokes Bay, with its almost manicured shingle, curves from the No 2 Battery Fort south to Fort Gilkicker, both fortifications being built in 1860 to protect the western approaches to Portsmouth docks. The narrow band of shingle, which shelves quite steeply to some sand at low tide, widens landward towards the south-east of the bay. The long shore drift currents continually move the shingle in this direction and has led to the build-up of a wide area of flat shingle stetching towards Fort Gilkicker. The beach, overlooking Ryde on the Isle of Wight, has a wide open feel about it. The promenade is level with the shingle and is backed by flat, grassed recreational areas which are in turn bordered by the trees and shrubs of the adjacent park and school. This well-managed beach, with easy access, good parking and facilities was awarded a Blue Flag in 1988. Popular for water sports, windsurfers can be seen dancing across the waves throughout the year. Lying just off the inshore rescue station are the two remaining legs of a pier which once provided a train-to-ferry link with Ryde. Dogs are banned from the beach. Dogs on the promenade must be kept on a lead and should not be allowed to foul.

Water quality Beach monitored by the water authority and found to meet the EC standard for clean bathing water in 1988. One outfall serving 200,000 people discharges primary treated sewage 1,100m below low water mark off Peel Common, to the north of Lee-on-the-Solent.

Litter The beach is cleaned regularly by the local authority. Heavy use of the Solent by shipping leads to problems on the beaches and marine debris is frequently washed ashore. Warning signs were posted earlier this year when oil was washed on to the beach after a tanker released contaminated bilge water off shore.

Bathing safety Safe bathing. Swimming and windsurfing are restricted to specific areas of the beach; these are signposted. First aid post near sailing club. Inshore rescue boat station at southern end of the bay.

Access Stokes Bay is signposted from the B3333 between Lee-on-the-Solent and Gosport. There is easy parking off the road behind the beach and level access on to the shingle.

Parking Car parks are signposted at each end of the beach and at its centre, with over 300 spaces. There is also some parking along the promenade.

Toilets At the car park adjacent to the No 2 Battery Fort and on the promenade near the sailing club.

Food Café on the promenade.

Seaside activities Swimming, windsurfing, sailing, canoeing, and diving. 2 public slipways. Children's paddling pool, miniature golf and tennis courts behind the beach.

Wet weather alternatives In Gosport there is a local museum, the submarine museum and Fort Brockhurst.

Wildlife and walks The Solent Way footpath can be followed south-east past Fort Gilkicker towards Portsmouth Harbour or north-west to Lee-on-the-Solent and beyond.

3 Cuckmere Haven, Westdean, East Sussex OS Ref: TV5298

A path from the Seven Sisters Country Park Centre leads through the lovely Cuckmere valley to this quiet pebble beach. The impressive white chalk cliffs of the Seven Sisters stretch away east to Beachy Head. Below them there are numerous rockpools which abound with marine life. This is an ideal spot for those who want to combine sun bathing with exploring the shore and surrounds. The nature trail, which starts from the lovely restored flint barn which houses the Country Park Interpretative Centre, is well worth following.

Water quality No sewage is discharged in the vicinity of this beach.

Litter A lot of plastic and metal cans and bottles, both washed up and left by visitors.

Bathing safety Safe bathing.

Access Pedestrian access only; a mile walk on a marked path through the Cuckmere Valley from the Country Park Centre at Exceat on A259 leads to the beach.

Parking Car park at Country Park Centre.

Toilets At Country Park Centre.

Food Pub at Exceat Bridge provides food.

Seaside activities Swimming and diving.

Wet weather alternatives The Country Park Centre and the Living World exhibition of living animals from the countryside and seashore.

Wildlife and walks A 1½ mile (2.5km) or 3 mile (5km) circular trail through the country park covers a selection of wildlife habitats, salt marsh, river meadows and the chalk grassland above the cliffs. Leaflets which describe the route are available at the Country Park Centre. The South Downs Way follows the cliffs and cuts though the valley. Survey work by the Marine Conservation Society showed that the shallow seas of this stretch of coast are particularly rich in marine life and the area has been designated as a Voluntary Marine Nature Reserve.

4 Eastbourne, East Sussex   OS Ref: TV6199

A lower and upper esplanade, separated by a colourful rock garden, are backed by the Marine Parade which is lined by gardens and overlooked by a number of elegant Regency hotels. Steps from the lower esplanade lead down onto the pebble beach which is ribbed with wooden groynes. Bands of pebbles trapped by the groynes give way to sand at low tide. A Martello Tower on a raised promontory bounds the main beach to the west and provides views along the promenade to the pier and to the white chalk cliffs of Beachy Head. To the east of the pier, the beach is less commercialised, curving away past the Redoubt Fort to Langney Point. A by-law banning dogs from the beach between Wish Tower and the Pier from 1st May to 30th September should be in force in 1989. Dogs will be permitted on other areas of the beach but owners will have to clean up after them.

Water quality Beach monitored by the water authority and found to meet the EC standard for clean bathing water in 1988. One outfall serving 87,000 people discharges macerated and screened sewage 710 yards (650m) below low water off Langney Point. Macerated sewage has been observed off the beach and there have been complaints about smell.

Litter Very little. Beach cleaned regularly.

Bathing safety The beach between groynes 1 to 18 and 20 to 25 is unsuitable for bathing due to the presence of rocks. Otherwise bathing from the beach is safe unless there is a red flag flying.

Access Steps and a ramp lead down from the esplanade to the beach. There are beach wheelchairs available from the bathing station on the lower esplanade.

Parking Pay-and-display car parks at the fishing station, Princes Park and Wish Tower. Free parking on the promenade, restricted in some areas between May 20 and September 20. Multi-storey car park in town centre.

Toilets Adjacent to band stand, pier, Wish Tower, Holywell, Redoubt and the fishing station.

Food Ice cream and refreshment kiosks on esplanade, cafés on pier and in town.

Seaside activities Swimming, sailing, windsurfing and angling. Hiring of windsurfboards is possible from the windsurfing school at the eastern end of the beach. West of the pier a wheeled gangway gives access across the sand to two converted fishing boats providing cruises around Beachy Head with fine views of the Seven Sisters beyond. Sovereign Centre – all weather recreation centre. Children's fun theme park, Punch and Judy and the pier provide traditional seaside entertainment. Land train on promenade. The annual pre-Wimbledon Women's Tennis Championship is held in early June in Devonshire Park.

Wet weather alternatives Lifeboat museum, invasion museum, Martello Tower 73 Museum, Redoubt Fortress Regimental Museum, Aquarium and Butterfly Centre. Band stand, pier amusements and tea dancing, leisure pool. Theatres, five-screen cinema, local history museum, arts centre and gallery in town.

Wildlife and walks To the east of the town rises Eastbourne Down (part of the Sussex Heritage Coast), 5 miles (8km) of coast covering 4,200 acres of unspoilt chalk upland from Eastbourne to Folkington. From Eastbourne you can walk over Beachy Head with its spectacular views back over the town and of the Beachy Head lighthouse and the Seven Sisters.

5 Pett Level, Winchelsea, East Sussex   OS Ref: TQ9116

A sea wall, along which the road runs, borders the beach stretching from Winchelsea beach to Cliff End. The 3½ mile (5.5km) groyne-crossed shingle beach has sand at low tide. The submerged remnants of a forest are revealed as the tide recedes; this is referred to locally as 'Moorlog' or 'Moorlag'. Lines of stones stretching out to sea give the area an air of mystery. Under the Winchelsea Cliffs is the western end of the Royal Military Canal which finally enters the sea at Cliff End. At the old mouth of the canal the Coastal Inspector for the beach has found musket balls and early pistol bullets. From Cliff End the cliffs stretch west to Rock-a-Nore, Hastings. Beach received Clean Beach Award from the Tidy Britain Group in 1988.

Water quality Beach monitored by the water authority and found to meet the EC standard for clean bathing water in 1988. No sewage is discharged in the vicinity of the beach.

Bathing safety Bathing is only safe in calm weather; beware of underwater obstruction.

Access Winchelsea beach signposted from A259 at Winchelsea. Steps down to the beach from the road along the sea wall.

Parking No car park, parking along road which runs along sea wall.

Toilets Public convenience adjacent to beach.

Food Café 450 yards (400m) from sea wall.

Seaside activities Swimming, windsurfing, sailing and fishing.

Wildlife and walks There are many local walks with Winchelsea and Camber Castle within easy reach. On the landward side of the sea wall are flat alluvial pastures. There is a collection of small ponds which attract many species of ducks and waders.

6 Camber Sands, Camber, East Sussex   OS Ref: TQ9618

This is a stretch of fine sand which extends from the mouth of the River Rother approximately 4 miles (6.5km) eastwards to Jurys Gap. For the first 2 miles (3.2km) the beach is purely sand and is backed by sand dunes which are fenced off under a conservation management scheme. The remaining stretch is a narrower shingle beach with sand exposed at low tide. The beach shelves very gently and the tide recedes up to half a mile (800m). The area is popular for shrimping and beach fishermen frequent the eastern end. This is a large and very popular beach with up to as many as 10,000 people using the beach on a sunny Sunday in summer. It received a Tidy Britain Group Clean Beach Award in 1988. Access further east towards Dungeness is restricted because of an MOD firing range.

Water quality Beach monitored by the water authority and found to meet the EC standard for clean bathing water in 1988. No sewage is discharged in the vicinity of the beach.

Litter The beach is raked daily and litter is removed by two litter pickers.

Bathing safety Safe bathing but beware of ridges in the sand that can be dangerous. The Coastal Inspector's office overlooks the beach and has immediate contact with the coastguard. St John Ambulance Brigade has a room in the car park near the beach which is manned on busy days to deal with minor injuries.

Access The beach road is signposted off the A259 east of Rye. Car parking is provided adjacent to the beach at Camber.

Parking 3 car parks (1 tarmac and 2 grass) with space for 1900 cars and 15 coaches.

Toilets 5 public toilets.

Food 2 cafés on beach.

Seaside activities Swimming, windsurfing and fishing. Amusements, trampolines, and deck chair hire facilities. Four holiday camps lie close to the beach.

Wet weather alternatives Amusement arcades.

Wildlife and walks The dunes behind the western car park are part of an SSSI (Site of Special Scientific Interest); the area is fenced as part of a conservation scheme.

7 St Margaret's Bay, St Margaret's at Cliffe, Kent   OS Ref: TR3644

A picturesque little cove sheltered by towering chalk cliffs, which form part of the white cliffs of Dover. A narrow lane leads past terraces of holiday homes to the promenade which backs the shingle, kept in place by iron groynes. This cove has been the starting point for many of the cross-Channel swims. The Pines, gardens on the slopes above the beach, are near tropical due to the mild climate of the area.

Water quality Beach monitored by the water authority and found to meet the EC standard for clean bathing water in 1988. No sewage is discharged in the vicinity of the beach.

Bathing safety Safe bathing except at high tide.

Access A narrow road twists to the sea, but it is easier to park on the cliff top and walk down the hill.

Parking Car park on cliff top.

Toilets Ladies and gents.

Food Public house, ice cream kiosk.

Seaside activities Swimming, diving, and fishing. Dover District Council operate a boat plot. Beach huts for hire.

Wildlife and walks The cove is on the Saxon Shore Way with cliff top walks to Dover and Kingsdown, but there is restricted access to some areas at times due to a Marine rifle range. There are good views from the cliff top where the rolling heathland is owned by the National Trust.

8 Margate, Kent   OS Ref: TR3571

The Isle of Thanet is fringed by a series of sandy bays between low chalk cliffs. The main sands which stretch out west from Margate harbour received a Clean Beach Award from the Tidy Britain Group in 1988. The bright lights of amusement arcades and the funfair along Marine Terrace overlook the promenade which edges the gently sloping crescent of sand. Margate has a long history as a popular seaside resort: it was here that the covered bathing machine was first used in the 18th century and it remains a traditional resort with lots to do both on and off the beach. Dog bins are provided on the promenade and poop scoops are available free from the council.

Water quality Beach monitored by the water authority and found to meet the EC standard for clean bathing water in 1988. A new outfall will be commissioned in the near future.

Litter The beach is cleaned daily by the local authority. The sale of glass bottles is banned.

Bathing safety Safe bathing. The beach is patrolled by lifeguards throughout the summer. Inshore rescue boat, life boat station and coastguard lookout.

Access From the promenade there are steps and ramps to the beach.

Parking Several car parks within easy reach of the beach, including those at Marine Terrace, Marine Parade, Fort Hill and off Trinity Square.

Toilets On the promenade with facilities for the disabled.

Food There is a wide range of cafés, restaurants and takeaways within easy reach of the beach.

Seaside activities Swimming, windsurfing, sailing. Amusement Park.

Wet weather alternatives Aquarium, show caves, shell grotto, lifeboat house, local history museum, Tudor house museum, winter gardens, and a sports and leisure centre.

9 Whitstable, Kent OS Ref: TR1166

This is a quiet resort retaining much of its traditional seafaring atmosphere around the harbour and in the narrow streets, alleyways and weather boarded cottages of the old town. Whitstable was famous for its oysters which are still produced and celebrated annually with an oyster week and carnival. Whitstable's main beach lies to the east of the harbour. Undulating grassy slopes lead gently down from Marine Parade to the promenade and sea wall which edge the pebble beach. A long bank of shingle known as The Street extends seawards from the west end of the beach. Half a mile of the bank is exposed at low water and is a good spot for collecting shells, but is dangerous to swim from. From the slopes at Tankerton there are good views east along the curving beach to Swalecliffe and Herne Bay, especially at sunset. Swalecliffe at the eastern end of the Tankerton slopes is used by water skiers as a launching area. The sport is very popular in the bay and the World Water Skiing Championships have been held here.

Water quality Beach monitored by the water authority and found to meet the EC standard for clean bathing water in 1988. One outfall serving 10,000 people discharges screened and macerated sewage 1,600 yards (1,500m) below low water mark. There have been complaints in past about problems with overflow of sewage in the local stream.

Bathing safety Bathing is safe except near The Street where there are unpredictable currents. Warning notices indicate where it is unsafe. There is a mobile coastguard lookout.

Access Steps and ramps from promenade.

Parking Free parking on Tankerton Road; car parks in harbour area charge.

Toilets At Beach Walk at the end of Tankerton Slopes, the harbour and Island Wall.

Food A wide variety of cafés, restaurants, ice cream kiosks and snack bars in the town within easy reach of the beach.

Seaside activities Swimming, windsurfing, sailing, water skiing and fishing. Bowling green, tennis courts and golf course.

Wet weather alternatives Heritage Museum, sports centre.

Wildlife and walks The Saxon Shore Way follows the banks of the Swale passing through the South Swale Local Nature Reserve on the edge of Graveney Marshes, just west of Whitstable. It continues through the town, along the shore to Herne Bay and the Bishopstone mud cliffs beyond.

10 Central Beach, Walton-on-the-Naze, Essex OS Ref: TM2521

There are some 10 miles (16km) of continuous beach extending from Walton to Clacton. Most of it developed for the entertainment of holidaymakers, the beaches are backed by fun fairs and amusements. Walton combines this aspect of the seaside with undeveloped cliff scenery to the north. Situated to the north-east of the Walton pier, the second longest in Britain, is one of the flattest and sandiest sections of beach on this stretch of coast. The expansive tide-washed sands are backed by a promenade. The sea wall extends north giving way to 40 feet (12m) steep sandstone and boulder clay cliffs. An 80 foot (24m) octagonal tower stands aloft the cliffs built as an aid to navigation. Beyond is the Naze, the most easterly part of the Essex coast. The Naze (Old English for Nose) is a grass and gorse covered promontory. It separates the quiet backwaters, Walton Creek and Hamford Water, from the North Sea. There are good views from the Naze towards Harwich and Felixstowe with their continually changing boating traffic.

Water quality Beach monitored by the water authority and found to meet the EC standard for clean bathing water in 1988. One outfall serving 21,000 people discharges primary and secondary treated sewage 55 yards (50m) below low water mark.

Bathing safety Safe bathing, full beach patrol together with Volunteer Services provide lifeguard cover.

Access Steps down from the promenade at regular intervals and ramps (one at The Colonnade and one near the tourist information centre) provide easy access.

Parking There are car parks at Bath House Meadow, Mill Lane and Saville Street all close to or within walking distance of the beach, also restricted parking along The Parade and some of the town's streets.

Toilets Opposite the tourist information centre, Bath House Meadow and Mill Lane (the latter two include facilities for the disabled).

Food An abundance of cafés and restaurants to choose from, as well as seafront and pier kiosks.

Seaside activities Swimming, sailing.

Wet weather alternatives Lifeboat house museum and exhibition centre.

Wildlife and walks From Mill Lane by the boating lake a public footpath takes you along the backwaters to the Naze and a Nature Reserve. There is a ½ mile (0.8km) nature trail. A network of paths around the islands of the backwaters provide pleasant walks where the migrating birds which frequent this area can be observed.

11 Aldeburgh, Suffolk   OS Ref: TM4757

This long strip of unspoilt shingle beach falls within the Suffolk Coast and Heath Area of Outstanding Natural Beauty and the Suffolk Heritage Coast. A wide sea wall protects the charming town from the continual attack of the North Sea. Aldeburgh is a 'working' beach – a considerable number of boats fish from the beach and most of their catch of crabs, lobster and a variety of fish are sold from huts on the beach. The local lifeboat can also be seen drawn up on the shingle. Shingle dunes and ridges stretch 2 miles (3.2km) north to Thorpeness. This Edwardian holiday village built around a man-made lake, The Meare, is a mixture of traditional weather-boarding combined with Tudor elegance. The working windmill standing on the heathland behind the beach is also the Heritage Coast visitors' centre and it is well worth a visit to find out more about this curious village and adjacent stretch of coast.

Water quality One outfall serving 2,500 people discharges macerated sewage ⅔ mile (1km) below low water mark.

Litter The beach is generally very clean, but subject to occasional spotting with tar and oil from passing ships. It is cleaned by the local authority.

Bathing safety The beach shelves quite steeply but evenly except at Thorpeness where some ridges and pits in the sea bed can be dangerous. It is dangerous to swim near the groynes.

Access Easy access from Aldeburgh promenade and across shingle dunes.

Parking Pay-and-display at each end of town adjacent to the beach, limited free parking in town near beach. Free car park at Thorpeness.

Toilets Public toilets at the Moot Hall and by coastgaurd station.

Food Several cafés, shops and pubs overlook the beach. Ice cream vendor on promenade. Tea shop and inn at Thorpeness.

Seaside activities Swimming, diving, windsurfing, sailing and fishing.

Wet weather alternatives Moot Hall Museum, Thorpeness Windmill and House-in-the-Clouds water tower, Heritage Coast Visitors' Centre. Snape Maltings concert hall on the banks of the River Alde, a few miles inland, is the home of the Aldeburgh Festival. Gallery, craft centre, shops and restaurants at the Maltings.

Wildlife and walks A very good map is available from tourist information centre which details the network of paths that covers Aldeburgh and its surrounding area. Aldeburgh lies on the Suffolk Coastal Path which runs from Felixstowe to Lowestoft. From the village of Snape the route follows the banks of the River Alde and joins the Sailors' Path. This crosses Snape Warren and the marshes north of the town to reach Aldeburgh beach, where shingle plants such as sea holly and the sea pea abound. The path continues north along the beach to Thorpeness and beyond. North Warren RSPB reserve includes The Meare at Thorpeness, the remnant heath, with dry reedbeds, scrub and birch woodland supporting a wide variety of birdlife.

12 Dunwich, Saxmundham, Suffolk OS Ref: TM4770

A one mile (1.6km) stretch of pebble beach that forms part of a long coastal strip that is continually under attack from the waves. Dunwich village, for example, was once a sizeable town but it is progressively falling into the sea.

Between Dunwich village and Minsmere, the RSPB reserve to the south, the shingle-ridged beach is backed by low sand cliffs and heathland owned by the National Trust. The heather and heath plants that thrive on the cliffs provide an attractive splash of colour when in full bloom. The steep banks of shingle which give way to sand at low tide curve northwards protecting the low lying meadows behind. Care is needed to ensure that these coastal defences remain undamaged. This is a quiet beach in an area frequented for the wildlife interest rather than for the holiday beach atmosphere.

Water quality No sewage discharged on to the beach.

Litter Some flotsam is washed up onto the beach.

Bathing safety War remains between low and high tide can be dangerous for swimmers.

Access The beach car park is signposted from the village; there is direct access on to the shingle from the car park.

Parking Car park adjacent to the beach.

Toilets In the car park.

Food Beach café at the car park.

Seaside activities Swimming, windsurfing and fishing.

Wet weather alternatives Museum of local history in Dunwich. Bird hides in the Minsmere Reserve are open to the public, free of charge.

Wildlife and walks There is a marked footpath around the edge of Dunwich Heath which gives the visitor a tour of all the various habitats that the 214 acre site contains. South of the heathland the 1,500 acre RSPB reserve includes reedbeds, lagoons, heath and woodland. Over 100 different species have been recorded breeding within the reserve which makes it one of the most important in Great Britain. There is a shop and information centre at the northern end of the reserve.

13 Southwold, Suffolk OS Ref: TM5076

Southwold once had a pier but all that remains is a short skeleton and the buildings on the promenade. But it is still the focal point for this 3 mile (5km) long beach of sand and shingle. To the north rainbow coloured beach huts line the sea wall which edges the groyne-ribbed beach of soft sand. The beach curves northwards below sand cliffs rising to replace the sea wall. South of the pier the groyne-ribbed beach of sand and shingle stretches to the harbour at the mouth of the River Blyth. Wheeled changing huts line the promenade below scrub covered slopes. The attractive town of Southwold sits aloft. Built around seven greens, it is shadowed by its lighthouse.

Water quality No outfalls discharge in the vicinity of the beach.

Bathing safety Safe bathing except near the groynes at the river mouth.

Access Direct from promenade via steps and a steep ramp.

Parking Three car parks with a total of 300 spaces adjacent to the pier and harbour.

Toilets On the promenade, including facilities for the disabled.

Food Café, bar, shop and takeaway at the pier.

Seaside activities Swimming, windsurfing, sailing and fishing. Amusement arcade. Boating lake.

Wet weather alternatives St Edmund Hall and museum.

Wildlife and walks There are walks along the river and across the meadows. The climb to the summit of Gun Hill is well worth the effort for the reward of some good views. The Suffolk Coastal Path runs north towards Lowestoft and south to Dunwich Forest and Minsmere, approximately 3 miles (5km) from Southwold.

14 Sea Palling, Norfolk   OS Ref: TG4327

10 miles (16km) of coastline that is undeveloped and not readily accessible. From Sea Palling the fine stretch of sandy beach to Waxham can be reached. This beautiful unspoilt beach has gentle sloping sands, fringed by substantial marram covered dunes. The beach is ideal for a quiet day by the sea; no facilities, no razzamatazz, just sand, sea and sky. 3 miles (5km) south, the Broads come within a couple of miles of the dunes, the only protection that the flat low lying land has against the sea. Beach cleaned daily during season; oil has been observed on sand in winter.

Water quality No outfalls in the vicinity of this beach.

Bathing safety Bathing can be dangerous on the ebb tide because of undertow currents.

Access From the village of Sea Palling a road leads to a concrete ramp over the dunes.

Parking Car park behind dunes provides spaces for 100 cars.

Toilets In Sea Palling village.

Food A tea shop and two pubs in the village serve food.

Seaside activities Swimming, windsurfing and fishing.

Wildlife and walks Fossils have sometimes been found in the area of the beach, also jet and amber. The more remote parts of the beach are popular for bird watching.

15 Happisburgh, Norfolk   OS Ref: TG3831

The stretch of coastline from Happisburgh (pronounced Hapsboro) east to Winterton is one of the cleanest in Norfolk. There is a continuous gently sloping sandy beach backed by clay cliffs and sand dunes. This attractive stretch of coastline remains undeveloped. Happisburgh, dominated by its red and white lighthouse and the 110 foot (33m) spire of St Mary's Church, is a good family beach, offering safe swimming for children between the groynes that hold the sands in place. The village is set back from the beach on the 50 feet (15m) clay cliffs, an advantage in an area where the ravages of the sea are much in evidence.

Water quality No outfalls in the vicinity of this beach.

Bathing safety Safe bathing. Inshore lifeboat. Coastguard's lookout.

Access A road leads from the village to the car parks above the beach. A concrete ramp leads past the inshore lifeboat hut to the beach.

Parking 2 car parks with 100 spaces.

Toilets On cliff top includes disabled facilities.

Food Ice cream van.

Seaside activities Swimming, windsurfing, diving, sailing, fishing.

16 Blakeney Point, Cley-next-the-Sea, Norfolk   OS Ref: TG0546

A 9 mile (15km) long shingle beach from Sheringham ends at Blakeney Point where a 3½ mile (5.5km) spit has been built out from Cley Eye. On the landward side of the point there are dunes and salt marshes which edge the Blakeney Channel. Low water reveals wide mud flats and creeks that are frequented by waders. The whole point (1,335 acres), is a National Trust-owned Nature Reserve, and is an area of geological, ornothological and botanical importance. The point itself can be reached by ferry, or on foot from Cley. The beach is very remote, particularily as you venture west from Cley, so take care and be prepared.

Water quality No sewage is discharged in the vicinity.

Bathing safety Shingle shelves steeply and therefore bathing can be dangerous.

Access By ferry from Marston and Blakeney or by foot along the shingle from Cley. A side road from Cley-next-the-Sea on the A149 leads down to the shore.

Parking Car park at ferry departure points and at the end of the shore road from Cley with spaces for 500 vehicles in total.

Toilets At each end of the beach.

Food Cafés at each end of the beach.

Seaside activities Swimming, windsurfing, sailing, water skiing and fishing. Sailing dinghies are available for hire.

Wildlife and walks The lifeboat house at the end of Blakeney Point now serves as the National Trust Warden's centre for the Nature Reserve. It contains information on how the point was formed and the large variety of wildlife to be found there. In the spring and autumn there are many migrant visiting birds and rare species can often be spotted. There is a wooden walkway from the centre to the main observation hide. Adjacent to Cley-next-the-Sea there is the Cley Nature Reserve run by the Norfolk Naturalists' Trust. There is an information centre.

17 Holkham Bay, Wells-next-the-Sea, Norfolk   OS Ref: TF8946

The endless sky seems to dominate this coastline. A clean and unspoilt curve of firm sand which is backed by extensive dunes planted with corsican pines looks over Holkham Bay. The tide retreats out 2 miles (3 km) over the flat sand and mud, and care must be taken as the tide rises swiftly, bringing the risk of being cut off.

Water quality Wells-next-the-Sea, further east, was monitored by the water authority and found to meet the EC standard for clean bathing water in 1988.

Bathing safety Safe bathing except at high tide; take care as the tide comes in very quickly.

Access Lady Anne's Road, a private road opposite Holkham Hall entrance, leads to the shore. There are also board walks across the dunes.

Parking Car park with 200 spaces on Lady Anne's Road.

Toilets None.

Food None.

Seaside activities Swimming.

Wet weather alternatives Holkham Hall and estate including pottery and tea shop.

Wildlife and walks The whole of the beach is part of the Holkham National Nature Reserve which covers 10,000 acres including the dunes and salt marshes. There is a great deal of interesting wildlife to be seen including a tern colony on the beach, which should not be disturbed. The Peddars Way long distance footpath follows this stretch of shore. There is a nature trail within the Holkham Hall grounds.

18 Brancaster, Norfolk   OS Ref: TF7743

The coastline between Hunstanton and Sheringham with its mixture of sand, mud flats, dunes and marshes is an Area of Outstanding Natural Beauty and forms part of the North Norfolk Heritage Coast. At Brancaster, an expanse of sand a mile (1.6km) wide is exposed as the sea retreats but it virtually disappears at high water with only a 10–20 yard (10–20m) strip of sand remaining. A concrete sea wall separates the tidal beach from the dunes inland. The beach is bounded on either side by extensive salt marshes owned by the National Trust. To the east, Brancaster Marsh stretches to the village of Brancaster Staithe with its near landlocked harbour. To the west of the beach are the salt marshes that form the Titchwell Marsh RSPB Reserve. Scolt Head Island lies offshore north-east of the beach, and at low tide the Wreck sands that extend west from the island, merge with the Brancaster beach. Visitors are advised not to walk across the harbour channel to the island. The beach is cleaned regularly.

Water quality No sewage is discharged in the vicinity of the beach.

Bathing safety The intertidal sand flats are dangerous and care is needed at all states of the tide; bathing is only safe close inshore.

Access Reached via the beach road which is liable to flooding at high tide. There are wooden walkways over the dunes to the beach.

Parking Car park with 1000 spaces 110 yards (100m) from the beach behind the dunes.

Toilets 220 yards (200m) from beach.

Food Refreshment hut provides teas, ice creams and post cards.

Seaside activities Swimming, windsurfing, sailing, fishing and bird watching. Golf course.

Wildlife and walks This stretch of coastline is famous for its flora and fauna and in particular for the numbers and variety of bird life. There are 12 designated nature reserves along this section of the Norfolk coast and together they cover some 6,000 acres. Part of Brancaster Bay falls within the Scolt Head National Nature Reserve. Scolt Head Island itself is noted for a variety of plants and animals, in particular for the large Sandwich Ternery at its western end. Access to the island is by boat from Brancaster Staithe harbour. There is a self-guiding nature trail around the island. Entry to the ternery is prohibited during the breeding season, May, June and July. Further details about the reserve can be obtained from the National Trust wardens at The Dial House, Brancaster Staithe. Titchwell Marsh, adjacent to Brancaster beach, is an RSPB reserve; 100 acres of the 420 acre site are enclosed by a sea wall to allow the water level and salinity to be controlled. This produces freshwater reed beds, and freshwater and brackish pools in addition to the original tidal marsh, shingle spit and foreshore. The area attracts a wide range of species. There is an information centre in the reserve.

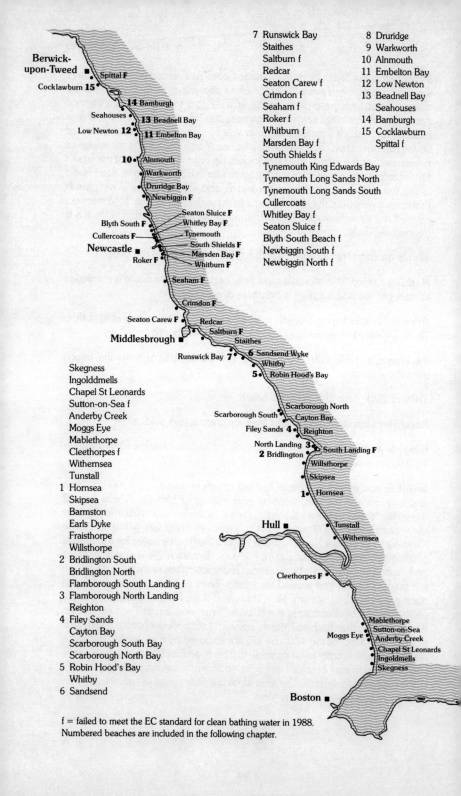

7 Runswick Bay
Staithes
Saltburn f
Redcar
Seaton Carew f
Crimdon f
Seaham f
Roker f
Whitburn f
Marsden Bay f
South Shields f
Tynemouth King Edwards Bay
Tynemouth Long Sands North
Tynemouth Long Sands South
Cullercoats
Whitley Bay f
Seaton Sluice f
Blyth South Beach f
Newbiggin South f
Newbiggin North f

8 Druridge
9 Warkworth
10 Alnmouth
11 Embelton Bay
12 Low Newton
13 Beadnell Bay
Seahouses
14 Bamburgh
15 Cocklawburn
Spittal f

Berwick-upon-Tweed ■
Spittal F
Cocklawburn 15
14 Bamburgh
Seahouses
13 Beadnell Bay
Low Newton 12
11 Embelton Bay
10 Alnmouth
Warkworth
Druridge Bay
Newbiggin F
Seaton Sluice F
Whitley Bay F
Blyth South F
Tynemouth
Cullercoats F
Newcastle ■
South Shields F
Marsden Bay F
Roker F
Whitburn F
Seaham F
Crimdon F
Seaton Carew F
Redcar
Middlesbrough ■
Saltburn F
Staithes
Runswick Bay 7
6 Sandsend Wyke
Whitby
5 Robin Hood's Bay
Scarborough North
Scarborough South
Cayton Bay
Filey Sands 4
Reighton
North Landing 3
South Landing F
2 Bridlington
Willsthorpe
Skipsea
1 Hornsea
Hull ■
Tunstall
Withernsea
Cleethorpes F

Skegness
Ingolddmells
Chapel St Leonards
Sutton-on-Sea f
Anderby Creek
Moggs Eye
Mablethorpe
Cleethorpes f
Withernsea
Tunstall
1 Hornsea
Skipsea
Barmston
Earls Dyke
Fraisthorpe
Willsthorpe
2 Bridlington South
Bridlington North
Flamborough South Landing f
3 Flamborough North Landing
Reighton
4 Filey Sands
Cayton Bay
Scarborough South Bay
Scarborough North Bay
5 Robin Hood's Bay
Whitby
6 Sandsend

Mablethorpe
Sutton-on-Sea
Moggs Eye
Anderby Creek
Chapel St Leonards
Ingoldmells
Skegness

Boston ■

f = failed to meet the EC standard for clean bathing water in 1988.
Numbered beaches are included in the following chapter.

The East Coast

Fabulous, spectacular, dramatic, remote, wild and mysterious have all been used to describe the East Coast. The beautiful sweeping bays of golden sand, unspoilt fishing villages and cliff-top castle ruins of Northumberland; the rugged cliffs and sandy crescents of Yorkshire; the magnificent chalk cliffs of Flamborough with mile upon mile of sand stretching south, backed by the fast retreating mud cliffs of Humberside; the everchanging sand banks of Lincolnshire. Unfortunately, less complimentary terms have also been used to describe parts of this coastline. Industry comes to the shore, with steel works, power stations, oil and chemical works. The coastal waters are used for dumping, sewage and industrial sludge. Waste from coal mines blackens the beaches of Tyne and Wear, Durham and Cleveland and smothers marine life. Sewage and industrial effluents are discharged and contaminate the waters, particularly around the Tyne and Tees. None of the beaches in the region totally escape the problem of marine litter.

Beaches monitored by the water authorities and found not to meet the minimum EC standard for clean bathing water in 1988:

Sutton-on-Sea, Cleethorpes, South Landing Flamborough, Saltburn-by-the-Sea, Seaton Carew, Crimdon Park, Seaham, Roker, Whitburn, Marsden, South Shields, Whitley Bay, Seaton Sluice, Blyth South Beach, Newbiggin-by-Sea and Spittal.

Beaches receiving Clean Beach Awards from the Tidy Britain Group in 1988:

Cleethorpes, Withernsea, Hornsea, Bridlington North and South, Scarborough South, Whitby, Filey, Seaton Carew, Crimdon Leisure Complex, Littlehaven Beach South Shields, Cullercoats and Tynemouth.

1 Hornsea, North Humberside   OS Ref: TA2047

From Barnston just south of Bridlington to the shingle of Spurn Point is the fastest eroding section of coastline in Britain. Tens of feet of the clay cliffs are lost annually. This makes access to the coastline difficult with the erosion of roads, paths and steps. Hornsea is one of the few places where there is a break in the cliffs and sea defences attempt to stop the advancing sea. A sea wall and promenade face the mile-long beach of sand and pebbles which virtually disappears when the tide rises. The beach is cleaned regularly. A park and various seaside amusements line the promenade. The quiet town of Hornsea is set back from the sea.

Water quality   Beach monitored by the water authority and found to meet the EC standard for clean bathing water in 1988. One outfall serving 10,500 people discharges screened and macerated sewage ⅔ mile (1km) below low water mark. One storm sewage overflow.

Bathing safety   Due to strong currents offshore, bathing is only safe close inshore. The central section of the beach is patrolled by lifeguards at weekends.

Access   Steps and ramp from promenade to sands.

Parking   Several car parks adjacent to the promenade.

Toilets   On promenade.

Food   3 cafés at central section of beach.

Seaside activities   Swimming, windsurfing, sailing and fishing. Golf course.

Wet weather alternatives   Hornsea Pottery with zoo and butterfly world just south of town. Museum of village life. Amusements.

Wildlife and walks   Hornsea Mere lies just south of the town. This 2 mile (3km) long lake is an RSPB reserve and its 5 acres (2 hectares) are an important wintering ground for wildfowl. There is a large population of reed

warblers to be found in the reed swamps. A public footpath along the south shore, through woods and open fields, provides good views of the area. There are boat launching facilities on the Mere.

2 Bridlington, North Humberside OS Ref: TA1866

'Good Old Brid' – a bustling holiday resort which won the English Tourist Board's title of Resort 2000 in 1986 and was awarded two Blue Flags in 1987 and two Clean Beach Awards in 1988. It combines the traditional seaside holiday entertainments with new up-to-date facilities, and there is easy access to the natural beauty of the adjacent Flamborough Head Heritage Coast. Two safe, sandy beaches are separated by Bridlington harbour; stone quays enclose a tidal harbour which is a continually changing scene of fishing and pleasure craft. The south beach extends for 5 miles (8km) with the busy promenade giving way to steep cliffs south of the town. North beach is the most popular for water sports as it is sheltered by the sheer white cliffs that sweep north to Flamborough Head.

Water quality Beach monitored by the water authority and found to meet the ECC standard for clean bathing water. One outfall at Bridlington South serving 50,000 people discharges screened sewage 1 mile (1.6km) below low water mark. Two storm water outfalls discharge storm overflow to the north beach at low water. There have been reports of solid sewage waste occasionally on the shore, probably resulting from these overflows.

Litter The beach is cleaned by the local council, but there are complaints about dog fouling.

Bathing safety Safe bathing.

Access Steps and ramps from Promenade.

Parking Sea front and adequate spaces within town.

Toilets On promenade.

Food Selection of cafés and restaurants along promenade.

Seaside activities Swimming, windsurfing, diving, fishing, sailing, water skiing and paragliding. Windsurfing and sailing facilities are available. Fishing tackle for hire and daily trips from the harbour.

Wet weather alternatives Old Town, Bayle Gate Museum, Harbour History Exhibition, Priory Church (organ recitals on Wednesdays during the season). Sewerby Hall (north of town, access by miniature train along cliffs). Leisure World – new water sports and entertainment complex. Amusement arcades.

Wildlife and walks There are cliff walks north and south of the town. For full details of the Flamborough Head Heritage Coast area, see the separate entry.

3 Flamborough Head, East Yorkshire   OS Ref: TA2270

Not a beach as such but a magnificent chalk headland with 300 feet (90m) vertical cliffs falling to the sea below. There are a series of sandy and rocky coves along the coastline and the area abounds in wildlife and geological interest. This stretch was defined as a Heritage Coast in 1979 because of its outstanding scenic quality. Thornwick Bay, North Landing, Selwicks Bay, South Landing and Danes' Dyke are all access points to the shore. It is not an area for swimming, but for sun bathing, exploring the rock pools below the cliffs, and enjoying the scenery. It cannot be beaten.

Water quality Both North and South Landing were monitored by the water authority, but only North Landing met the EC standard for clean bathing water in 1988.

Bathing safety Dangerous.

Access Paths or steps to each beach; difficult access at Selwicks Bay with steep descent to the shore.

Parking All beaches have car parks for between 100 and 200 cars.

Toilets All have toilets.

Food Cafés at North Landing, Selwicks Bay and Danes' Dyke.

Seaside activities Diving and fishing.

Wet weather alternative Sewerby Hall, Flamborough Head Lighthouse, Heritage Coast Information Centre (South Landing).

Wildlife and walks A network of footpaths rings the headland and provides views of the magnificent cliff scenery with natural arches, stacks and caves. There are nature trails at Danes' Dyke and at South Landing which include the rocky foreshore. There is a series of guided walks and full details of the trails and the walks are available from the Heritage Coast Information Centre at South Landing. The headland includes a variety of habitats that lead to an extensive range of wildlife and in particular bird life. There are cliffs, rocky shores, fields and woods. The cliffs at Bempton are an RSPB reserve, the only nesting site on mainland Britain for a gannet colony. Guillemots, razorbills, puffins, kittiwakes and fulmars can all be seen from the footpaths and observation platforms within the reserve.

4 Filey Sands, Filey, North Yorkshire   OS Ref: TA1180

5 miles (8km) of wide flat golden sands at Filey are sheltered by Filey Brigg, a rocky promontory that extends a mile (1.6km) out to sea. From the headland you can enjoy good views north to Scarborough and south to Flamborough Head. Below the gently sloping grass covered cliffs, the beach curves to the Coble Landing at the north end of the town. Traditional coble fishing boats are drawn up behind the protective wall and the fishermen are often seen busy

mending their nets. South of the landing a promenade and gardens face the beach which all but disappears at high tide. The Georgian residences of this elegant resort overlook the bay.

Water quality Beach monitored by water authority and found to meet the EC standard for clean bathing in 1988. 2 outfalls serve 2,500 people discharging macerated sewage 220 yards (200m) below low water mark.

Litter Cleaned regularly. Received Clean Beach Award from the Tidy Britain Group in 1988.

Bathing safety Bathing requires caution as there are strong cross currents.

Access Ramps at the southern end of the promenade and the Coble Landing lead onto the sand.

Parking There are 3 pay-and-display car parks at West Avenue (880 spaces), Station Avenue (280) and Country Park (3,000). There is street parking on the Promenade and on Church Hill.

Toilets 'Superloo' at Cargate, toilets at Coble Landing and Royal Parade.

Food Various kiosks and pub at Coble Landing, Margate Hill and Royal Parade.

Seaside activities Swimming, surfing, windsurfing, sailing, diving and fishing (very good off Filey Brigg; boats available for hire). Boating, putting and amusements. Edwardian Festival in June.

Wet weather alternatives Amusement arcades at Coble Landing, Filey Folk Museum, and shows at the Sun Lounge. Indoor swimming pool.

Wildlife and walks The Cleveland Way starts at Filey Brigg and follows the coast north to Redcar. The Wolds Way runs from Filey to the River Humber via the Wolds. There is a 70 acre (28 hectare) country park on the cliff top north of the town.

5 Robin Hood's Bay, North Yorkshire   OS Ref: NZ9505

A wide sweeping bay framed by crumbling red cliffs stretches from Ness Point and the village of Robin Hood's Bay south to the 600 foot (180m) headland of Old Peak with its scattered housing of Ravenscar. Magnificent views of the bay with its series of shingle and sand beaches can be obtained from the undulating farmland on the cliff top. There is a remnant cliff line inland. A 40 feet (12m) high sea wall protects the cluster of fishing cottages that make up Robin Hood's Bay village, famous for its ancient smuggling activities. Vehicle access to the older parts of the village is restricted and to get to the beach you have to park at the top of the hill and walk down through the village. Elsewhere there is limited access to the shore of this huge bay. Boggle Hole, where Mill Beck cuts through the cliffs, is a sheltered shingle and rock cove. Stoupe Beck Sands is an 875 yards (800m) stretch of sand in the middle of the bay. This area of the bay is very isolated with no facilities; the beach is reached by a paved track through a wooded valley. The headland at Ravenscar and the rocky shore below are owned by the National Trust and offer excellent views north along the coast. There is a National Trust information centre and shop.

Water quality Beach monitored by the water authority and found to meet the EC standard for clean bathing water in 1988.

Litter Very little litter, but there is often a lot of seaweed washed up that can cause a problem.

Bathing safety Safe bathing but beware of sharp rocks.

Access The main access to the beach is from Robin Hood's Bay village. There is a regular bus service to the village and parking above.

Parking Pay-and-display car park at the top of the hill.

Toilets By the beach.

Food Various cafés, kiosks and pubs.

Seaside activities Swimming, diving and fishing.

Wildlife and walks The area is famed for its geology and fossils – there is a geological trail from Ravenscar. The Cleveland Way follows the bay and there is a network of paths on the cliffs. There is much to interest the beachcomber with rock pools full of life.

6 Sandsend Wyke, Sandsend, N. Yorkshire   OS Ref: NZ8612

For those looking for a quieter beach than Whitby, try Sandsend Wyke at the opposite end of the bay. 2 miles (4km) of sand and pebble beach stretch north-west from Whitby to Sandsend. There is easy access from the road that runs parallel with the beach along the sea wall. Impressive grass and rocky cliffs rise on either side of the village.

Water quality Beach monitored by the water authority and found to meet the EC standard for clean bathing water in 1988. One outfall serves 450 people discharging raw sewage at low water mark.

Bathing safety Beware of strong currents and take care not to get cut off; the beach disappears at high tide.

Access From the A174 that runs parallel to the beach.

Parking Pay-and-display car park next to beach at Sandsend with 100 spaces; also private car park.

Toilets Adjacent to beach.

Food Ice cream kiosk, a few shops and a pub.

Seaside activities Swimming.

Wildlife and walks Two streams flow through a wooded valley at Sandsend, Mickleby Beck and East Row Beck where there are pleasant walks. The Cleveland Way runs along the shore and can be followed over the cliffs, along the line of a disused railway line passing a large alum quarry.

7 Runswick Bay, Runswick, North Yorkshire   OS Ref: NZ8016

From the picturesque hillside village of Runswick, the broad sandy beach backed by steeply sloping clay cliffs curves south-east to the rocky headland that bounds the bay. The crescent of sand gives way to rocky shore at either end. The old village of Runswick nestles at the base of the cliffs with a new one perched above. There is easy access to the beach and the area is not over commercialised although there are some beach huts and chalets on the scrub-covered cliffs. There are good views across the bay from the village of Kettleness on the southern headland.

Water quality Beach monitored by the water authority and found to meet the EC standard for clean bathing water in 1988. One outfall serving 480 people discharges raw sewage at low water mark.

Bathing safety Safe bathing.

Access Ramp to the beach.

Parking Pay-and-display at the bottom of the hill with 104 spaces.

Toilets By car park.

Food Cafés and shops in village.

Seaside activities Swimming, sailing and fishing.

Wildlife and walks The area is excellent for walking with the Cleveland Way skirting the bay. By following the route north for 2 miles (3km) you reach the tiny harbour of Mulgrave now falling into disrepair below the cliffs. Further north at the mouth of a tiny rocky inlet is Staithes Harbour. The village with its closely packed houses and network of alleyways nestles in the steep valley.

8 Druridge Bay, Cresswell, Northumberland   OS Ref: NZ2993

A 5 mile (8km) curving sweep of golden sand is fringed by dunes with rocky outcrops at either end, at Cresswell and Hadston Carrs. Cresswell is the easiest point of access and may be busy on a sunny afternoon, but a short walk along the shore will bring you to miles of quiet sand. There are views north along the bay to Coquet Island and its lighthouse. The bay is threatened by a proposed CEGB nuclear power station and an opencast mine at East Chevington.

Water quality Beach monitored by the water authority and found to meet the EC standard for clean bathing water in 1988. 1 outfall serves 5,500 people with macerated sewage discharged at low water mark.

Bathing safety Swimming with extreme caution as the tides and currents are strong and unpredictable.

Access A road from Ellington on the A1068 leads to Cresswell. It is a short walk from the car park across the dunes.

Parking Near Cresswell there is a car park with 100 spaces; at Cresswell Ponds there is space for 10 cars, and on Druridge Links a National Trust car park has 150 spaces.

Toilets In Cresswell village and at Druridge Country Park at the northern end of the bay.

Food Café in village, mobile ice cream vans.

Seaside activities Swimming, sailing and fishing.

Wildlife and walks At the northern end of the beach is Druridge Country Park. There are also nature reserves at Druridge and Hauxley. Cresswell Ponds have been designated as a Site of Special Scientific Interest. South of the bay is the sharply contrasting Lynemouth beach, blackened by coal dust washed from waste tips that line the beach.

9 Warkworth, Northumberland   OS Ref: NU2606

Between Warkworth Harbour at the mouth of the Coquet Estuary and the Aln Estuary there lies 3¾ miles (5.2km) of fabulous sandy beach. The beach, margined by sand dunes, extends northwards for 2 miles (3km) to merge with Alnmouth Links. The town of Amble lies on the southern banks of the estuary and here fishing cobles may be seen in the harbour and yachts moored in the river or at the Braid Marina — winner in 1987 and 1988 of a European Blue Flag for ports, awarded for environmental quality, and good facilities. Coquet Island lies one mile (1.6 km) offshore, sheltering the harbour entrance. The island is an RSPB reserve and boat trips are available from the harbour. The view back across the estuary, with the backdrop of Warkworth Castle, is most impressive. The near perfect mediaeval village of Warkworth, an idyllic spot with dramatic castle, Hermitage and unique fortified bridge, is set a mile inland and is almost enclosed by a meander of the river Coquet. Warkworth beach is signposted from here. The picnic site by the beach has panoramic views of the Coquet Estuary. There is access to Alnmouth Links south of Bilton on the A1068 but there is very limited parking behind the dunes.

Water quality Beach monitored by the water authority and found to meet the EC standard for clean bathing water in 1988. One outfall serving 8,000 people discharges screened and macerated sewage at Amble.

Litter Some marine litter and fishing debris is washed on to the beach.

Bathing safety Bathing is dangerous at high tide. There is an inshore rescue boat and coastguard station in the harbour.

Access North of Warkworth, a turning off the A1068 is signposted.

Parking Car park at picnic site with space for 50 cars.

Toilets In car park.

Food None. Tea rooms in village a mile away.

Seaside activities Swimming and golf course (Warkworth), river and sea fishing from Amble.

Wildlife and walks The picnic site and surrounding area at Warkworth beach is managed by the Northumberland National Park and the National Trust own the land to the north. A coastal path stretches the 3¾ (5.2km) from Warkworth to Alnmouth and is described in a leaflet available locally. A walk to the south takes you through dunes to the long breakwater serving Warkworth harbour and some interesting salt marshes which were designated as a Site of Special Scientific Interest in 1988. Coquet Island, with its prominent lighthouse, is frequented by colonies of breeding sea birds — puffins, terns and eider. These may be viewed from boat trips around the island organised by the RSPB and bookable at the Amble Tourist Information Office.

10 Alnmouth, Northumberland   OS Ref: NU2410

A sandy beach one mile (1.6km) long, winner of 1987 Clean Beach Award, stretches from the picturesque village of Alnmouth north to the Marsden Rocks. At low tide over a quarter of a mile (400m) of excellent sand is exposed. The beach is bordered by a large car park and golf course, behind which lies the village. Alnmouth was a port of some importance during the 18th century, but due to a change in the course of the river little can be seen of the old harbour. However, the old granaries have been carefully converted into pubs, shops, eating places and accommodation, retaining its unspoilt character.

Water quality   Beach monitored by the water autority and found to meet the EC standard for clean water in 1988. No sewage is discharged in the vicinity of the beach.

Bathing safety   There are dangerous currents at some states of the tide.

Litter   Little marine litter is washed on to the beach.

Access   Alnmouth is signposted off the A1068 south of Alnwick. A road through the golf course north of the village leads to the beach car park.

Parking   Parking for 150 cars 220 yards (200m) from the beach.

Toilets   In the village.

Food   Numerous cafés and restaurants in the village.

Seaside activities   Swimming, surfing, windsurfing, fishing and sailing in estuary. Two links golf courses north of village.

Wildlife and walks   There is an excellent coastal walk north from Alnmouth along the rocky shore with a series of small sandy bays to explore. Fulmars glide effortlessly along these cliffs where a wide range of sea birds can be seen. At Howick Haven you can either continue north along the low cliffs to the fishing village of Craster or turn inland following the wooded valley for a mile (1.6km) to the grounds of Howick Hall, where the gardens are open in summer.

11 Embleton Bay, Northumberland   OS Ref: NU2329

This scencially outstanding bay is bounded to the south by the craggy headland on which stand the dramatic ruins of Dunstanburgh Castle. The steep basalt cliffs are known as Gull Crag because of the numerous nesting sea birds, especially kittiwakes and fulmars. The excellent sandy Embleton beach, bordered by sand dunes and a golf course, stretches north from the boulder strewn shore below the Crag to merge with the Newton Haven beach at the northern end of the bay.

Water quality   No sewage is discharged on to the beach.

Litter   A clean beach; but with some marine debris washed up, particularly in winter.

Bathing safety Bathing is safe on the incoming tide; there are undercurrents on the ebbing tide.

Access From Embelton village on the B1339 follow the road leading to the Golf Course or Dunstan Steads Farm. A path leads directly on to the beach and connects with the coastal footpath.

Parking Roadside parking for approximately 100 cars.

Toilets In the village.

Food In the village.

Seaside activities Swimming.

Wildlife and walks This stretch of coastline is owned by the National Trust. There are excellent views across the bay from the Heritage Coast path to the south. The path continues along the rocky foreshore to Craster, a classic fishing village with miniature harbour, rows of neat cottages and the stone sheds where the world-famous Craster kippers are smoked.

12 Newton Haven, Northumberland OS Ref: NU2525

Newton Haven's half-mile (800m) crescent of dune-fringed sand lies at the northern end of Embleton Bay. Low tide exposes a wide beach which is fringed by dunes. Sheltered by a grass headland to the north and an offshore reef, the beach is popular for water sports. The beach is overlooked by the village of Low Newton, an attractive square of fishermen's cottages and a pub, now owned by the National Trust. Behind the dunes lies Newton Pool, a freshwater lagoon which is a nature reserve.

Water quality Beach monitored by the water authority and found to meet the EC standard for clean bathing water in 1988. There is no sewage discharged in the vicinity of this beach.

Litter Some oil drums and fishing debris are washed up, particularly in winter.

Bathing safety Bathing is safe on the incoming tide; there are undercurrents on the ebbing tide.

Access From the car park on the approach road to Low Newton, signposted off the B1339 from High Newton. It is a short walk down to the village with direct access to the beach. A path leads along Low Newton beach to Embleton Bay.

Parking There is a car park 300 yards (300m) from Low Newton and on the road sides with space for about 100 cars. Parking in the village is for residents and disabled badge holders only.

Toilets Adjacent to beach.

Food Pub with snacks and tea room in High Newton ⅔ of a mile (1km) away.

Seaside activities Swimming, windsurfing, sailing, diving, canoeing and fishing. Newton Sailing School provides tuition hourly or weekly and has dinghies, canoes and windsurfboards for hire.

Wildlife and walks There are bird hides at Newton Pool (one with disabled access) and a wide variety of species can be seen, particularly in winter. The Heritage Coast Path stretches south round Embleton Bay to Dunstanburgh Castle and north arouind Newton Point to the wide sweep of Newton Links and Beadnell Bay.

13 Beadnell Bay, Beadnell, Northumberland   OS Ref: NU2229

The golden sands of this superb dune-edged beach sweep south on a 2 mile (3km) long curve to the rocky outcrop of Snook Point. A stream meanders across the flat sands in the centre of the bay and to the south is a good area for collecting shells. At the northern end of the beach is the tiny harbour of Beadnell, still used by the traditional east coast fishing cobles. Standing on the quay are huge 18th century limestone kilns. These impressive structures have been restored and are owned by the National Trust.

Water quality Beach monitored by the water authority and found to meet the EC standard for clean bathing water in 1988. One outfall serving approximately 2,000 people discharges macerated and screened sewage at low water mark.

Litter A very clean beach.

Bathing safety Bathing is safe on the incoming tide; there are dangerous undercurrents on the ebb.

Access A road from the B1340 in Beadnell village leads to the harbour. Short walk from either car park to sand.

Parking Large car park at north end of bay near harbour with 200 spaces. Small car park at Newton Links at south end of bay with space for 30 cars.

Toilets In Beadnell car park.

Food Ice cream van at car park.

Seaside activities Swimming, windsurfing, sailing, diving, water skiing and canoeing. Outdoor sports hire centre at car park.

Wildlife and walks This stretch of coastline provides some splendid walking. To the south a path around the edge of the bay leads to Newton Haven, the lovely Embleton Bay and the romantic ruins of Dunstanburgh Castle. To the north, the rocky shore gives way to sand that stretches to Seahouses.

14 Bamburgh and Seahouses, Northumberland   OS Ref: NU1834

A 150 foot (45m) rock outcrop towers above beautiful long sandy beaches and provides the magnificent setting for Bamburgh Castle. From the castle rock there are spectacular views of the sandy beach stretching north to Holy Island and south to Seahouses. Seaward lies the panorama of the Farne Islands. Their rocky cliffs fall steeply to the water below. It was from the Longstone lighthouse on Outer Farne in 1838 that Grace Darling set off to rescue the crew of the stricken steamer 'Forfarshire'. The row that made her a national heroine is remembered in the Grace Darling Museum in Bamburgh. Today the trip to the Islands is made from the little harbour at Seahouses. Inland, Bamburgh village nestles below the castle among undulating fields. Between Bamburgh and Seahouses are 4 miles (6.5km) of super beach with sand which squeaks when walked over. Backed by the St Aidan's and Shoreston Dunes, the sands give way to rocky shore at Seahouses where the rock pools are full of marine life.

Water quality Both Bamburgh and Seahouses were monitored by the water authority and found to meet the EC standard for clean bathing water in 1988. 2 outfalls at Bamburgh: one serving approximately 1,000 people, discharges macerated sewage through the tidal tank at low water mark; the other serves 100 people and discharges untreated sewage at low water mark. One outfall at Seahouses serving 6,000 people discharges screened and macerated sewage through a tidal tank 110 yards (100m) below low water mark.

Litter A little wood, plastic and fishing debris is washed onto the beach. Litter is cleared by the National Trust. The beach is sometimes spotted with oil.

Bathing safety Bathing is safe only on the incoming tide due to undercurrents as the tide ebbs. Beware of offshore winds. Lifebelts are available at Seahouses.

Access There is access from both Bamburgh and Seahouses on the B1340, with easy access to beach across dunes.

Parking Bamburgh: Large car park in Bamburgh has over 200 spaces. 3 dune car parks with approximately 25 spaces in each, plus space for about 50 cars along the road above dunes.
Seahouses: Car park in village has 500+ spaces. Space for 30 cars parking on verge of B1340 north of Seahouses.

Bamburgh

Toilets In village.

Food Café and hotel in village, and ice cream vans on or near beach.

Seaside activities Swimming, surfing, windsurfing, diving, sailing and fishing.

Wet weather alternatives Castle, Grace Darling Museum and grave in village.

Seahouses

Toilets In village.

Food In village.

Seaside activities Swimming. Golf course. Amusements..

Wet weather alternative Marine Life Centre.

Wildlife and walks This fantastic section of coastline falls within the North-umberland Heritage Coast and is also designated an Area of Outstanding Natural Beauty. Below the lofty position of Bamburgh Castle, a walk north along the shore leads to Budle Bay. The saltmarsh, mud and sand flats are part of the Lindisfarne Nature Reserve which covers the whole of the Fenham Flats, Holy Island Sands and most of the Island itself. The area provides feeding for thousands of waders and wildfowl. It is dangerous to cross the sands; access to the island is by the causeway which is covered for at least 11 hours each day. With its Castle and Priory, the island is steeped in history and its distinctive conical shape leaves a lasting impression on the memory. The beaches around the island are wide and sandy but unsafe for swimming because of strong currents. The Farne Islands to the south of Holy Island are of international importance for their large colonies of sea birds and grey seals. The 30 islands that make up the Farnes are a National Trust Nature Reserve and landing is permitted on Inner Farne and Staple Island. Boats make the hour-long trip from the harbour at Seahouses in good weather. Further information about the service is available from the National Trust shop in Seahouses. Access is restricted during the bird breeding season from mid-May until mid-July.

15 Cocklawburn, Scremerston, Northumberland   OS Ref: NU0349

The retreating tide exposes rock pools in the rocks which bound this ⅔ mile (1km) long section of sandy beach. This is the accessible end of an extensive sandy beach which stretches south as Cheswick Sands towards Holy Island. The further south-east you venture along the beach, the quieter it becomes. Wide flat sands revealed at low tide join Holy Island with the mainland. They should not be crossed by foot, even at low tide – use the causeway road from Beal. The influence of man is much in evidence at the Cocklawburn beach with the remains of lime kilns and waste heaps on the edge of the beach. The modern activity of man imposes on the beach at times too, with the sound of trains from the railway line to Edinburgh which runs parallel with the shore.

Water quality One outfall serving 300 people discharges raw sewage 22 yards (20m) above the low water mark.

Bathing safety Safe bathing on the incoming tide; undercurrents on the ebbs tide and offshore winds make swimming dangerous.

Access Turning east from the village of Scremerston, a lane leads down to and then runs parallel with the shore. The beach is reached by a short walk through the dunes.

Parking Cars can be parked at several places along the lane on grassland behind the dunes. There is space for approximately 200 cars.

Toilets None.

Food None.

Seaside activities Swimming, surfing, windsurfing and fishing.

Wildlife and walks The dunes that margin the beach support excellent flora and an area at the southern end of the beach is a Northumberland Wildlife Trust Nature Reserve. The limestone outcrops are favoured by cowslips, cranesbills and vetches which add to the variety of plants to be found. A path north along the rocky shore leads to the mouth of the river Tweed where fishermen netting salmon can often be seen.

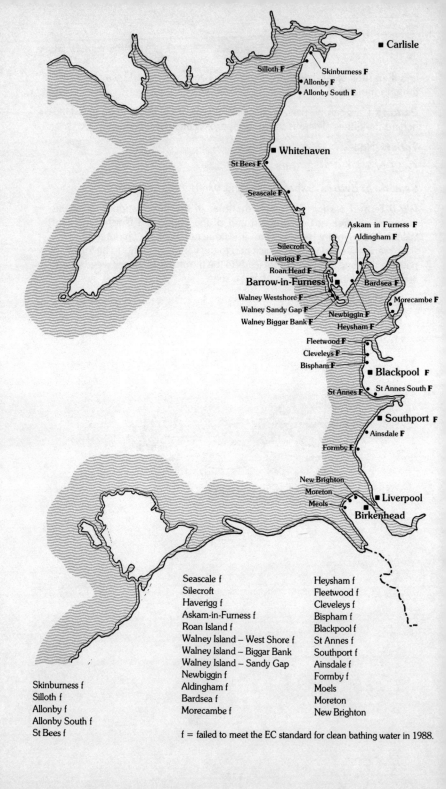

■ Carlisle

Silloth F   ■ Skinburness F
            • Allonby F
            • Allonby South F

■ Whitehaven

St Bees F •

Seascale F •

                    Askam in Furness F
                    Aldingham F
Silecroft
Haverigg F
Roan Head F
Barrow-in-Furness   Bardsea F
                                    Morecambe F
Walney Westshore F
Walney Sandy Gap F   Newbiggin F
Walney Biggar Bank F   Heysham F

            Fleetwood F
            Cleveleys F
Bispham F
                    ■ Blackpool F

St Annes F   • St Annes South F

                    ■ Southport F
            • Ainsdale F
Formby F •

      New Brighton
      Moreton
      Meols   ■ Liverpool
            Birkenhead

Seascale f   Heysham f
Silecroft   Fleetwood f
Haverigg f   Cleveleys f
Askam-in-Furness f   Bispham f
Roan Island f   Blackpool f
Walney Island – West Shore f St Annes f
Walney Island – Biggar Bank   Southport f
Walney Island – Sandy Gap   Ainsdale f
Newbiggin f   Formby f
Aldingham f   Moels
Bardsea f   Moreton
Morecambe f   New Brighton

Skinburness f
Silloth f
Allonby f
Allonby South f
St Bees f

f = failed to meet the EC standard for clean bathing water in 1988.

North-West England

The North-West does have some lovely stretches of coastline with much to offer the visitor. Bird watching on Morecambe Bay with the Lake District as a back drop; the traditional illuminations, pier and trams of Blackpool; the Victorian elegance of Southport and wide sandy beaches and dunes of Formby. Unfortunately, the whole region suffers from major pollution problems which affect nearly all its shores. The Irish Sea is heavily polluted, it is the most radioactive sea in the world and it is more chemically contaminated than the North Sea. The Mersey Estuary and Liverpool Bay are particularly badly affected. For example, 1.8 lb (4 kg) of mercury and cadmium, and 202 lb (450 kg) of lead are released into the bay each day, mostly from industrial and

contaminated sewage discharged to the Mersey and its tributaries. In addition, at least 1.5 million tonnes of sewage sludge and 3.5 million tonnes of dredged spoil (sediments dredged from the estuary usually contaminated with heavy metals and other persistent toxic chemicals) are dumped into Liverpool Bay each year.

Unsightly ribbons of foam are an ever-increasing phenomenon along the beaches of North Wales and the north-west. These result from excessive algal growth triggered by the very high nutrient inputs from sewage. Refuse dumped from the boats and ships which use the waterway is continually washed ashore. In 1988, only five of the designated Eurobeaches in the region complied with the EC standard for bathing water quality: Silecroft, Walney Island, Moels, Moreton and New Brighton. But with reports of litter and sewage problems even on these beaches, no beach from the north-west area is featured in the guide. Although some work is being undertaken to improve the situation, without more action it will be many years before there are significant improvements.

Beaches monitored by the water authority and found not to meet the minimum EC standard for bathing water cleanliness in 1988:

Skinburness, Silloth, Allonby, Allonby South, St Bees, Seascale, Haverigg, Askam-in-Furness, Roan Island, Walney West Shore, Newbiggin, Aldingham, Bardsea, Morecambe, Heysham, Fleetwood, Cleveleys, Bispham, Blackpool, St Annes, Southport, Ainsdale and Formby

Beaches receiving Clean Beach Awards from the Tidy Britain Group in 1988: Blackpool between the north and south piers, Fleetwood, Southport, Silloth on Solway.

Eyemouth
1 Coldingham
2 Pease Bay
Dunglass
Thortonloch
Whitesands
Belhaven
Dunbar East
Peffersands
Seacliff
Milsey Bay f
Yellowcraig
North Berwick f
Broadsands f
3 Gullane
Gosford
Longniddry
Fisherrow f
Portobello f
Silverknowes
Cramond
Aberdour Silversands
Burntisland
Pettycur
Kinghorn f
Leven – East
Leven – West f
Lundin Links
Lower Largo f
Largo
Shell Bay
4 Elie and Earlsferry
Pittenweem
Anstruther
Crail
St Andrews East f
5 St Andrews West
6 Tentsmuir Point
Broughty Ferry f
Monifieth f
Carnoustie
Arbroath f
7 Montrose
8 St Cyrus
9 Stonehaven
10 Muchalls
Aberdeen Ballroom
Aberdeen Footdee
Balmedie

11 Cruden Bay
Peterhead
12 Strathbeg
Fraserburgh f
Banff f
Inverboyndie Bay
13 Sandend
14 Cullen
Lossiemouth East f
Lossiemouth Silversands
15 Burghead
Nairn f
Invergorden f
Belleport Pier & boating jetty
16 Dornoch
17 Sinclair's Bay
18 Duncansby Head
Dunnet Bay f
Thurso
Sandside Bay
Farr Bay
19 Coldbackie
20 Balnakiel Bay
21 Sandwood
22 Scourie
23 Clashnessie Bay
24 Clachtoll
25 Achmelvich
26 Achnahaird
27 Achiltibuie
28 Gruinard Bay
29 Gairloch
30 Applecross
31 The Coral Beaches
32 Morar
33 Camusdarrach
34 Sanna Bay
35 Calgary Bay
36 Erraid
37 Machrihanish
38 Brodick Bay
39 Blackwaterfoot
Saltcoats f
Irvine f
Troon
Prestwick
Ayr f
Turnberry f
Girvan f
Sandyhills
40 Southerness

f = failed to meet the EC standard for clean bathing water in 1988.
Numbered beaches appear in the following chapter.

Scotland

If you are looking for a clean beach in Britain you are most likely to find one in Scotland. That is not to say that Scotland does not have problems around the coast. There are Scottish beaches that have failed to meet the EC bathing water quality standard. Sewage sludge is dumped off the Clyde, Forth and Tay Estuaries. Industrial waste is discharged into the Clyde and Forth. Nuclear installations at Chapelcross, Hunterston, Torness and Dounreay contribute to pollution of the sea. There is development of the coastline detrimental to scenic value. The West coast lochs are studded with the floating cages of the rapidly expanding fish farming industry. The offshore structures of the North Sea oil and gas industry that dot the horizon have resulted in the growth of onshore terminals. The view along the Cromarty Firth is dominated by a string of massive platforms. By contrast there is probably some of the most spectacular coastal scenery in the country, including the long sand dunes of the east coast, and the rocky shore of Fife with its series of picturesque fishing villages. There are also the cliffs and stacks of Caithness, and of course the west coast, Highlands and Islands, sea lochs, towering mountains and fantastic sunsets. There are hundreds (if not thousands) of beaches, tiny sandy bays, mostly remote, deserted and beautiful. Many can only be reached by the keen walker but without a doubt the effort is well worth while. The beaches that follow are relatively easily accessible for a day at the sea or as a starting point to explore the delights of this coastline further. The sands of the Western Isles have not been included in the section; if you take the boat to the outer islands, good beaches abound. If you are looking for peace and solitude combined with traditional hospitality then try Scotland.

Beaches monitored by the River Purification Boards and found not to meet the minimum EC standard for bathing water quality in 1988:
North Berwick, Milsey Bay, Fisherrow, Portobello, Kinghorn, Kirkcaldy, Leven West, Lower Largo, Broughty Ferry, Monifieth, St Andrews East, Arbroath, Fraserburgh, Banff, Lossiemouth East, Nairn East, Saltcoats, Irvine, Ayr, Turnberry and Girvan.

Beaches receiving Clean Beach Awards from the Tidy Britain Group in 1988:
Montrose, Aberdeen, Fraserburgh, Ayr, Girvan, Troon and Prestwick.

1 Coldingham, Berwickshire   OS Ref: NT9066

A half mile crescent of sand bounded by rocky outcrops below the headlands which shelter either end of the bay. A grass and shrub-covered bank backs the beach and from the top you obtain a good view of the whole beach. Old bathing huts edge the sands and the path leading down to the beach. To the north of the bay is the superb rocky coastline of St Abb's Head. The beach is cleaned by the local authority.

Water quality Beach monitored by the River Purification Board and found to meet the EC standard for clean bathing water in 1988. One outfall serving 200 people discharges raw sewage.

Bathing safety Unsafe bathing at times at each end of the beach. The beach is patrolled by lifeguards during the summer.

Access The B6438 from Coldingham leads to St Abb's, a side road leads to the bay. A 110 yard (100m) path runs parallel with the beach descending from the car park to the sands. There is a 15 minute walk to the beach from the village where buses are available.

Parking Car parking for 40+ vehicles adjacent to the hotel, 222 yards (200m) from the beach and in Coldingham village.

Toilets At the beach.

Food Café off path to beach.

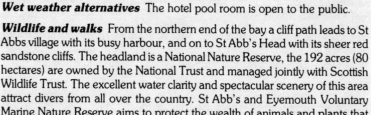

Seaside activities Swimming, diving, and fishing.

Wet weather alternatives The hotel pool room is open to the public.

Wildlife and walks From the northern end of the bay a cliff path leads to St Abbs village with its busy harbour, and on to St Abb's Head with its sheer red sandstone cliffs. The headland is a National Nature Reserve, the 192 acres (80 hectares) are owned by the National Trust and managed jointly with Scottish Wildlife Trust. The excellent water clarity and spectacular scenery of this area attract divers from all over the country. St Abb's and Eyemouth Voluntary Marine Nature Reserve aims to protect the wealth of animals and plants that abound in these waters. There are often conducted shore walks by the warden of the reserve during the summer months.

2 Pease Sands, Cockburns Path, Berwickshire   OS Ref: NT7971

The deep wooded valley of Pease Burn opens out onto the sandy cove of Pease Bay. Framed by red cliffs, a shrub and grass-covered bank fringes the landward side of the sands beyond which is a large caravan and mobile home park. ¾ mile (1.2km) of good sandy beach is very much dominated by the caravan site that rings the bay.

Water quality Beach monitored by the River Purification Board and found to meet the EC standard for clean bathing water in 1988. One outfall serving 1,000 people discharges secondary treated sewage.

Bathing safety Safe bathing.

Access A steep road from the A1107, just south of its junction with the A1, leads down to the bay.

Parking Car park with 100+ spaces directly off beach.

Toilets At car park.

Food Small shop adjacent to beach.

Seaside activities Swimming and fishing.

Wildlife and walks Good walks are available in Pease Dean. A cliff path can be followed north of the beach passing the tiny village and harbour of Cove and leading to the Dunglass Gorge.

3 Gullane, East Lothian   OS NT4882

This is an absolutely beautiful and completely unspoilt 1½ mile (2.5km) sweep of sandy beach. The extensive flat sands exposed at low tide are backed by Gullane Bents, a series of 15 foot (5m) high dune ridges behind which scrubland slopes up 68 feet (20m) to flat grassland. Here there is parking and a picnic area, overlooked by the houses of Gullane village. The curve of sand is bounded at either end by outcrops of black pillow lava. To the west of the bay is the Aberlady Nature Reserve and to the east there is a series of tiny sandy bays only accessible by foot along the coast path. Muirfield golf course overlooks this lovely bay and the view across the beach is frequently seen as a backdrop to televised tournaments.

Water quality Beach monitored by River Purification Board and found to meet the EC standard for clean bathing water in 1988. No outfall discharges in the vicinity of the beach.

Litter All litter is cleared daily in summer.

Bathing safety Bathing is safe from this beach which is patrolled by lifeguards.

Access The beach is signposted from Gullane village on the A198, there is a mile walk down through the dunes to the beach.

Parking Car park with 500 places on grassland behind Gullane Bents.

Toilets Block at centre of beach sign-posted 110 yards (110m) from the beach.

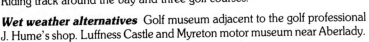

Food None, closest is in Gullane village.

Seaside activities Swimming and windsurfing. Riding track around the bay and three golf courses.

Wet weather alternatives Golf museum adjacent to the golf professional J. Hume's shop. Luffness Castle and Myreton motor museum near Aberlady.

Wildlife and walks The beach has a large lug worm population as evidenced by the casts left on the sand. Rock outcrops at either end of the beach contain pools rich in marine life including mussels, crabs, anemones and numerous snails. The rocks at the west end of the beach are covered in barnacles but very little seaweed. Inland the dunes are stabilised by marram grass and the dune slacks (areas between the sand ridges) have a rich and diverse vegetation. To the west of the beach lies the Aberlady Bay Nature Reserve. Its low dunes and salt marsh are a haven for birds, but access to the reserve is restricted at all times.

4 Elie and Earlsferry, Fife   OS Ref: NO4900

Elie and Earlsferry are typical of the East Fife coast with its series of small fishing villages. Charming whitewashed and orange-tiled cottages cluster around small sheltered harbours along this rocky coast. Once two separate communities on either side of this small bay, Elie and Earlsferry are now completely linked. They overlook sheltered beaches of red sand with a natural harbour quay to the east. At each extreme of the bay there are rocky outcrops.

Water quality Beach monitored by the River Purification Board and found to meet the EC standard for clean bathing water in 1988. Two outfalls serving

1,000 people discharge raw sewage at low water mark. New treatment facilities and outfall is under construction.

Bathing safety Safe bathing.

Access Lanes to beach.

Parking 120 spaces at the harbour.

Toilets At harbour and adjacent to the beach.

Food Pubs and cafés close to the beach.

Seaside activities Swimming, surfing, diving, windsurfing, sailing and fishing.

Wildlife and walks Walks west to Chapel Ness take you past the site of the chapel that gave the headland its name. There are excellent views back across the bay and seawards to Bass Rock, with North Berwick Law beyond. Continuing further west brings you to the caves at Kincraig Point and then to the wide sweeping sands of Largo Bay.

5 West Sands, St Andrews, Fife   OS Ref: NO5016

The extensive west sands are said to be the finest on the east coast of Scotland. They stretch a mile (1.6km) north of the town towards the mouth of the Eden estuary where a sand spit has developed. The gently sloping, but rather wind-swept beach is backed by low dunes and the fairways of the five golf courses that have made St Andrews famous as the home of golf. During the summer the beach is cleaned by the local authority three times a week, in winter once a week.

Water quality Beach monitored by the River Purification Board and found to meet the EC standard for clean bathing water in 1988. The east sands stretching south of St Andrews were also monitored but failed to meet the standard. One outfall serving 16,000 people discharges primary sewage at low water mark. Failure of the treatment works to meet the consent limit was due to build-up of sludge within the plant; we are informed that action is being taken to prevent this reoccurring.

Bathing safety Strong currents towards the river mouth make some areas of the west beach unsafe for swimming.

Access A road from the town runs parallel to the shore. There are car parks at each end of the beach and it is a short walk from them to the sands.

Parking Spaces for 1000 cars in two car parks one at each end of the beach.

Toilets Adjacent to the beach.

Food Ice cream kiosks, cafés and tea rooms close to beach.

Seaside activities Swimming, sand yachting, surfing, windsurfing and sailing. Windsurf boards are available for hire from the west beach. Five golf courses including the Royal and Ancient's Old and New courses make this the home of Scottish golf.

Wet weather alternatives The town of St Andrews with its castle, cathedral, university and wynds (narrow winding lanes) is a delight to explore.

Cathedral museum, Queen Mary's House, Crawford Arts Centre, Sea Life Centre, Leisure Centre, theatres and cinemas. There are guided tours of the university during the summer.

Wildlife and walks Following the cliff path south-east of the town takes you along the St Andrews coastal walk, passing shingle bays and rocky coves. The walk continues as far as Crail via Fife Ness headland. Extreme care is required on some sections of the path which are eroded.

6 Tentsmuir Point, Tayport, Fife   OS Ref: NO5024

A large area of the extensive sand dunes north of the Eden Estuary dunes has been stabilised by the conifers planted in the 1920s by the Forestry Commission. The coastline can still be reached along roads cut through the forest giving access to parking and picnic areas beyond the forest. A wild and remote spot with a wide flat sandy beach backed by high sand dunes which are continually moving seawards.

Water quality No sewage is discharged in the vicinity of this beach. The beaches at the mouth of the Tay failed to comply with the EC bathing water quality standard in 1988 and poor water quality from the estuary may affect this beach.

Bathing safety Beware of offshore currents.

Access A turning off the road north-east of Leuchars leads to the forest. There are paths to the beach from the car park.

Parking Forestry Commission car park behind dunes.

Toilets At the car park.

Food None.

Seaside activities Swimming.

Wildlife and walks A large area of the shore, including dunes and developing scrub woodland, is a National Nature Reserve. There is a ranger service based at the car park where a nature trail commences. Wildlife is abundant. The area is a feeding ground for numerous waders and wildfowl and there is a rich vegetation. This is an excellent spot for walking with views across the offshore sand banks and away north across to the Tayside coast.

7 Montrose Links, Montrose, Tayside   OS Ref: NO7358

From the mouth of the South Esk 4 miles (6.5km) of magnificent beach stretches north to the mouth of the North Esk. At low tide there is 200 yards (200m) of firm clean sands backed by a 30 feet (9m) high dune ridge. Access is from the southern end of the beach where the delightful little town of Montrose is separated from the beach by 2 links golf courses. At the entrance a stretch of sea wall edges the beach, protecting the car park and facilities 20 feet (6m) above. On a beach with so much space there should never be an overcrowding problem, and the further north you walk along it the quieter it should be. The beach received a Clean Beach Award from the Tidy Britain Group in 1988.

Water quality Beach monitored by the River Purification Board and found to meet the EC standard for clean bathing water in 1988. An outfall serving 8,000 people discharges macerated sewage at low water mark, another serving 6,000 people discharges untreated sewage at low water mark.

Litter The beach is cleaned regularly by the local authority.

Bathing safety Safe bathing except near the river mouths at each end of the beach. Lifeguards patrol the beach during the summer.

Access The beach is signposted from the A92. A road through the golf course leads to car parks at the south end of the beach. Steps lead down onto the sands.

Parking 2 car parks adjacent to beach with approximately 350 spaces.

Toilets At the car park.

Food Café at the car park.

Seaside activities Swimming, windsurfing and fishing. Children's amusement play area. Small amusement arcade.

Wet weather alternatives Museum, amusement arcade.

Wildlife and walks The whole area is a nature reserve. Low tide reveals extensive mud flats which are an important feeding ground for wintering birds.

8 St Cyrus, Grampian   OS Ref: NO7565

From the cliff-top path at St Cyrus there is a superb view along this lovely beach that forms the northern half of Montrose Bay. Below the steeply sloping lava cliffs of Milton Ness, 2 miles (4km) of golden sand sweep south to the mouth of the River Esk. The cliffs retreat slightly inland and there is a ridge of dunes at their base which gives way to salt marsh close to the river. The cliffs, dunes and beach fall within the St Cyrus Nature Reserve and this has ensured that the beach remains natural and undeveloped.

Water quality Montrose at the southern end of the bay was monitored by the River Purification Board and found to meet the EC standard for clean bathing water in 1988. One outfall serving 820 people discharges macerated sewage at low water mark.

Bathing safety Bathing is safe away from the river mouth at the southern end of the beach. Beware of rocks at the northern end of the bay.

Access The main entry to the beach is at St Cyrus on the A92 where there is a car park with a paved pathway leading along the cliff top. There is also access to the southern end via a side road from the A92 which leads to parking at

Nether Warburton where board walks cross the salt marsh to the dunes.

Parking Car parks at St Cyrus and Nether Warburton.

Toilets None.

Food None.

Seaside activities Swimming.

Wildlife and walks The whole beach forms part of the St Cyrus National Nature Reserve. The reserve with its cliffs, dunes, salt marsh and beach contains a wide range of wildlife. Over 300 wild flower species have been recorded and 47 bird species are said to breed here, with many more visiting species. Grey seals can be seen off shore, as well as traditional salmon netting at the river mouth. Walks along the cliff tops provide wonderful views over Montrose Bay.

9 Stonehaven, Grampian OS Ref: NO8786

At a break in the rugged sandstone cliffs at Stonehaven the waters of Cowie and Carron flow to the sea. Nestling between the Downie and Garron headlands, Stonehaven retains the atmosphere of a traditional fishing village, its quaysides busy with boats. The fishing has declined but the twin-basin harbour is used by pleasure craft in summer. A ¾ mile (1km) sand and pebble beach curves away north of the harbour below the rolling farmland rising beyond the town. The beach is not popular for swimming but often busy with people taking advantage of the promenade facilities. Steep 200 feet (60m) cliffs rise on either side of the bay and offer excellent walking with splendid views over the cliffs and Stonehaven Bay.

Water quality Beach monitored by the River Purification Board and found to meet the EC standard for clean bathing water in 1988. A new outfall was built in 1987.

Bathing safety Some currents can make swimming dangerous.

Access From promenade.

Parking Ample on seafront and adjacent to the leisure centre.

Toilets On seafront.

Food Café.

Seaside activities Swimming and windsurfing. Sailing, diving and fishing trips from the adjacent harbour. Cliff-top golf course. Open air heated swimming pool and leisure centre.

Wet weather alternatives Dunnottar Castle, Tolbooth museum of local history, indoor pool and leisure centre, amusement arcades.

Wildlife and walks The promenade leads north to the fishing village of Cowie. North from Cowie, a grass cliff path beside the golf course provides glorious sea views across Stonehaven Bay. 2 miles (3km) along the cliff-top is a steep valley which leads down to two secluded pebbly coves at Skatie Shore. South from Stonehaven, a mile (1.6km) walk along the cliffs leads to the War Memorial giving panoramic views of the coast and inland. Continuing south for 2 miles (3km), the path leads to Dunnottar Castle. This impressive castle stands on an isolated sandstone cliff 170 feet (50m) above the sea. The connection between the castle rock and mainland was cut through to allow easier defence. A further 4 miles (6.5km) south lies the Fowlsheugh Bird Reserve, one of the largest bird colonies with 2 miles (3km) of cliff providing a home to thousands of birds. Parking at Crawton village provides easy access.

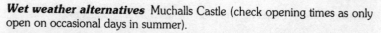

10 Muchalls, Nr Stonehaven, Grampian   OS Ref: NO9292

This is a spectacular stretch of coastline whose rock formations include stacks, arches and caves with an underground waterfall. There are several rock and pebble coves below the steep cliffs but take care as some are cut off at high tide with no escape routes. Swimming is out of the question due to dangerous rocks offshore. The cliff-top scenery, interesting coves and rock pools make the area worth a visit.

Water quality No outfalls discharge in the vicinity of the beach.

Bathing safety There are unsafe rocks off shore.

Access There are two access routes. One is a very steep path; the other is a road down from Muchalls village under the railway to the shore.

Parking In village.

Toilets None.

Food Pub and hotel in village.

Seaside activities Fishing.

Wet weather alternatives Muchalls Castle (check opening times as only open on occasional days in summer).

Wildlife and walks A cliff-top path gives fine views of the cliff formations to the north and the numerous nesting sea birds that frequent the rocky ledges. Rock pools on the shore contain a wealth of interest for the beach walker but remember to keep an eye on the tide.

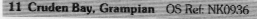

11 Cruden Bay, Grampian   OS Ref: NK0936

The red granite cliffs of Buchan are very impressive. Predominantly steep and rocky, they form a series of holes, stacks and rocky inlets. The largest indent is Cruden Bay where the cliffs give way to a 2 mile (3km) sandy beach fringed by dunes and golf links. On the low headland at the northern end of the beach is the village of Cruden Bay and Port Erroll with its small harbour. The waters of Cruden flow across the northern end of the bay separating the harbour from the beach. Cruden is an excellent spot to combine a coastal walk with relaxation on the sands. Along this stretch of coast, debris from fishing boats and oil and gas supply boats causes litter problems. The beach is cleaned by the local authority.

Water quality Beach monitored by the River Purification Board and found to meet the EC standard for clean bathing water in 1988. 1 outfall serving 2,200 people discharges macerated sewage some way from the beach.

Bathing safety There are some currents, therefore bathing with care is advised.

Access There is parking in Cruden village, signposted off the A975 and a bridge leads on to the beach.

Parking There is a car park with 50–60 places.

Toilets In village at north end of the beach.

Food Café and shops in the village.

Seaside activities Swimming, windsurfing, sailing, diving and fishing. Championship golf course.

Wildlife and walks The route north of the bay passes the ruins of Slains Castle above the original harbour of Cruden and follows the cliffs to the village of Bullers of Buchan. The path follows the edge of a narrow inlet with a sheer 100 feet (30m) drop to the water below. The precipitous drops along the route mean that great care is needed when using this path; don't take small children on this route. South of the bay a cliff-top walk leads to the ruins of Old Slains Castle 3¾ miles (6km) away. The cliff ledges provide nesting sites for thousands of sea birds. To the north of Bullers of Buchan, the cliffs are a Scottish Wildlife Trust nature reserve, where herring gulls, greater and lesser black backed gulls, kittiwakes and guillemots can be seen.

12 Strathbeg Bay, Grampian   OS Ref: NK0663

This little-frequented beach has 3¾ miles (6km) of sand and substantial dunes stretching from the rocky Cairnbulg Point south, past the fishing villages of Inverallochy and St Combs to Rattray Head. This beach is not particularly scenic, but if you seek solitude on a remote and peaceful beach the wind-swept sands of Rattray should meet your requirements. The lighthouse off the headland indicates the presence of a reef which causes swift currents and makes swimming dangerous. To the south of Rattray Head, a further 7 miles (11km) of deserted sandy beach stretches to Peterhead, but the shore is dominated by the St Fergus gas terminal.

Water quality No sewage is discharged in the vicinity of this beach.

Litter Marine litter is frequently washed onto the shore.

Bathing safety Care is required as the currents off Rattray Head are dangerous.

Access There is a path through the dunes at St Combs, off the B9033 south east of Fraserburgh and another at Rattray Head, reached via a road off the A952 south of Crimmond.

Parking There is a car park at St Combs and very limited parking at Rattray Head.

Toilets None.

Food None.

Seaside activities Swimming, sailing, diving and fishing.

Wildlife and walks The Loch of Strathbeg RSPB reserve lies just behind the dunes. It is the largest dune slack pool in Britain and an important site for wintering wildfowl. Admission is by permit only, available from the warden.

13 Sandend, Grampian   OS Ref: NJ5566

From Fraserburgh to Inverness is a stretch of coast known as the Banffshire Riviera. It is characterised by towering cliffs, small sheltered sandy bays and fishing villages. Clear waters wash this most attractive sandy beach. ⅔ mile (1km) of dunes fringe the beach landwards and the bay is framed by high cliffs.

Water quality No sewage is discharged in the vicinity of the beach.

Bathing safety Heavy surf on occasions.

Access Sandend is signposted off the A98, it is a short walk from the car park to the beach.

Parking Car park with 100 spaces.

Toilets Public conveniences in village.

Food Small shop and restaurant.

Seaside activities Swimming, surfing, windsurfing, sailing, diving and fishing.

Wildlife and fishing East of the bay the coast path climbs over the cliffs on to the headland which offers excellent sea and coastal views. The path continues to Portsoy, a charming fishing village with a small harbour which has won awards for its architectural restoration. West of Sandend the cliff path can be followed to the ruins of Findlater Castle with its impressive position 165 feet (50m) above the waves. Below the ruins is the lovely secluded Sunnyside Beach, its sweep of golden sand nestling below the steep cliffs.

14 Cullen Sands, Cullen, Grampian OS Ref: NJ5167

The dipping Cullen quartzites form a spectacular rocky coastline and create the extremely scenic Cullen Bay. From the curving quays of the harbour, sheltering below the cliffs at the eastern end of the bay, an arc of rock-studded sand sweeps west to the isolated stacks known as the Three Kings. Beyond, the Boar's Craig rises and the sands give way to rocks below the cliffs of Portknockie headland. Here there are caves, known as the Preacher's and the Whale's Mouth, to explore and numerous rock pools to investigate. Hire a deck chair and relax, or stretch your legs to enjoy the wonderful scenery around the bay. The railway once passed through Cullen but all that remains is a series of graceful viaducts. They separate the narrow streets of Seatown that cluster around the harbour from the upper town with its open square and wider streets.

Water quality Beach monitored by the River Purification Board and found to meet the EC standard for clean bathing water in 1988. One outfall serving 1,500 people discharges sewage below low water mark.

Bathing safety There are strong cross tides so care is required when bathing.

Access From Seatown and from the road to the golf course.

Parking Car park close to harbour.

Toilets Public toilets at the harbour are open all year.

Food Tea room, café and hotel in Seatown.

Seaside activities Swimming. Bathing huts and deck chairs for hire. Putting, bowls, tennis and a golf course. Sea-angling and boat trips from the harbour.

Wildlife and walks From the harbour a path leads east along the shore to the excellent sandy cove of Sunnyside Bay. The path climbs to the cliff top and continues to Findlater Castle, a 15th century ruined castle sitting on a rocky promontory 165 feet (50m) above the sea. A return journey can be made along the cliff top, giving excellent views along the coast and across to Sutherland and Caithness. Alternatively you may head east to Sandend Bay, another of the lovely coves along this coastline complete with its own small harbour. West from Cullen there is a well marked path alongside the golf course. The path leads up from the rocky shore to the quiet fishing village of Portknockie on the cliff top. There are superb views of this magnificent rocky coast; just off-shore lies Bow Fiddle rock, where erosion of the dipping rock strata has produced an arch resembling a violinist's bow. Further west from Portknockie the cliff path leads to Findochty with its sheltered sandy cove and harbour; there are superb views of the Moray Firth and Black Isle.

15 Burghead Bay, Burghead, Grampian   OS Ref: NJ1169

The solid fishing cottages that make up Burghead stand on a low rocky promontory overlooking the 6 mile (10km) curve of Burghead Bay. At the western end of these long flat sands is Findhorn, situated at the mouth of the large, tidal Findhorn Bay. The quiet but somewhat windswept beach of fine sand and pebbles is rimmed by dunes, on which there is a Forestry Commission conifer plantation. A road has been made through the mature pines and there are parking and picnic facilities. Wartime concrete defences once stood on grassland well back from the beach, but the retreating beach means that they now stand on the tidal sands.

Water quality No significant sewage discharges in the vicinity of the beach.

Bathing safety There are strong currents at the western end where the River Findhorn flows out of Findhorn Bay. Bathing is not recommended in the bay but is safe from the beach of Burghead.

Access At either end of the bay at Findhorn or Burghead and also by paths from Roseisle Forest.

Parking At Findhorn dunes and picnic site, Roseisle Forest picnic site and at Burghead.

Toilets At Findhorn and Roseisle picnic sites (including disabled facilities). Public toilets at the harbour in Burghead.

Food Pubs, hotels and fish and chips available at Findhorn and Burghead. Wholefood café at Findhorn Bay Caravan Park.

Seaside activities Swimming, diving, fishing, windsurfing and waterskiing. The bay is a sailing centre with racing throughout the summer. Rowing, sailing and motor boats are available for hire at Burghead, also sea-angling trips from the harbour.

Wet weather alternatives Forres Museum, Burghead Well and local history museum. Findhorn Foundation (a spiritual community based southeast of Findhorn village. They run a craft shop and take conducted tours during the summer).

Wildlife and walks There is a walk from Burghead to Findhorn along the shore, where rock and sand pools contain a variety of marine life. 1 miles (3km) south-west of Burghead is the Forestry Commission Roseisle Forest. Pathways from the beach lead to glades in the Corsican and Scots pines planted in the 1930s. Continuing along the shore the walk leads on to the Findhorn peninsula where the extensive tidal bay provides excellent birdwatching.

16 Dornoch, Highland   OS Ref: NH7989

The excellent Royal Dornoch Links golf course attracts many visiting players but the lovely sandy beach remains quiet and uncommercialised. The approach to the beach from Dornoch is unassuming; the low lying lands do not permit any view of the beach until you cross the dunes. To the south of the beach is the entrance to the Dornoch Firth which stretches almost 20 miles (32km) inland. The 330 yard (300m) wide sands stretch 3 miles (5km) north narrowing towards Loch Fleet, a small sea-loch. There is access to the beach from the village of Dornoch, and at the northern end at Embo. Further north in Sutherland the main A9 hugs the shore which is only a ribbon of sand.

Water quality Sewage is treated by septic tank and discharged at Blackburn away from the beach.

Bathing safety There are currents at the north and southern ends of the beach; safe bathing in the main bay at Dornoch.

Access One road from the Square in Dornoch leads to the shore and golf courses, another takes you to Embo; there is a short walk across dunes to the sand.

Parking Dornoch: Two car parks, one overlooking the sea with spaces for 20 cars, the other close by has a further 20 spaces. Embo: car park with 25 spaces.

Toilets New toilet block at caravan site backing beach.

Food None (At Embo: Grannie's Helian Hame Café and fish and chip shop – seasonal).

Seaside activities Swimming. Royal Dornoch Golf Course, local pipe band parade during the summer and Highland Games during August.

Wet weather alternatives Dornoch Cathedral. Local social club is open for supervised games during the season.

Wildlife and walks Loch Fleet, a sea-loch at the northern end of the beach, is the last of the Firth indents into this coastline going north. The loch and the Alderwoods behind the mound embankment are nature reserves which contain a wide variety of wildlife. The Scottish Wildlife Trust Reserve Warden runs a series of guided walks during the summer. These include an exploration of the woodland and estuary or the sand dunes and sea shore. Otherwise, access to the reserve is restricted. In the nearby Skelbo Wood, the Forestry Commission has laid out several forest trails; the walks start from the Commission's car park off the B9168.

17 Sinclair's Bay, Wick, Highland   OS Ref: NO3561

There are only two breaks in the high sandstone cliffs of the eastern coast of Caithness, Freswick and Sinclair's Bay. The huge indent of Sinclair's Bay is by far the more attractive: 4 miles (6.4km) of sandy beach are backed by impressive dunes. At the southern end of the bay the sand gives way to a rocky shore backed by the craggy sandstone cliffs of Noss Head. The ruins of Castle Girnigoe and Castle Sinclair seem almost to grow directly out of the cliffs. A road from Wick leads to the castles where the prospect across the bay and north along the cliffs towards Duncansby Head is outstanding. Unfortunately, as with many locations on the east coast of Scotland, the oil industry impinges on the shore. Part of the bay is used for the welding of oil pipes. This is not evident from the Keiss end of the bay where there is parking and an easy walk down to the sands. Below the dunes 10 yards (10m) of large stones and cobbles stretch down to the large sandy beach.

Water quality Monitored by the River Purification Board and found to meet the EC standard for clean bathing water in 1988. Three outfalls, each serving between 200-250 people; only one discharging treated sewage.

Litter Complaints about litter problems on the land adjacent to the beach have been received.

Bathing safety Bathing with care as there can be strong currents.

Access From the car park at Keiss, on the A9 north of Wick, there is a short walk to the beach down gentle steps.

Parking Car park adjacent to Keiss Golf Course with approximately 40 spaces.

Toilets None.

Food None.

Seaside activities Swimming, horse riding and jogging.

Wildlife and walks Seals and porpoises can often be seen in the bay. A steep path from the castles on Noss Head leads down to the rocky shore where there are rock pools to explore.

18 Duncansby Head, John o'Groats, Highland   OS Ref: ND4173

Travellers taking the A9 north beyond Inverness are normally heading for John o'Groats as the most northerly point. Not to be missed is Duncansby Head, without doubt one of the finest stretches of coastline in Britain. The road from John o'Groats takes you to the Duncansby lighthouse. From the small car park the view to the Orkney islands is hard to beat. On a clear day the panorama laid out before you can be breathtaking. Just offshore beyond the white foaming waters are the Pentland Skerries and Stroma, on which you can see many abandoned dwellings. Beyond these, Swona, South Ronaldsay, Hoy and the mainland of Orkney complete the picture. Tucked below the headland, just off the lighthouse approach road, is a tiny beach. A mere 100 yards (100m) in length, the narrow strip of sand is shadowed by the red sandstone of the headland. A delightful spot, this may not be the beach to seek out for a day by the sea, but after enjoying a stroll in the headland, relax a while and watch the seals that bob around offshore. This is one of many little beaches along the north coast between the Duncansby and Dunnet headlands, although most are difficult to get to and are not as attractive, lacking the backdrop of sheer red cliffs.

Water quality No sewage is discharged in the vicinity of this beach.

Bathing safety The beach shelves steeply and swimming is dangerous.

Access Duncansby Head is signposted from the A9 south of John o'Groats. A short walk from the parking area down the hill across turf leads on to the sands.

Parking Car park at Duncansby Lighthouse with approximately 25 spaces.

Toilets None.

Food None.

Wildlife and walks A short walk over the headland passes a narrow inlet or geo whose cliff walls rise nearly 200 feet (60m) above the waves. A short distance further and you are rewarded with the marvellous view of Duncansby Stacks, their steeple-like outlines pointing skywards. These are also known as Muckle Stack. Boat trips around this stretch of coast are available from John o'Groats.

19 Coldbackie, Tongue, Highland   OS Ref: NC6160

The half-moon of Coldbackie Sands faces Tongue Bay at the mouth of the Kyle of Tongue, one of the three deep indents into the north coast. The undulating turf-covered moorland which dominates this corner of Scotland, slopes down to the grass-covered dunes which flank the beach. Below Meall Mor, a round hill which shadows the western side of the beach, low grass-covered cliffs flank the beach. From the road above the beach a bank of dunes descends to the sands.

Water quality *No sewage is discharged in the vicinity of this beach.*

Bathing safety Safe bathing.

Access From the A836 north of Tongue, banks of dunes descend to the beach. There is no proper footpath but it is an easy walk down to the sand.

Parking There is limited car parking in a layby off the main road above the beach.

Toilets None.

Food None.

Seaside activities Swimming.

Wildlife and walks The 1000 feet (300m) peaks of Cnoc an Fhreiceadan and Ben Tongue rise behind the beach. From the road a footpath inland skirts the sides of the hills, passing a tiny loch to reach Tongue and the shores of the Kyle.

20 Balnakeil Bay, Durness, Highland   OS Ref: NC3869

There are in fact three beaches at Durness all worthy of note. All three have clean white sands, are unspoilt and are quiet, even at the height of summer. To the east of Faraid Head Peninsula, below the steep limestone cliffs on which Durness stands, are the twin beaches of Sango Bay and Sangobeg. The best beach, however, is on the western side of the peninsula, Balnakeil Bay, a long curve of white sand and dunes. There is easy access at the southern end of the beach close to the ruined Balnakeil church. The extensive wind-sculptured dunes stretch north along the low rugged headland. The bare and treeless landscape is dominated by wild windswept moorland. It is in sharp contrast to the coastline made up of warm red sandstone cliffs, folded and faulted limestone, collapsed caverns, geos, rocky shores and sandy bays.

Water quality No sewage is discharged in the vicinity of the beach.

Bathing safety Safe bathing although in this part of the country some might find it rather cold.

Access The road from Durness village leads to a car park behind the beach, and from here an easy path leads to the sand.

Parking Car park with 30 spaces.

Toilets Portaloo at car park.

Food None.

Seaside activities Swimming.

Wet weather alternatives ½ mile (800m) inland is a craft village in the building of a disused early warning station. The workshops are open to the public during the summer months.

Wildlife and walks There are walks on the cliffs surrounding the bay, with much evidence of 1000 years of human activity, including slight remains of an ancient fortress on the Faraid Headland. Steps lead down from Durness village to the beach at Sango Bay where the high arched entrance to the Smoo Cave can be found. The Allt (river) Smoo flows from the cave and the first of the three chambers can be entered. The Highland Regional Ranger Service organises guided walks in the area, and further information can be obtained-from the information centre in Durness. The remote north-western tip of Scotland, Cape Wrath, can be reached by a small ferry across the Kyle of Durness followed by a minibus service to the Cape. The bus takes you across the wild moorland to the Cape Wrath Lighthouse and there is fantastic cliff scenery along this most isolated stretch of coastline. The most spectacular cliffs are along the northern coast, where in places the sheer cliffs fall 800 ft (250m) to the waters below.

21 Sandwood Bay, Highland OS Ref: NC2364

Sandwood Bay must be one of the most remote beaches in Britain, but equally one of the most magnificent. Lying on the west coast of Scotland between Kinlochbervie and Cape Wrath, a 4 mile (7km) walk from Blairmore brings you to this outstanding beach with its huge sand dunes and gently sloping pink sands, studded with rock outcrops. Towering sandstone cliffs extend away on either side of the bay, and to the west is a most impressive rock stack. For those who do not want to venture to such an isolated and exposed beach, there are a series of pocket-handkerchief-sized sandy beaches that surround Blairmore, the starting point for the walk to Sandwood.

Water quality No sewage is discharged in the vicinity of this beach.

Bathing safety Very dangerous.

Access The B801 leads along Loch Inchard to Kinlochbervie, and beyond this a steep and twisting road continues to Sheigra. Sandwood can only be reached on foot, 4 miles (7 km) along the track which turns off the road between Blairmore and Sheigra.

Parking Limited parking at Blairmore.

Toilets None.

Food None.

Wildlife and walks The walk to Sandwood crosses the peat moorland of Sutherland before making a steep descent to the bay. This area is both wild and beautiful, but anyone thinking of walking here should be fully aware of the dangers of this remote and difficult terrain. Only those completely prepared should undertake the trip.

22 Scourie, Highland OS Ref: NC1544

Unlike most of the crofting villages along the west coast, Scourie has some facilities to cater for the visitor. It boasts two hotels, a shop, a post office and a camp site, thus enabling the tourist to stop a while and enjoy this most picturesque district. Scourie is set at the head of a 1 mile (1.5km) rocky inlet, on the banks of a small river draining from a loch a short distance inland. There is a lovely sheltered beach on the southern flank of the bay. The wide, gently sloping sands are backed by a narrow storm beach, where small boulders and pebbles edge the sand. The irregular hummocks of this grey-green rocky landscape come down to the water's edge in the outer bay. This exposed rocky coast is coloured by bands of lichens and encrusted with barnacles and seaweed below high water mark, where there are many rock pools to explore. This is a deservedly popular spot.

Water quality Monitored by the River Purification Board and found to meet the EC standard for clean bathing water in 1988. Two outfalls, each serving 100-200 people, discharge primary treated sewage.

Bathing safety Safe bathing.

Access There are gently sloping grass slopes down to the sand.

Parking Parking space available adjacent to the beach.

Toilets In village.

Food Hotel and shop in village.

Seaside activities Swimming.

Wildlife and walks A stroll around the loch, village and its quayside can be a most pleasant way to spend an afternoon. Alternatively follow the path north of the bay to Tarbet. Handa Island, lying just across the South of Handa, is an RSPB reserve. The numerous ledges on its vertical cliffs provide nesting sites for thousands of sea-birds including guillemots, kittiwakes and fulmars. The island can be visited by boat from Tarbet daily, except Sunday, from April to August.

23 Clashnessie Bay, Lochinver, Highland   OS Ref: NC0631

Steep rocky cliffs, wide bays dotted with tiny islands, clean clear waters, beautiful sunsets, sea birds and seals: the perfect ingredients to make a good beach. Clashnessie is an attractive and safe beach. The 660 yards (600m) of gently sloping pink sands are framed by red sandstone cliffs. There are superb views north towards Oldany Island and east along the rugged cliffs of the Stoer Peninsula.

Water quality No sewage is discharged in the vicinity of the beach.

Bathing safety Safe bathing.

Access A side road from the B869 at Clashnessie leads down to the shore, and then there is a short walk down to the beach.

Parking Car park at beach with 10-15 spaces.

Toilets None.

Food None.

Seaside activities Swimming.

Wildlife and walks To the east there is a cliff-top walk onto the Stoer Point with views of the fine cliff scenery including the Old Man of Stoer, an isolated sea stack rising 200ft (60m) above the waves. Further along the coast stands the Stoer lighthouse. A good variety of birds can be seen on the beach and cliffs. There are also a number of walks on the wide flat moors inland.

24 Clachtoll, Lochinver, Highland   OS Ref: NC0427

This is one of a series of sandy coves along this stretch of coastline, north of Loch Inver, which is scenically stunning. Clachtoll is a small cove, 275 yards (250m) of beautiful white shell sand backed by machair banks and grey and red cliffs. The quiet beach is washed by clear waters and seals can often be seen close to the shore.

Water quality No sewage is discharged in the vicinity of this beach.

Bathing safety Safe bathing within the bay.

Access The B869 runs along this stretch of coast. A short walk across dunes leads to the beach.

Parking Car park with 20 spaces.

Toilets Toilets and showers at beach car park.

Food Take-away meals and snacks at the camp site.

Seaside activities Swimming, windsurfing, diving, sailing, canoeing and fishing. Boats can be hired for fishing. Details are available from the local Ranger.

Wet weather alternatives Teas and games at Stoer village hall.

Wildlife and walks There is a diverse range of plant and animal life around the bay, and an interesting variety of birds and mammals, including seals and whales, can be seen. Many rare plants can also be found. There is a wealth of material for those interested in conservation and the history of the area. Full details are available from the interpretative centre at the beach, and coastal walks can be arranged by the Ranger.

25 Achmelvich, Lochinver, Highland   OS Ref: NC0625

This is a small sandy cove at the southern end of Achmelvich Bay which can be reached fairly easily. The white sands of the bay are backed by an area of machair grassland. This type of vegetation is very fragile and easily eroded, so great care must be taken not to cause damage in this area. Steep grey, rocky cliffs rise on either side of the sands, creating a marvellous setting for the bay. Dogs are permitted on the beach under strict control; they are not allowed on the surrounding land.

Water quality No sewage is discharged in the vicinity of this beach.

Bathing safety Safe bathing.

Access A side road off the B869 north of Lochinver leads to Achmelvich. The car park gives direct access to the turf sloping to the sand.

Parking Car park with 60 spaces.

Toilets Public toilets in car park.

Food None.

Seaside activities Swimming, surfing, windsurfing, diving, sailing and fishing.

Wildlife and walks There is a 1 mile (2.5km) nature trail along the coast to the small sandy bay of Alltan na Bradhan. The walk leads from the machair grassland over the sand hills and then passes through heath and bog vegetation. A leaflet describing the whole trail is available from the Countryside Ranger Centre at the rear of the car park at Achmelvich. This area also has interesting geology. With a combination of red sandstone and grey Lewisian Gneiss (pronounced nice) with igneous dyke intrusions – dark rock squeezed in bands up through the surrounding rock.

26 Achnahaird, Enard Bay, Highland   OS Ref: NC0214

Flat windswept moorland with outcrops of grey Gneiss leads down to the shore of Enard Bay, a magnificent island dotted prospect. On the western side of the Rudha Mor headland is the narrow inlet of Achnahaird Bay. The bay, in the southern corner of Enard Bay, stretches nearly a mile inland and low tide reveals an expanse of flat white sand. On the western side of the inlet there are extensive dunes which give way to salt marsh at the head of the bay. Irregularly layered sandstone cliffs flank the eastern side of the inlet and a stream meanders across the centre of the sands.

Water quality No sewage is discharged in the vicinity of this beach.

Bathing safety Bathe with caution.

Access A side road from Achnahaird village leads to parking behind the beach. There is access to the sands on a path down the rocks (can be difficult) or through the camp site behind the dunes.

Parking There is limited parking behind the dunes.

Toilets None.

Food None.

Seaside activities Swimming.

Wildlife and walks The shores of Enard Bay are part of the Inverpolly National Nature Reserve, a huge area of moorland, including the huge bulk of Suilven. There is a visitors' centre at Knockan some way inland, where there is an interpretative centre, a nature trail and a geology trail. This helps to introduce the visitor to an area that abounds in wildlife including red deer and otters. 100 bird species and 300 types of plant have been recorded within the reserve. Achnahaird Bay combines a wide variety of vegetation types: dunes, salt marsh, rocky and sandy shore. The salt marsh attracts waders and wildfowl. There is a comprehensive range of wildlife supported by the diverse habitats. The rocky shore is banded with lichen and there are rock pools among the barnacle encrusted rocks.

27 Achiltibuie, Badentarbat Bay, Highland   OS Ref: NC0309

Smooth heather-clad slopes descend to the crofting village of Achiltibuie which straggles 3 miles (5km) along the shore of Badentarbat Bay. The beach, which curves round the bay, lacks the sand so common on the west coast but to compensate is a marvellous view across the bay to the Summer Isles, a patchwork of islands and rocky skerries lying just offshore and providing the most wonderful seascape. From the pier at the northern end of the bay, the shingle and cobble beach stretches south to the rocky headland of Rubha Dunan.

Water quality No sewage is discharged in the vicinity of this beach.

Bathing safety Bathe with caution as there may be some currents that cause problems for the swimmer.

Access The road through the village continues along the edge of the bay and the sand can be reached across the grass which slopes below the road.

Parking On the grass between the road and the beach.

Toilets None.

Food Shops in village.

Seaside activities Swimming and fishing.

Wildlife and walks The Summer Isles fall within the Ben More Coigach Nature Reserve (Scottish Wildlife Trust – Royal Society for Nature Conservation). 6,075 hectares include the peak which gives the reserve its name, and whose purple and red slopes dominate the views inland from Achiltibuie. There is good walking along the Coigach Peninsula west of the bay. The Summer Isles can be viewed at closer range by taking a boat trip from the pier at Achiltibuie.

28 Gruinard Bay, Laide, Highland   OS Ref: NG9092

There are several excellent beaches dotted around Gruinard Bay, all of which overlook the lovely Gruinard Island, centrepiece of the bay. The island was used for anthrax experiments during the last war and has been out of bounds ever since. It is now being cleaned up, so hopefully the warning signs that have prohibited landing for so long will soon disappear. The A832 skirts the southern and eastern shores of the bay giving easy access to the three lovely cove beaches on the eastern shore. Their pink sands are set among sandstone rock outcrops. In contrast, the south eastern shore at Little Gruinard has the bulging hummocks of Lewisian Gneiss as a most attractive backdrop. Gruinard Hill provides the best views of the bay, the island, and of the Summer Isles on the horizon. Wooded slopes above the beach provide a sharp contrast to the grey rocky outcrops. At Laide, the road runs parallel with the beach behind the machair turf, which slopes to the sand of this 1 mile (2km) beach. This picturesque bay, like most of the west coast beaches, is relatively quiet and unspoilt. A holiday spent walking the coast or exploring the lochans that speckle the surrounding countryside is an ideal way to escape and relax. Facilities for the tourist are limited and there is restricted parking. In many parts of the bay parking along the back-shore causes severe erosional problems for the machair grass. It is important that the grass cover is maintained and parking should be limited accordingly.

Water quality No sewage is discharged in the vicinity of this beach.

Bathing safety Safe bathing.

Access The A832 follows the shore round most of the bay with easy access to the beach.

Parking There are two car parks in the south eastern corner of the bay near Little Gruinard and a third at Laide.

Toilets In Laide.

Food Hotel and shop in Laide.

Seaside activities Swimming and fishing.

Wildlife and walks There are trips around the bay available during the summer months which allow the visitor to take a closer look at Gruinard Island and enjoy the spectacular panoramas across the bay towards the mountains inland.

29 Gairloch, Highland   OS Ref: NG7679

Set among the stunning mountains of Wester Ross, Gairloch, although it is no more than a sizeable fishing village, is one of the few 'holiday resorts' on the west coast. It overlooks a fine sandy beach which curves north from the rocky promontory at Charlestown, round Strath Bay at the head of the loch, extending west of Gairloch to Big Sand. The bay enjoys the mild climate resulting from the North Atlantic Drift, and gardens nearby are filled with plants more commonly found in more southern locations. The A832 follows the shore at the head of the beautiful Loch Gairloch, where there are rocky outcrops of Gneiss. The outer section of the bay is red sandstone with safe, sandy beaches at Shieldaig and Badachro on the southern shores, and Big Sand on the northern shore. There is a large caravan site behind the extensive beach which is sheltered by Longs Island just offshore.

Water quality Three outfalls discharge primary treated sewage into river Sand.

Bathing safety Safe bathing.

Access The A832 runs parallel with the shore between Charlestown and Gairloch. There are paths to the beach.

Parking Parking at Big Sand, in Gairloch and off the A832 to the south.

Toilets In Gairloch.

Food In Gairloch.

Seaside activities Swimming, windsurfing, sailing and fishing.

Wet weather alternatives Gairloch Heritage Museum.

Wildlife and walks From Badachro there is a footpath which leads south-west inland. It passes a small loch and leads to the cliffs of Redpoint, where there are superb views across the Minch to the Hebrides. For those less able, there is road access and a car park at Redpoint. A further mile to the south, there is a beautiful and remote sandy beach backed by dunes. The path continues to the south-east along the shores of Loch Torridon to Diabaig. This walk follows a spectacular length of coast which can only be reached on foot.

30 Applecross, Highland   OS Ref: NG7144

The dramatic and tortuous 'Pass of the Cattle' climbs over 2,000ft (620m) as it twists its way from the A896, at the head of Loch Kishorn, across the wild mountains and moorlands to Applecross. There is a wooded approach to the cluster of white cottages which make up this remote village, on the southern shore of a wide bay. The sweeping sandy beach lies below limestone cliffs from which there are superb views across the Inner Sound to Raasay and Scalpay, with the Cuillin Hills of Skye on the distant horizon. Having crossed desolate moorland, negotiated precipitous roads and revelled in vast panoramic views, one could be at the edge of the world. This lovely beach with its magnificent setting provides an ideal spot to rest and unwind.

Water quality No sewage is discharged in the vicinity of this beach.

Bathing safety Safe bathing.

Access The Pass from Loch Kishorn should not be attempted by the cara-vanner or the faint-hearted; the alternative route which approaches the village along the coast from Loch Torridon is an easier drive. The village stands on the shore with easy access to the sands.

Parking Limited at Applecross.

Toilets None.

Food Shop in village.

Seaside activities Swimming and fishing. Picnic site behind the beach.

Wildlife and walks There are good walks along this beautiful stretch of coast with eider duck, mergansers and other sea birds to be seen in the bays.

31 The Coral Beaches, Dunvegan, Skye   OS Ref: NG2354

A pleasant, easy, half-mile walk across grassland takes you to two small beaches which are beautiful and totally unspoilt. Known locally as the Coral Beaches, they are in fact white sand made up of broken shells. Grass banks slope gently down to the sand. The bays, each about 220 yards (200m) in length, are separated by a low grassy promontory around which there are rocky outcrops. There are lovely views across Loch Dunvegan whose clean clear waters wash the beach.

Water quality No sewage is discharged in the vicinity of this beach.

Bathing safety Safe bathing.

Access The road north from Dunvegan becomes a narrow lane beyond Claigan. From the lane ending there is a well defined path across the grassland to the sand.

Parking Limited parking along the lane.

Toilets None.

Food None.

Seaside activities Swimming and snorkelling.

Wildlife and walks There is excellent walking to the Coral Beaches and along the beautiful peninsula beyond. Numerous seals can be seen in the waters of the loch. They are often visible close inshore, and a short boat trip from Dunvegan takes you to the rocky islands where they can be seen basking on the shore. They are unconcerned by the little boat which passes within feet of them.

32 Morar, Highland   OS Ref: NM6793

This stretch of coastline between Mallaig and Arisaig has to be one of the most memorable in Scotland. When you try to imagine the silver sands of the west coast you probably create a picture closely resembling this stretch of shore. The green crofting land, dotted with white cottages, slopes down to the white sands of the bays. A couple of miles south of Mallaig, with its busy harbour with links to the Islands, is the wide sheltered Morar Bay. ⅔ mile (1km) of white sands fringe the wide 'Y'-shaped bay which is set below undulating hills. The bay was originally the mouth of a sea loch similar to many others that penetrate this coastline. The long finger of Loch Morar was cut off from the sea by an uplift of the land and glacial deposits. A fast flowing river drains the fresh water lake over a weir, which is all that remains of once impressive falls which were sacrificed to a hydro-electric power scheme. The river meanders across the southern edge of the bay to the narrow sea opening.

Water quality There have been reports that some sewage from Morar village and other villages along this coast end up on the sands.

Bathing safety Bathing is only safe close inshore due to strong undercurrents 110 yards (100m) from the shore.

Access The main road runs parallel with the beach and it is a short walk across the turf banks down to the sand. The railway runs alongside the road and some trains will stop at Morar.

Parking Along the road above the beach.

Toilets None.

Food None.

Seaside activities Swimming and sailing.

Wildlife and walks At the southern end of the bay a turning off the main coast road leads along the shore of Loch Morar. Beyond the tiny hamlet of Bracora the road gives way to a path which can be followed through some spectacular scenery to Tarbet on Loch Nevis. Walking the shoreline around Morar there are stunning views east to the Inner Hebrides.

33 Camusdarrach Beach, Highland   OS Ref: NM6592

This beach was made famous in Bill Forsyth's film, *Local Hero*. The mile (1.6km) of gleaming white sands backed by dunes and undulating grassland is popular, but remains beautiful and unspoilt. There is easy access to the beach by paths from the road above the beach. A series of delightful secluded bays can be reached by walking over the hills edging the shore, forming rocky outcrops. The area is popular with tourists and in summer many caravans appear. The approach to the beach is vulnerable to erosion and visitors should use the paths to avoid damaging the dunes. Those staying late at this beach will enjoy the most breathtaking sunsets, as the sun sinks behind the rugged mountains of Skye.

Water quality There is no sewage outfall to this beach. Beach monitored by the River Purification Board and found to meet EC standard for clean bathing water in 1988.

Bathing safety Safe bathing but beware of some offshore currents.

Access Camusdarrach is situated just south of Morar Bay. The road runs parallel with the shore between Morar and Arisaig. There are paths giving access at various points across the low turf-banks that descend to the beach.

Parking At various points along the road, cars can park on the turf behind the beach.

Toilets None.

Food None.

Seaside activities Swimming and windsurfing. Golf course.

Wildlife and walks All along the western coast there is much to interest for the naturalist; underwater there is a rich and varied marine life which can only be glimpsed from the shore. The bobbing heads of seals are common; the outline of the basking shark a rarer occurrence. On the rocks that edge these beautiful beaches cormorants, shags, gannets and terns may be seen.

34 Sanna Bay, Sanna, Highland   OS Ref: NM4368

On the northern side of Ardnamurchan Point, the most westerly point of mainland Britain, are the lovely white sands of Sanna Bay. This is a beautiful and unspoilt beach backed by impressive marram-covered dunes and ringed by craggy hills. There are a series of island skerries off Sanna Point at the northern end of the bay, as well as rocky outcrops along the beach, dividing the bay into three sections. The sands are washed by clean clear seas. The south side of the bay is covered by extensive rocks encrusted with barnacles and many types of seaweeds. To the south is a second sandy cove which is shadowed by cliffs and the Ardnamurchan Lighthouse; from here, excellent views are obtained seawards to Rhum and Eigg.

Water quality No sewage is discharged in the vicinity of the beach.

Bathing safety Offshore currents necessitate bathing with caution.

Access The B8007 from Kilchoan leads to the southern end of the bay, Portuairk, and from here it is a short walk across the dunes to the beach.

Parking Limited parking behind the dunes.

Toilets None.

Food None.

Seaside activities Swimming, sailing and fishing.

Wildlife and walks There is a string of small sandy bays along the north coast of Ardnamurchan, only accessible on foot. These deserted beaches offer much to interest the naturalist.

35 Calgary Bay, Mull   OS Ref: NM3652

Calgary Bay has been described as Mull's most beautiful bay. It might best be considered as a small sea loch with a sandy beach at its head. The gently sloping white sands are backed by small dunes and flat machair grassland. Rocky shores extend at right angles from both sides of the beach. There are areas of both flat rock and boulders amongst which are numerous rock pools rich in animal and plant life. Steep cliffs and grassy slopes rising behind the rocky shore enclose the bay. This lovely beach is understandably popular with visitors in the summer. Emigrants from this area may well have founded the Canadian city which bears the same name.

Water quality No sewage is discharged in the vicinity of this beach.

Bathing safety Safe bathing.

Access The B8073 from Tobermory leads south to Calgary. The road skirts the grassland behind the beach and continues along the southern shore.

Parking There is a car park at the northern end of the beach and a small parking area at the southern end.

Toilets At the southern end of the beach, on the road behind the dunes.

Food None.

Seaside activities Swimming and fishing.

Wildlife and walks From the car park at the northern end of the beach, a track leads to an old pier. The track continues for a short distance as a footpath above the rocky shore where a series of lava dykes can be seen as grey bands where the molten lava has pushed up between the surrounding rocks.

36 Erraid, Fionnphort, Mull   OS Ref: NM3120

Mull has 300 miles (480km) of breathtaking coastline including sheer cliffs, stacks and arches. There are also tiny bays nestling below the cliffs with a backdrop of brooding mountains. The Ross of Mull, a long low peninsula to the south of the island, has some of the best coastal features. There are cliffs of basalt columns, the Carsaig Arches at Malcolm's Point, numerous caves and secluded sandy bays which can only be approached on foot. The extensive sands at the western tip of the Ross are much more accessible. A road from Fionnphort, the departure point for the ferries to Iona, proceeds south along the Sound of Iona to extensive sandy beaches sheltered by Erraid Island. Between the island and the mainland, the Sound of Erraid is a sandy beach at low tide backed by sand dunes and machair grassland. At either end of the Sound are rocky outcrops, and a host of islets and skerries lie just offshore. The grassland behind the beach is used for camping and as a result the beach can be quite crowded in summer. Those wanting to get away from the busier beaches should seek out the bays along the southern coast. There is easy access to Ardchiavaig, with limited parking.

Water quality No sewage is discharged in the vicinity of this beach.

Bathing safety Bathing can be dangerous due to the numerous skerries and associated currents.

Access A side road from the A849 at Fionnphort leads south to Fidden skirting the dunes south to Knockvologan.

Parking Parking space is available behind the dunes. There is a car park in Fionnphort.

Toilets None.

Food None.

Seaside activities Swimming.

Wildlife and walks The lovely island of Iona is well worth a visit; boat trips leave from Fionnphort. There are sites of great historical interest including the St Oran Chapel and the Iona Cathedral. The island has much to offer scenically with its beautiful shoreline, clear blue seas, and white sands set amongst fringing green grassland.

37 Machrihanish, Campbeltown, Strathclyde   OS Ref: NR6521

A ribbon of pale sand edges the underdeveloped west coast of the Mull of Kintyre, from West Loch Tarbert to Machrihanish. All along this western shore there are sea views north to the mountains of Jura and the low lying Islay. Ireland, only 20 miles (12.5km) away, is clearly visible on a good day. 3½ miles (6km) of sandy beach studded with rocky outcrops sweep north from the headland at Machrihanish. Pounding surf washes the gently sloping sands which are backed by mountainous dunes. There is a golf course at the southern end of the beach and an airfield on the flat grassland stretching inland from the dunes. This delightful beach is popular in summer.

Water quality One outfall serving 200 people discharges untreated sewage at low water mark.

Bathing safety Dangerous undertows just offshore can cause problems for bathers.

Access There is access from either end of the beach with a short walk to the sands. The B843 from Campbeltown leads to Machrihanish at the southern end of the beach. The A83 hugs the western shore from Tarbert to Machrihanish Bay where it swings inland crossing the Mull towards Campbeltown.

Parking There is off-the-road parking at Machrihanish and at Westport off the A83 at the north end of the beach.

Toilets None.

Food None.

Seaside activities Swimming, surfing and fishing.

Wildlife and walks The plain that spans the peninsula from Campbeltown on the east coast to Machrihanish is in contrast to the tree-clad slopes to the north and the windswept Mull to the south. The Mull coast has cliffs dotted with caves, and most of its length can only be reached on foot – it is well worth the effort. There are often seals, basking sharks or porpoises to be seen offshore.

38 Brodick Bay, Brodick, Isle of Arran   OS Ref: NS0237

Below the bare granite summit of the majestic Goat Fell, wooded slopes descend to the water's edge of Brodick Bay north shore. The busy pier on the rocky southern shore at Brodick is the main landing point for the island. The rocky shore gives way to a mile-long (1.6km) arc of sand and pebble beach extending around the head of the bay. The beach is bisected by a river which meanders across flat grassland behind the beach before crossing the sands. The beach has a most beautiful setting, overlooked by the impressive Brodick Castle. The bay enjoys a particularly mild climate which is reflected in the Castle Gardens where thriving semi-tropical plants can be found.

Water quality 2 outfalls serving 700 people discharge untreated sewage, one below and one above low water mark. There have been reports of sewage solids and litter washing onto the beach.

Bathing safety Safe bathing.

Access The car park at Brodick is adjacent to the beach. A few steps from the car park take you to the sands.

Parking Parking for 100 cars at Brodick and Claddach.

Toilets At Brodick and Brodick Country park.

Food Several small cafés.

Seaside activities Swimming, windsurfing, canoeing and fishing. Canoes, rowing boats, windsurfboards and fishing tackle are all available for hire. Golf course.

Wet weather alternatives Brodick Castle, Heritage Museum and Transport Museum.

Wildlife and walks On the northern side of the bay is the Brodick Country Park. Its 173 acres include the formal gardens and woodland of Brodick Castle which have a notable rhododendron collection. There is a self-guided nature trail and access to a path climbing Goat Fell. There is a permanent Ranger Naturalist Service and a series of guided walks are organised during the summer months, including a seashore life walk. A walled Victorian garden has been restored and in addition there is an ice house, Bavarian summer house and a children's adventure play area.

39 Blackwaterfoot, Arran   OS Ref: NR 8928

The northern half of Arran is scenically outstanding, with lush glens cutting deep in to the massive granite mountains. This area has been classed as a National Scenic Area. Beaches attractive to the tourist predominate around the south of the island and include Lamlash Bay sheltered by Holy Island, Whiting Bay and Blackwaterfoot. The latter, on the western shore of the island, has 1.miles (2km) of sand and shingle with rocky outcrops containing rock pools that are worth exploring. Sand dunes and a links golf course stretch south around the bay.

Water quality No sewage is discharged in the vicinity of this beach.

Bathing safety Safe bathing.

Access There is a short walk from car park to the beach.

Parking There is a car park next to the golf club and Kinloch Hotel has 200 spaces.

Toilets At Blackwater harbour.

Food Kinloch Hotel.

Seaside activities Swimming.

Wet weather alternatives Kinloch Hotel has a swimming pool, squash court, sauna and solarium.

Wildlife and walks The lane past the golf course leads towards Drumadoon Head were there is a most impressive sill, produced when molten rock is forced upwards through other rocks. The path continues north along the line of a raised beach to the King's Cave. The path can be followed along the wooded slopes to Tormore and Machrie Bay. There is much evidence of man's past activities in the area with standing stones and hut circles on the hillside.

40 Mersehead Sands, Southerness, Dumfries   OS Ref: NX9855

An endless sky seems to dominate these wide flat sands that face the Solway Firth. From Southerness Point 6 miles (10km) of flat sands backed by low dunes stretch west to the cliffs of Port O'Warren and Sandyhills. On the low rocky headland of Southerness stands a lighthouse which once directed boats into Dumfries. East of the headland the sands narrow to the Arbigland estate. Behind the dunes is the holiday village of Southerness.

Water quality Sandyhills was monitored by the River Purification Board and found to meet the EC standard for clean bathing water in 1988. One outfall serving 200 people discharges secondary treated sewage to the tidal water course.

Bathing safety Due to the very flat nature of the beach the tide flows in very quickly and swimming is therefore only safe close inshore.

Access This very large beach can be accessed from both ends, from Sandy-hills on the A710 or at Southerness signposted to the east from the A710.

Parking Car park with 50 places at Southerness.

Toilets Near beach.

Food Café (seasonal opening).

Seaside activities Swimming and fishing.

Wet weather alternatives Paul Jones Cottage. (Paul Jones was a local boy who became a famous admiral in the American Navy. The cottage is where he was born and brought up.)

Wildlife and walks The wide sand flats are a rich feeding ground for numerous waders and sea ducks.

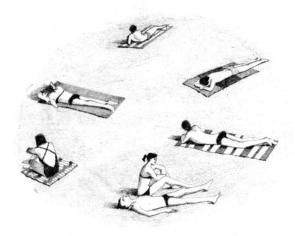

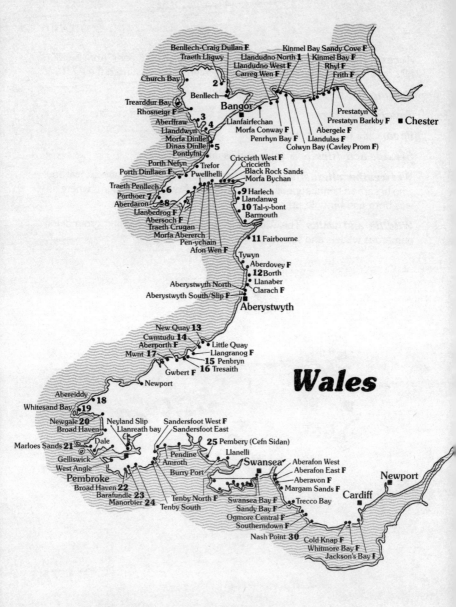

Benllech-Craig Dullan **F**
Traeth Lligwy

Church Bay

Treardur Bay
Rhosneigr **F**
Aberffraw
Llanddwyn
Morfa Dinlle
Dinas Dinlle
Pontlyfni
Porth Nefyn
Porth Dinllaen **F**
Traeth Penllech
Porthoer **7**
Aberdaron
Llanbedrog **F**
Abersoch
Traeth Crugan
Morfa Abererch
Pen-ychain
Afon Wen

Benllech

2

3
4
5

Trefor
Pwellheli

6

8

Kinmel Bay Sandy Cove **F**
Llandudno North **1**
Llandudno West **F**
Carreg Wen

Kinmel Bay
Rhyl **F**
Frith **F**

Prestatyn
Prestatyn Barkby **F** ■ Chester

Llanfairfechan
Morfa Conway **F**
Penrhyn Bay **F**
Abergele **F**
Llandulas **F**
Colwyn Bay (Cavley Prom **F**)

Bangor

Criccieth West
Criccieth
Black Rock Sands
Morfa Bychan

9 Harlech
Llandanwg
10 Tal-y-bont
Barmouth

11 Fairbourne

Tywyn
Aberdovey **F**
12 Borth
Llanaber
Clarach **F**

Aberystwyth North
Aberystwyth South/Slip **F**

Aberystwyth

New Quay **13**
Cwmtudu **14**
Aberporth **F**
Mwnt **17**

Little Quay
Llangranog **F**
15 Penbryn
16 Tresaith

Gwbert **F**

Newport

Wales

Abereiddy
Whitesand Bay
19 **18**

Newgale **20**
Broad Haven
Marloes Sands **21**
Gelliswick
West Angle
Pembroke
Broad Haven **22**
Barafundle **23**
Manorbier **24**

Neyland Slip
Llanreath bay
Dale

Sandersfoot West **F**
Sandersfoot East

25 Pembery (Cefn Sidan)
Llanelli

Pendine
Amroth
Burry Port

Tenby North
Tenby South

Swansea

Aberafon West
Aberafon East **F**
Aberavon
Margam Sands

Newport

Cardiff

Swansea Bay **F**
Sandy Bay **F**
Ogmore Central **F**
Southerndown **F**

Nash Point **30**

Trecco Bay

Cold Knap **F**
Whitmore Bay **F**
Jackson's Bay **F**

Rhossili Bay **26**

Port Eynon **27**
Oxwich Bay **28**
Three Cliffs Bay **29**

Bracelet Bay
Limeslade Bay
Langland Bay
Caswell Bay

Prestatyn
Prestatyn Barkby f
Rhyl Splash Point f
Rhyl f
Frith f
Kinmel Bay f
Kinmel Bay/Sandy Cove f
Abergele f
Llandulas f
Colwyn Bay – Cayley Prom f
Colwyn Bay – Rhos Abbey
Colwyn Bay
Penrhyn Bay f
1 Llandudno North Shore
Llandudno West Shore f
Morfa Conwy f
Carreg Wen f
Llanfairfechan f
Benllech
Benllech – Craig Dullan f
2 Traeth Lligwy
Church Bay
Trearddur Bay
Rhosneigr Beach Road f
Rhosneigr Porth f
3 Aberffraw North
4 Niwbwrch (Llanddwyn)
Morfa Dinlle
5 Dinas Dinlle
Pontllyfni
Trefor
Porth Nefyn
Porth Dinllaen f
6 Traeth Penllech
7 Porthoer
Porth Twyn
8 Aberdaron
Abersoch f
Llanbedrog f
Treath Crugan
Pwllheli* f
Pwllheli*
Morfa Aberech
Pen-y-Chain f
Afonwen f
Criccieth West f
Criccieth
Black Rock Sands
Morfa Bychan
9 Harlech
Llandanwg

10 Tal-y-bont
Barmouth
11 Fairbourne
Tywyn
Aberdovey East f
Aberdovey f
12 Borth
Llanaber
Clarach f
Aberystwyth North
Aberystwyth Slip f
Aberystwyth South* f
Aberystwyth South*
Llangronog f
Little Quay
13 New Quay
New Quay South
14 Cwmtudu
15 Penbryn
16 Tresaith
17 Mwnt
Aberporth East f
Aberporth Slip f
Gwbert f
Newport
Newport South
18 Abereiddy
19 Whitesand Bay
20 Newgale
Newgale North
Newgale South
21 Marloes Sands
Broadhaven
Dale
Gelliswick f
Neyland Slip f
Llanreath Bay f
West Angle Bay
22 Broad Haven
23 Barafundle
24 Manorbier
Tenby South Opp. Kiln Park
Tenby South Atlantic Hotel
Tenby South St Catherines
Tenby South
Tenby North f
Tenby North Lifeboat
Saundersfoot
Saundersfoot West f
Saundersfoot Slip f
Saundersfoot East

Amroth
Amroth East
Amroth West
Pendine West
Pendine
25 Pembery (Cefn Sidan)
Burry Port f
Llanelli f
Jersey Marine f
26 Rhossili Bay
27 Port Eynon Bay
28 Oxwich Bay
29 Three Cliffs Bay
Caswell Bay
Langland Bay
Limeslade Bay
Bracelet Bay
Swansea Bay f
Aberafan East f
Aberafan West
Aberavon
Margam Sands f
Rest Bay
Sandy Bay f
Trecco Bay
Ogmore Central f
Southerndown f
30 Nash Point
Cold Knap f
Whitmore Bay f
Jacksons Bay f

f = failed to meet the EC standard for clean bathing water in 1988.
Numbered beaches appear in the following chapter.

*Two sites on the same beach were monitored, but with different results.

Wales

Sand dunes of Anglesey, pounding surf on the Lleyn, miles of sand, cliffs and secluded coves of West Wales and the beautiful Gower – this is the coast of Wales. There are numerous lovely beaches which are comparable with the best anywhere in the country and they have the added advantage of not being too crowded. Unfortunately there are individual beaches throughout the region that have failed to meet the minimum EC standard for clean bathing water due to the inadequate disposal of sewage from their shores. The north and south coasts suffer from the close proximity of large industrial centres. The large conurbations of South Wales – Swansea, Cardiff, Port Talbot and Newport – all contribute to the pollution of the south coast with discharges of sewage, and also waste from heavy industry, such as steel and chemical works. The north coast is affected by pollution from Merseyside and the Wirral. Milford Haven has suffered from oil pollution problems from the terminals and refineries that line its shore. Further west, away from the centres of population, beaches remain on the whole clean and unspoilt; definitely worth exploring.

Bathing beaches monitored by the water authority and found not to meet the minimum EC standard for clean bathing water in 1988:

Prestatyn Barkby, Rhyl, Kinmel Bay, Abergele, Colwyn Bay–Cayley Prom., Llandudno West Shore, Morfa Conwy, Carreg Wen, Llanfairfechan, Benllech–Craig Dullan, Abersoch, Llanbedrog, Pwllheli, Pen–y–Chain, Afonwen, Criccieth West, Aberdovey, Aberystwyth Slip and South, Llangranog, Aberporth, Gwbert, Gelliswick, Neyland Slip, Llanreath Bay, Tenby North, Saundersfoot Slip and West, Burry Port, Llanelli, Jersey Marine, Swansea Bay, Aberafan East, Margam Sands, Sandy Bay, Ogmore Central, Southerndown, Cold Knap, Whitmore Bay, Jacksons Bay.

Beaches awarded a European Blue Flag in 1988:

Pembery Sands (Cefn Sidan).

Beaches receiving Clean Beach Awards from the Tidy Britain Group in 1988:

Dinas Dinlle, Borth, Aberystwyth North, New Quay, and Barry Island.

1 North Shore, Llandudno, Gwynedd   OS Ref: SH7882

Punch and Judy, donkey rides, a cable car and a country park – everything you might want for a family holiday. From the huge limestone headland of the Great Orme 2 miles (3km) of sandy beach curve to the Little Orme. The beach is fringed by a wide promenade overlooked by elegant Victorian houses characteristic of this most traditional seaside resort. An ornate pier extends 750 yards (700m) from the western end of the beach below the towering bulk of the Orme. The lower wooded slopes include the Happy Valley Gardens from which a cable car can take you to the summit, 675 feet (200m) above the beach. There are superb views of the bay, the North Wales coast towards the Menai Strait and Snowdonia inland.

Water quality North Shore monitored by the water authority and found to meet the EC standard for clean bathing water in 1988. The West Shore fails to comply with the standard. One outfall serving 34,000 people discharges screened and macerated sewage at low water mark.

Litter Very clean.

Bathing safety Safe bathing. Promenade inspector patrols the beach.

Access Steps and slipways from the promenade.

Parking Free parking along the full length of the promenade.

Toilets On promenade. Aberconwy participates in the National Key Scheme for Disabled Toilets; keys available from the Tourist Information Centre or Social Services Department.

Food Refreshments available on pier but not on promenade.

Seaside activities Swimming, diving, surfing, windsurfing, sailing, water skiing and fishing. Pitch and putt on promenade, golf course, bowling and tennis. Boat trips around the bay leave the jetty adjacent to the pier.

Wet weather alternatives The Dungeon Waxworks and amusements on the pier. Moystn Art Gallery, Aberconwy Leisure Centre, Dolls' Museum, Model Railway, Charden House Museum, indoor swimming pool.

Wildlife and walks The Great Orme is a Country Park and a nature reserve, the 2 miles (3.2km) by 1 mile (1.6km) headland is easily accessed. Marine Drive provides a scenic route around its base. The road is a one-way system starting from close to the pier, and a toll is charged. The summit, where there is a visitors' centre, can be reached by road, cable car or tram. A leaflet available at the centre guides the walker round a 3 mile (5.6km) nature trail. The area is rich in wildlife with particularly interesting vegetation. There is limestone grassland, limestone pavements with woodland plants in the grykes (crevices between the pavement stones), and heathland plants on the deeper soils of glacial deposits. A range of resident and visiting birds can also be seen.

2 Traeth Lligwy, Moelfre, Anglesey   OS Ref: SH4987

A hard flat sandy beach ⅔mile (1km) wide is revealed at low tide, ideal for sand castles and ball games. There are some areas of mud on the sand surface but signs indicate the areas to avoid. Gently sloping, grass-covered cliffs ring the bay to the south of the dunes that back the centre of the beach. A cliff path along the low rugged cliffs that rise to the north of the beach leads to the adjacent Dulas Bay. This more secluded bay has a fine sandy beach which can only be reached on foot.

Water quality Beach monitored by the water authority and found to meet the EC standard for clean bathing water in 1988. One outfall serving 894 people discharges raw sewage at Moelfre. The stream which crosses the beach may well be polluted; presence of solids and an unpleasant smell at times.

Litter Beach fairly clean.

Bathing safety Safe bathing but beware of offshore winds.

Access Two lanes off the A5025, one at the Moelfre roundabout and one slightly further north, lead to the bay. The car park is adjacent to the sand.

Parking Two privately run car parks with 500 spaces, rough surfaced.

Toilets One block at car park.

Food Refreshment caravan.

Seaside activities Swimming.

Wildlife and walks Cliff-top paths can be followed in both directions from the beach. Walking south, the path over the headland provides excellent views of the rocky coastline. It leads to the picturesque little fishing village of Moelfre. Above the beach, in the rolling green field which slopes down to the shore, there are the remains of a 4th-century fortified village, Din Lligwy, and also a megalithic burial chamber.

3 Aberffraw, Anglesey OS Ref: SH3568

A wide flat sandy beach bounded landwards by a series of sand dune ridges behind which flat grassland extends inland. This makes the dunes a prominent feature in a landscape that seems to be dominated by the sky. Aberffraw village is set back from the beach on the higher ground that rises to the west. The beach extends about 900 yards (1000m) from low cliffs at the western end, below which the river flows. The beach is cleaned during the summer.

Water quality Beach monitored by the water authority and found to meet the EC standard for clean bathing water in 1988. One outfall serving 534 people discharges screened and macerated sewage at high water mark west of the beach.

Bathing safety Safe bathing.

Access A lane off the A4080 just south of Aberffraw leads to the car park behind the dunes. Easy walk through dunes to beach.

Parking Parking for several hundred cars −1 mile (800–1600m) from beach, on grassed common land.

Toilets In village.

Food In village.

Seaside activities Swimming.

Wildlife and walks The marram grass covered dunes are well developed; depressions between the ridges (wet slacks) abound with wild flowers and low scrub, for example creeping willow. There is a 2 mile (3km) walk along the cliffs from Aberffraw leading to the church of Llangwyfan. This area was the site of Llewelyn the Great, Prince of Gwynedd's summer palace.

4 Llanddwyn, Newborough, Anglesey OS Ref: SH4163

From the rocky Llanddwyn Island, a lovely sand beach curves 3 miles (5km) east to Abermenai Point, the end of a sand spit at the mouth of the Menai Strait. The beach is backed by the extensive sand dunes of Newborough Warren. At the western end there is a conifer wood planted by the Forestry Commission. This remote gently shelving beach is usually quiet and has superb views of Snowdonia and the Lleyn Peninsula.

Water quality Beach monitored by the water authority and found to meet the EC standard for clean bathing water in 1988. No sewage is discharged in the vicinity of this beach.

Bathing safety Safe bathing except at the eastern end; currents at the entrance to the Menai Strait can cause problems.

Access Road from Newborough village leads to a Forestry Commission car park within their plantation, and a path leads to the beach.

Parking Car park with space for several hundred cars in cleared forest areas behind beach.

Toilets At car park.

Food None.

Seaside activities Swimming and sailing.

Wildlife and walks There is a forest trail starting from the car park. The dunes of Newborough Warren behind the beach and Llanddwyn Island are both nature reserves. There is restricted access to the dunes to prevent damage. The island can be reached by a causeway, and you get good views back along the beach and to the mountains in the distance. There is a ruined church and navigation beacon on the island. There are extensive cockle beds on the Strait side of Abermenai Point. Across the sand flats, a footpath leads through the Warren to Newborough Village.

5 Dinas Dinlle, Gwynedd   OS Ref: SH4456

3 miles (4.8km) of wide open beach stretches from Dinas Dinlle (a 100 foot (30m) hill which dominates the surrounding flat coastal plain) north to the mouth of the Menai Straits. The hill shadows the small village of the same name, with its string of bungalows, cafés and shops facing the beach. A moderately steep bank of large pebbles gives way to sand at low tide. The adjacent grassland, on which stands the Caernarfon airport, is protected by a low sea wall. Good surfing conditions frequently prevail. There is easy access to this unspoilt beach which received a Clean Beach Award from the Tidy Britain Group in 1988.

Water quality Beach monitored by the water authority and found to meet the EC standard for clean bathing water in 1988.

Litter The beach is cleaned regularly.

Bathing safety Safe bathing except at the northern end.

Access Dinas Dinlle is signposted from the A499 south of Caernarfon. The road runs along adjacent to the beach, with easy level access from or through gaps in the low sea wall.

Parking Parking along the whole length of the road, with about a mile (1.6km) of pebbled parking areas.

Toilets Blocks at either end of the beach and one at the centre.

Food Several shops and cafés at the southern end of the beach.

Seaside activities Swimming, surfing, and fishing.

Wet weather alternatives Airport viewing pavilion.

6 Traeth Penllech, Tudweiliog, Gwynedd OS Ref: SH2034

A super beach, a wide sandy arc stretching over ⅔ mile (1km) below the rocky, grass-topped cliffs that fall steeply to the shore. A long strip of soft sand remains at high water, and wide flat sands studded with rocks towards the southern end are exposed at low tide. Traeth Penllech forms part of a larger indented bay on the northern coast of the Lleyn Peninsula. There are good views from the cliff-top to the headlands in either direction. By following the cliff-top path, small sand and shingle coves can be reached. The relentless waves that wash this coast make for excellent surfing conditions.

Water quality No sewage is discharged in the vicinity of this beach.

Bathing safety Safe bathing.

Access From the B4417 take the road through Penllech, turning left at the T–junction. There is parking off this road, above the beach. A steep path down a narrow valley leads to the beach.

Parking During the summer there is parking in a private field off the road north-east of Pen-y-graig.

Toilets None.

Food None.

Seaside activities Swimming, surfing, windsurfing, diving and fishing.

Wildlife and walks The area is popular with divers because of its rich marine life; the rock pools below the cliffs give a hint of what can be seen below the waves. A path along the cliff top, above which choughs may be seen, leads to other delightful little sandy coves.

7 Porthoer, Gwynedd OS Ref: SH1630

This is the last and most accessible in a series of long secluded bays along the north coast of the Lleyn Peninsula. This small cove is ringed by steep grass-covered cliffs, typical of this whole coastline. It is also called 'Whistling Sands' because the white sands seem to whistle or squeak as they are walked on. To really get away from it all, try Porth Iago and Porth Colmon further north.

Water quality There is no sewage discharged in the vicinity of this beach.

Bathing safety Safe bathing.

Access From the B4413 south of Pey-y-groeslon lanes lead down to car park just before Carreg. Steep path down from cliff-top.

Parking Car park on cliff-top 220 yards (200m) from beach.

Toilets At car park.

Food Café on beach.

Seaside activities Swimming and fishing.

Wildlife and walks Low tide reveals rockpools at the western end containing a wide variety of marine life.

8 Aberdaron, Gwynedd   OS Ref: SH1726

A sheltered sandy bay, except when a south or south-west wind blows and the waves come crashing in. The mile long (1.6km) sandy beach, below the cluster of houses that make up the fishing village of Aberdaron, completely disappears at high tide. Take care not to get caught below the rocky cliffs that fringe the bay and extend south to the toe of the Lleyn.

Water quality Beach monitored by water authority and found to meet the EC standard for clean bathing water in 1988. No sewage is discharged in the vicinity of the beach.

Bathing safety Safe bathing.

Access Ramp to beach.

Parking Adjacent.

Toilets Adjacent.

Food Cafés and two pubs in village.

Seaside activities Swimming, windsurfing, diving, fishing and sailing.

Wildlife and walks Cliff-top walks lead south to the 500 ft (150m) hill Mynydd Mawr that rises above the end of the peninsula. There are spectacular views of the rocky coast and of Bardsey Island, 2 miles (3km) offshore. Westwards, the cliff paths lead to the cove of Porth Ysgo, inaccessible by road. Boat trips to Bardsey Island leave from Aberdaron.

9 Harlech, Gwynedd   OS Ref: SH5831

From Harlech, with its castle perched on a rocky cliff 60m above the coastal plain, there are superb views over the dunes and golf links below and across Tremadoc Bay to the Lleyn Peninsula. 4 miles of soft sands, edged by a wide belt of dunes, extend from Harlech Point south to Llandanwg. There is masses of room on the extensive flat rather windswept sands. The fragile dunes have suffered from erosion, and restoration work is being undertaken to help them recover; please assist this work by avoiding any further damage. There is also access to the beach at Llandanwg, where board walks lead across the dunes to the beach. The church of old Llandanwg village can be seen half buried by sand.

Water quality Harlech and Llandanwg are monitored by the water authority and were found to meet the EC standard for clean bathing water in 1988. One outfall at Harlech serving 1,291 people discharges primary treated sewage at low water mark. One outfall at Llandanwg serving 258 people discharges macerated and primary treated sewage at low water mark.

Litter Some marine debris is washed onto the shore.

Bathing safety The estuary and the area around Harlech point are unsafe for bathing due to strong currents. Further south, the beach is safe for bathing. HM Coast Guard search unit post at the car park.

Access The beach is signposted from the A496 at Harlech. The road leads to car parking behind the dunes. A path leads through dunes.

Parking Car park with 300 spaces behind the dunes.

Toilets At the car park.

Food None.

Seaside activities Swimming, surfing, windsurfing, diving, sailing, canoeing, and fishing. St David's Golf Course.

Wet weather alternatives Harlech Castle, indoor swimming pool, galleries and craft shop in Harlech.

Wildlife and walks The northern end of this beach and the shore of the estuary fall within the Morfa Harlech nature reserve; access is by permit only. The Snowdonia National Park Information Centre is situated in the town.

10 Tal-y-Bont, Gwynedd   OS Ref: SH5921

A first-class beach; miles and miles of golden sand backed by dunes – 15 miles (24km) in all, unspoilt and set against the magnificent scenery of North Wales. The beach stretches from Shell Island Peninsula in the north, so called because of the variety of shells to be found there, to Llanaber and Barmouth in the south. A road just north of Tal-y-bont leads to car parking behind the dunes. There are a lot of caravan parks along this section of coastline. At Tal-y-bont they remain hidden behind the dunes but it does mean that the sands can be popular in summer. However, the wide flat sands revealed at low tide provide plenty of space.

Water quality No sewage is discharged in the area of Tal-y-bont.

Litter Beach cleaned by the local authority.

Bathing safety Safe bathing. Emergency phone at the car park.

Access Beach signposted off the A496 north of Tal-y-bont, road leads to a car park behind the dunes. Good paths through the dunes to the beach.

Parking National Park car park behind the dunes has 120 spaces.

Toilets At the car park.

Food None, cafés in village.

Seaside activities Swimming, surfing, windsurfing, canoeing and fishing.

Wildlife and walks The dunes at the north end of the beach form the Morfa Dyffryn Nature Reserve; access is by permit only.

11 Fairbourne, Gwynedd   OS Ref: SH6116

Fairbourne has a magnificent setting at the mouth of the beautiful Mawddach estuary with the back drop of the Welsh mountains. 2 miles of sandy beach stretches north from the small resort of Fairbourne to the mouth of the estuary. The promenade gives way to the dunes of Morfa Mawddach, a sand spit . A narrow gauge railway runs from Fairbourne along the beach to the point, where a ferry will take the visitor across the estuary to the old quay of Barmouth on the opposite shore.

Water quality Beach monitored by the water authority and found to meet the EC standard for clean bathing water in 1988. One outfall discharges macerated primary treated sewage 440 yards (400m) below low water mark.

Bathing safety Safe bathing except near the estuary mouth.

Access Beach signposted from the A493 through the town. Direct access from the promenade.

Parking Extensive car parking near the beach.

Toilets On the beach.

Food Refreshment kiosks and cafés on the seafront. Restaurant at the point.

Seaside activities Swimming, windsurfing, sailing, canoeing and fishing. Amusements. Narrow gauge railway. Windsurfing boards available for hire.

Wet weather alternatives Fairbourne railway and Butterfly Safari.

Wildlife and walks There is excellent walking country within easy reach of Fairbourne, with footpaths leading along the estuary. The panorama walk above Barmouth provides superb views of mountains, river and sea.

12 Borth, Dyfed   OS Ref: SN6190

The popular seaside resort of Borth extends along a shingle spit that separates the sea from the bog inland. The beach received a Clean Beach Award from the Tidy Britain Group in 1988. Below the promenade there are shingle ridges at the top of the beach and excellent sands are exposed at low water. Cliffs rise to the south with a rocky foreshore at their base. To the north the beach extends 2 miles (3km) to the dunes of Ynyslas at the mouth of the Dyfi Estuary.

Water quality Beach monitored by water authority and found to meet the EC standard for clean bathing water in 1988. No sewage is discharged at Borth but Aberdovey on the far shore of the Dyfi Estuary failed to meet the EC standard for clean bathing water and this may effect Ynyslas.

Litter The beach is cleaned regularly by the local authority.

Bathing safety Safe bathing except towards Dyfi estuary. Inshore rescue boat.

Access Direct from promenade in Borth or 10 minutes walk from Ynyslas.

Parking Car park with 200 spaces at Borth and for 200-300 cars at Ynyslas.

Toilets On the promenade.

Food Cafés and hotels.

Seaside activities Swimming, surfing, windsurfing, sailing and fishing. Golf course to north of Borth.

Wildlife and walks The footpath onto Craig-y-Wylfa headland leads to the War Memorial which has notable views of the Dyfi Estuary and the Cambrian Mountains beyond. The Credigion Heritage Coast path going south, which leads to the secluded bays of Wallog, Clarach and Aberystwyth is an arduous one. The bog land of Cors Fochno and dunes of Twyni Mawr and Twyni Bach comprise the Dyfi National Nature Reserve, an interpretative centre, and nature trails north of Ynyslas show how the dunes were formed. A submerged forest is exposed on the wide flat sands at low water.

13 New Quay, Dyfed   OS Ref: SN3959

This traditional fishing town perched on the steep slopes above the harbour has three beaches. Traeth y Dolau to the north of the harbour is backed by contorted shale cliffs. The harbour beach, bounded by the stone pier, and Traethgroyn, stretching around the curve of New Quay Bay, are both gently sloping sandy beaches. At low tide Llanina Point to the north can be rounded to reach Cei Bach beach, a quiet mile (0.8km) of sandy beach, backed by a shingle ridge and shrub-covered slopes. New Quay received a Clean Beach Award from the Tidy Britain Group in 1988.

Water quality Beach monitored by the water authority and found to meet the EC standard for clean bathing water in 1988. One outfall serving 6,000 people discharges macerated sewage from a tidal tank at low water mark off New Quay Head.

Bathing safety Safe from all beaches.

Access Short walk along the road which slopes from the town to the beach.

Parking Car parks with 60 spaces in town.

Toilets Close to the beach.

Food Hotels, motels and cafés.

Seaside activities Swimming, surfing, windsurfing, sailing and fishing. Boats and surf boards for hire.

Wet weather alternatives Bird hospital and lifeboat station.

Wildlife and walks Ceredigion Heritage Coast Path provides walks with views of dramatic cliff scenery. Ceredigion District Council produce leaflets describing the many beaches from Borth in the north to Gwbert-on-Sea in the south.

14 Cwmtudu, New Quay, Dyfed   OS Ref: SN3558

A small secluded cove among the rugged cliffs south west of New Quay, it lies at the mouth of the wooded Afon Fynnon Ddewi valley. A group of houses nestle in the valley. The shingle beach has small amount of sand at low tide and is edged by cliffs with striking rock formations. Caves among the folds and faults were once used by smugglers.

Water quality No sewage is discharged in the vicinity of this beach.

Bathing safety Safe.

Access Signposted from the A487 south of New Quay. Several miles' drive along lanes to the cliff top car park, hence steep path down to the cove.

Parking Car park with 30 spaces.

Toilets None.

Food Café.

Seaside activities Swimming.

Wildlife and walks The Ceredigion Heritage Coast Path, 100 yards (100m) up the road from the beach, leads around the headland to the north and gives views over the bay. Earth banks above the craggy inlet are the remains of an Iron Age fort. From here the path continues along the coast for 3 miles (4.8km) to New Quay Headland and Birds Rock.

15 Penbryn, Dyfed   OS Ref: SN2953

A wooded valley cuts through the steep cliffs to reach the beach: ¾ mile (1.2km) of golden sand with small dunes on either side of the river Hoffnant. The headland to the east is blue-grey shale and mudstone smoothed at its base by the waves. Access to the sandy bay beyond the headland is possible at low tide, but beware of the rising tide as there is no escape at high tide.

Water quality No sewage is discharged in the vicinity of the beach.

Bathing safety Safe bathing.

Access Penbryn is signposted from the A487. Short walk from the car park.

Parking National Trust car park with 150 spaces.

Toilets None.

Food Café, half a mile from the beach.

Seaside activities Swimming.

Wildlife and walks Footpath to the west of the sand dunes leads to St Michael's Church which commands good views of the Hoffnant valley. A track way from Llanborth car park leads up between hedges and banks to give coastal views westwards.

16 Tresaith, Dyfed OS Ref: SN2752

A fine wide sandy bay enclosed by steep shale cliffs and shrub covered slopes. A valley slopes gently down to the cluster of white houses that overlook the beach. The Afon Staith cascades down the cliff face to the east of the beach beyond which you can reach a small secluded bay framed by interesting rock structures, caves, outcrops and the deep vertical fissure known as the Devil's Cut. At low tide the beach merges with the sands of Penbryn.

Water quality One outfall serving 180 people discharges macerated sewage 80 yards (75m) below low water mark.

Bathing safety Safe bathing. Lifeguards in July and August.

Access Tresaith is signposted from the A487.

Parking Car park with 50 spaces at top of hill on edge of village.

Toilets Close to the beach.

Food Hotel and café.

Seaside activities Swimming, windsurfing, sailing and fishing.

Wildlife and walks The Ceredigion Heritage Coast Path leads 1 mile (1.6km) south to Aberporth passing a series of rocky inlets.

17 Mwnt, Cardigan, Dyfed OS Ref: SN1952

A natural suntrap, this beautiful undeveloped sandy beach is quite easily accessible and can be very popular in summer. The 330 yards (300m) of gently sloping sands are fringed by folded and faulted shale and mudstone cliffs. The beach is shadowed by the imposing form of Foel y Mwnt, a conical hill on the headland. The tiny white-washed church of The Holy Cross nestles in a hollow at its foot. The only other obvious sign of man is the remnant of a limekiln adjacent to the path down to the beach; limestone was landed in the bay and fired ready for use by the local farmers.

Water quality No sewage is discharged in the vicinity of this beach.

Bathing safety Safe bathing inshore; care is required as surface currents, due to waves breaking on the headland, deflect across the bay.

Access Mwnt is signposted from the B4548 north of Cardigan. Lanes lead to the car park. Steps and a steep path down the cliff to the beach.

Parking Nature Conservancy Council car park with 200 spaces.

Toilets At the beach entrance.

Food Refreshments available in the summer.

Seaside activities Swimming.

Wildlife and walks National Trust cliff-top walks. A pack detailing walks in the Cardigan area is available from local tourist information centres. Foel y Mwnt hill on the headland provides good views of the bay south to Cardigan Island and the narrow rocky inlet to the north. On the cliff tops above the beach there is a small remnant dune system where marram grass covers the wind-blown sand.

18 Abereiddy Bay, Abereiddy, Preseli, Dyfed OS Ref: SM8031

One of many small bays that have known a very different and more active past. The slate that gives the small beach its dark grey sand was quarried, and the remains of the workings can still be seen at the northern end of the beach. A small harbour on the north side of the headland where the rock has been cut away forms a deep blue pool: mile (0.8km) along the coast path north, there is the sandy bay of Traeth Llfyn. Here the sheltered beach is enclosed by steep cliffs.

Water quality No sewage is discharged in the vicinity of this beach.

Bathing safety Dangerous undercurrents and undertows off parts of the beach; life saving equipment and an emergency phone are available.

Access Lanes from the A487 north of St David's lead to the hamlet of Abereiddy.

Parking Large car park next to beach.

Toilets At car park.

Food None.

Seaside activities Swimming, diving, canoeing, surfing and fishing.

Wildlife and walks The Pembrokeshire Coast Path leads in both directions along this most impressive and unspoilt stretch of rocky coastline.

19 Whitesand Bay, St David's, Preseli, Dyfed OS Ref: SM7327

Gorgeous sunsets framed in the wide arc of Whitesand Bay, from the remote rocky headland of St David's to St John Point, are an added attraction of this lovely beach. There are splendid views away to Ramsey Island and the Bishops and Clerks; the South Bishop can be identified on the far horizon by its lighthouse. The wide white sands stretch for ⅔ mile (1km). Large pebbles are thrown to the top of the beach by waves that frequently crash onto this beach, much to the delight of many surfers. At the northern end of the beach a rocky promontory separates the small cove of Pwlleuog from the main beach. The two merge at low tide, but take care, as the smaller cove is cut off by the tide and there is no escape. Open fields slope down to the shore from the imposing craggy hill Carn Llidi, which provides good walking with excellent sea views.

Water quality Beach monitored by the water authority and found to meet the EC standard for clean bathing water in 1988. No sewage is discharged in the vicinity of this beach.

Bathing safety Dangerous and unpredictable currents off parts of the beach and at some states of the tide; warning signs indicate where to bathe. Flags indicate when it is safe to bathe. Lifeguards patrol the beach during the summer. Weaver fish.

Access Road off A487 north of St David's, signposted to Whitesand, leads directly to car park a few yards from the sand.

Parking Car park behind beach, with approximately 160 spaces.

Toilets At car park.

Food Café/shop at car park.

Seaside activities Swimming, surfing, canoeing, diving, windsurfing and fishing.

Wildlife and walks The coast path to the north provides an interesting circular walk, taking in St David's Head with the remains of a fort and a burial chamber, and returning round Carn Llidi Hill. A guide describing the route is published by the Pembrokeshire Coast National Park and can be obtained at information offices locally. Ramsey Island lies just south of the bay, and boat trips from Whitesand (12-person inflatables, May-September) take you round the island to view the sea-bird breeding colonies.

20 Newgale Sands, Newgale, Preseli, Dyfed   OS Ref: SM8522

A high bank of shingle edges this beach; it protects the low lying land behind and conceals from the approaching visitor the 2 miles (3km) of wide sandy beach revealed at low tide. Cliffs rise at either end of the beach where the sand gives way to rocky foreshore. Framed by green hills, the village of Newgale sits on the slopes at the northern end of the beach. The extensive sands are safe and easily accessible. Facing west, over St Brides Bay, it has the advantages of lovely sunsets and good surfing conditions.

Water quality Beach monitored by the water authority and found to meet the EC standard for clean bathing water in 1988. No sewage is discharged in the vicinity of this beach.

Bathing safety Safe bathing.

Access The A487 runs from Newgale along behind the shingle bank. Access directly on to shingle from the car park.

Parking Large car park adjacent to the beach, at the junction of the A487 and the Nolton Haven road.

Toilet At the car park.

Food In the village.

Seaside activities Swimming, surfing, windsurfing, canoeing and fishing.

Wildlife and walks The Pembrokeshire Coast path can be followed from either end of the beach. To the north it follows the cliffs towards Solva, an attractive rocky inlet popular for sailing. To the south the path continues along St Brides Bay towards Nolton Haven. There are excellent views along this stretch of coast.

21 Marloes Sands, Marloes, Preseli, Dyfed   OS Ref: SM785075

'Magnificent Marloes', a mile (1.6km) of wide flat golden sands, stretch from the imposing bulk of Gateholm Island in the north west to Red Cliff and Hooper's Point to the south-east. Beds of rock laid flat on a sea bed long ago are tilted and seem to be pushing up through the sands. Their jagged outlines point skywards along the length of this glorious bay. The steep cliffs that bound the beach reflect these dipping strata; do not attempt to climb them as they are dangerous. The barnacle and seaweed-covered rocky outcrops allude to the fact that the whole beach disappears at high water. There is only one access point to the beach where a tiny stream flows through a narrow valley, so take care not to get cut off at the extremities of the beach by the incoming tide.

Water quality No sewage is discharged in the vicinity of this beach.

Bathing safety Beware of currents and rocks. Safe bathing. Life-saving equipment is available. Take care as some areas of the beach are quickly cut off by the rising tide. The cliffs are dangerous; do not climb.

Access From Marloes village a lane, signposted Marloes Sands, takes you to the National Trust car park. From here take the lane to the YHA, and just beyond the Youth Hostel a foot path to the beach is marked. Walk across the field and a path leads steeply down to the beach.

Parking National Trust car park with about 50 spaces.

Toilets None.

Food None.

Seaside activities Swimming and fishing.

Wildlife and walks The coast path that follows the cliff-top round the bay provides excellent views of the sands. There is a 2 mile (3km) nature trail starting from the National Trust car park. Walkers using the trail are guided by a leaflet produced by the West Wales Trust for Nature Conservation (WWTNC). To the south-west, the coast path leads to West Dale Bay and a series of secluded sandy beaches around the Dale Peninsula that can only be reached on foot. To the north-east, the path heads towards Martin's Haven. A National Park guide, available from the WWTNC Information Centre describes a 1 mile (1.6km) walk around the headland. Boat trips run from Martin's Haven to Skomer Island, renowned for its sea birds, wild flowers and seal colonies.

22 Broad Haven South, Bosherston, Dyfed   OS Ref: SR9893

A classic golden beach with a clear stream meandering across a wide flat 'V' of golden sands, backed by dunes and with rocky cliffs rising at either side. A distinct rocky outcrop lies just offshore. This unspoilt beach is only accessible by foot across the dunes but still gets busy in summer. It is perfect for relaxation or for exploration. There are lily ponds in the nature reserve behind the dunes and surprises around every headland. Beach cleaned regularly.

Water quality No sewage is discharged in the vicinity of this beach.

Bathing safety Safe bathing. Lifesaving equipment available.

Access A lane from Bosherston leads to the National Trust car park; a path leads to the beach, and there is also a steep path to the beach from Bosherston a mile (1.6km) inland.

Parking National Trust car park on headland above beach, National Park car park in Bosherston.

Toilets At car park in summer.

Food None.

Seaside activities Swimming.

Wildlife and walks Separated from the beach by the dune ridge are the Bosherston lily pools, three lakes created in the late 18th century by damming three narrow valleys behind the beach. Water lilies abound along with a varied freshwater wildlife. Paths and causeways form circular walks around the area, starting at the car park in Bosherston. To the south of the bay, the coast path proceeds along the cliff-top to the tiny rocky inlet where St Govan chapel stands at the foot of a long flight of steep steps up the cliffs. Further south there is a 130 foot (40m) deep cleft in the cliff known as the Huntsman's Leap: a local huntsman is said to have died of fright after realising what his horse had just leapt! The path continues along this most beautiful rocky coastline towards the Elugug Stacks, a series of impressive limestone stacks, about 3 miles (4.8km) away. A large arch carved by the waves from the limestone cliffs is known as 'the Green Bridge of Wales'.

23 Barafundle Bay, Stackpole, Dyfed   OS Ref: SR9995

The National Trust owns an 8 mile (13km) section of the coast around Stackpole, including the beautiful Barafundle Bay. The beach can only be reached by foot with a mile (1.2km) walk along the cliff top from Stackpole Quay. One of many tiny harbours that once proliferated in West Wales, the stone quay in this tiny inlet has been restored by the National Trust. From the cliff top path you have your first glimpse of the bay, an impressive view of soft golden sands backed by high dunes, with steep limestone cliffs rising on either side. The cliffs, with distinctive dark bands at their base due to the encrusting sea weeds, barnacles and lichens, extend to Stackpole Head which shelters the bay.

Water quality No sewage is discharged in the vicinity of this beach.

Litter Clean; a small amount of litter is washed up. Cleaned daily in summer.

Bathing safety Safe bathing. Lifesaving equipment at top of steps down cliff.

Access A lane east of Stackpole, signposted to Stackpole Quay and Barafundle, leads to the car park at Stackpole Quay. A 10 minute walk along the coast path, signposted from the car park, leads to the bay; follow the steps down the cliff to reach the sands.

Parking National Trust car park at Stackpole Quay with about 230 spaces.

Toilets At car park.

Food None.

Seaside activities Swimming.

Wildlife and walks The coast path from Stackpole Quay crosses the beach and, climbing through the trees, the path tracks around Stackpole headland, passes Rame Blow Hole, and on to Broad Haven Bay. There are excellent views of the rocky coastline, and north-east the ranks of red sandstone headlands extend to the horizon. Walking south-east there are views down onto tiny sandy coves which cannot be reached due to the steep limestone cliffs that tower above.

24 Manorbier Bay, Manorbier, Dyfed   OS Ref: SS0698

Numerous surfers take advantage of the waves that pound into this lovely cove. Bracken covered hills slope down to the red sandstone rocks that frame the narrow bay. The gently sloping, soft, pink sands are scattered with large flat sandstone pebbles. Behind the beach an open wooded valley extends inland, watched over by Manorbier Castle and church. The well-preserved Norman castle stands on a hillock on the western side of the valley and is open to the public. The church with its castellated tower sits on the eastern valley slope completing a most attractive picture. Beach cleaned daily.

Water quality One outfall serving 520 people discharges secondary treated sewage at low water mark off western end of beach.

Bathing safety Swimming can be dangerous due to heavy surf; lifesaving equipment is available at the car park.

Access A lane to the beach is signposted from Manorbier village, and leads to the car park, with a flat path to the beach about 550 yards (500m) away.

Parking Car park in valley behind beach with about 150 spaces.

Toilets At car park.

Food None at beach; shops and pubs in village.

Seaside activities Swimming, surfing, surf canoeing and diving.

Wet weather alternatives Manorbier Castle.

Wildlife and walks The Pembrokeshire Coast Path skirts the bay. To the east, the path climbs the headland to the King Quoit, a burial chamber with a 15 foot (4.5m) cap stone supported by two standing stones and estimated to be 5,000 years old. Beyond, it leads to Skrinkle Haven, a small sandy cove that can only be reached down a very steep path. West of the bay the path follows the cliff-top to reach another sandy cove, Swanlake Bay. There is good diving from Manorbier Bay, which has a good example of a rocky exposed shore.

25 Pembrey Sands, Llanelli, Dyfed OS Ref: SN3802

A marvellous beach with 7 miles (11km) of sand edged by a belt of sand dunes, known locally as Cefn Sidan. It was awarded a Blue Flag in 1988. The beach falls within the Pembrey Country Park which also covers the extensive grassland and forest behind the dunes. The middle of the beach near the visitors' centre can be very busy on a warm sunny afternoon, but the extremities remain relatively quiet although they are often used for marine sports. Land yachting by the local club is well worth watching. Whether you want to relax on the sand and enjoy the clear views to the Gower on the horizon or be more active, the country park has lots of facilities, both natural and man-made, to keep the whole family happy. Dogs are not permitted in the central ¾ mile (1.2km) section of the beach.

Water quality Beach monitored by the water authority and found to meet the EC standard for clean bathing water in 1988. One outfall serving 3,832 people discharges treated sewage above high water mark.

Bathing safety Safe bathing. Lifeguards patrol the beach near the main access point from June to September.

Access Country Park signposted from the A484. Buses 173 and 174 from Llanelli to the Country Park stops at the end of the road off the A484. Board walks from the car parks lead through the dunes to the beach.

Parking Several car parks behind dunes with about 1,000 spaces.

Toilets One toilet block with facilities for the disabled.

Food Permanent kiosk with outdoor seating provides snacks, drinks and ices.

Seaside activities Swimming, windsurfing, canoeing and fishing. Pitch and putt, miniature and narrow gauge railway, adventure play area, dry ski slope and golf. Events are regularly staged on the beach, for example sand sculpture competitions and treasure hunts.

Wet weather alternatives Kidwelly Castle and Industrial Museum, Pembrey Motor Sports Centre. The Country Park Information Centre presents displays and exhibitions about the surrounding beach and country park (open all year).

Wildlife and walks There are four self-guided nature trails around the country park: woodland walk, floral trail, the yellow post walk (which includes the beach, dunes, forest and grassland), and the leisure route, suitable for wheel chairs and push chairs. There is a permanent orienteering course, a programme of guided walks by the Ranger service and a nature quiz for children. Full information is available from the visitors' centre.

26 Rhossili Bay, Rhossili, West Glamorgan   OS Ref: SS4287

A spectacular 3 miles (5km) sweep of golden sands edges Rhossili Bay, stretching from Worms Head north to Burry Holms. The sands are shadowed by Rhossili Down, whose grass slopes rise 600 feet (200m) above the beach and are popular with hang gliders. The southern end of the beach is ringed by steep cliffs which fall away northwards where the Down is replaced by sand dunes. Contrary to its name, Worms Head is in fact an island and is only linked to the mainland at low tide. The remains of a wreck can sometimes be seen at low tide. This lovely beach and the adjacent Down are owned by the National Trust.

Water quality Beach monitored by the water authority and found to meet the EC standard for clean bathing water in 1988. No sewage is discharged from this beach.

Bathing safety Safe bathing.

Access The B4247 leads to Rhossili village. There is a good path down the cliffs to the beach.

Parking Car park in village.

Toilets At the car park.

Food In the village.

Seaside activities Swimming, surfing and fishing.

Wildlife and walks Worms Head island and the adjacent stretch of coast are a National Nature Reserve. The limestone cliffs are rich in flora, and nesting birds can be seen on the nature trail. The limestone rocky shore of the Gower is one of the best examples in Britain. There is a network of paths on the headland and the adjoining Down where superb views can be obtained.

27 Port Eynon, West Glamorgan   OS Ref: SS4685

The rocky headland of Port Eynon Point to the south shelters this sandy cove which was designated a Blue Flag beach in 1987. The road from the post office leads down to the shore where a short section of newly built promenade gives access to the beach. On either side, high dunes back the wide flat sands. High cliffs rise on either side of the bay with rocky outcrops at their base. On the eastern side of the bay stands the newly excavated remains of a salt house and workings. The wide, gently sloping sands are safe for bathing, and an ideal spot for building sand castles or playing cricket. The beach is cleaned daily in summer and twice weekly in winter. There are plans to restrict the access of dogs in 1989.

Water quality Beach monitored by the water authority and found to meet the EC standard for clean bathing water in 1988. One outfall serving 1,200 people discharges primary and secondary treated sewage at low water mark off Overton Mere, east of Port Eynon Point.

Bathing safety Warning notices indicate where it is safe to bathe. The beach is patrolled by lifeguards from May until September.

Access From the village a road leads to main access point where there is direct access to the sands. There are also board walks and marked paths through dunes to the beach.

Parking Car park behind the dunes with 500+ spaces.

Toilets At beach entry point.

Food Shop and café at beach entrance.

Seaside activities Swimming, surfing, windsurfing, diving, canoeing and fishing. A boat ramp leads from the car park to the tidal sand, providing easy access to the beach for boats.

Wildlife and walks The South Gower Coast Nature Reserve stretches from Port Eynon to Worms Head at Rhossilli, comprising 6 miles (10km) of rocky shore with faulted and folded grey limestone cliffs. There is interesting limestone flora and nesting birds can be seen on some ledges. The limestone rocky shore of the Gower is one of the best examples in Britain. A footpath onto Port Eynon Point climbs the cliff from the eastern end of the beach, leading to the Culver Hole, a deep cleft in the cliff which has been sealed off with a wall. There is a nature trail from the Rhossilli Bay car park at the opposite end of the Nature Reserve.

28 Oxwich Bay, Oxwich, West Glamorgan   OS Ref: SS4986

A superb beach, from the steep tree-clad slopes of Oxwich Point a sweep of very fine soft sand backed by high dunes curves 1 miles (3km) round the bay to Great Tor – a stretch of towering rocky limestone cliffs. At low tide wide flat sands are revealed. There is only one indentation into the crescent of sand, where the dunes are interrupted by the river Nicholaston Pill which meanders through marshland before crossing the beach. The main access is from Oxwich village where there are full facilities. The North Devon Coast can be seen on the horizon and in the evening it appears as a string of lights. At low tide Oxwich Bay links with Threecliff Bay to the east giving 3 miles (5km) of continuous south-facing sands.

Water quality Beach monitored by the water authority and found to meet the EC standard for clean bathing water in 1988. No sewage is discharged in the vicinity of this beach.

Bathing safety Safe bathing; lifeguards from May to September.

Access Narrow lanes lead to Oxwich village at the western end of the bay. A car park next to the dunes faces directly onto the beach. The ramp for launching boats could be used for easier access to the hard tidal sand. There is also access to the other end of the beach; a 15-minute walk from Penmaen along the footpath marked Tor Bay leads to a steep path down the cliff.

Parking Large car park at Oxwich village, plus limited parking at Penmaen. In summer, additional space is provided in a farmer's field at Penmaen.

Toilets Two blocks at Oxwich car park.

Food The Oxwich Bay Hotel which stands at the eastern end of the beach provides meals and bar snacks. There is a kiosk for refreshments at the car park, and cafés and a shop within the village.

Seaside activities Swimming, windsurfing, sailing, diving, canoeing and fishing. A slipway across the sand enables boats to be launched and makes the bay popular with water skiers. There is a windsurfing school on the beach.

Wildlife and walks The Oxwich National Nature Reserve covers most of the beach, backshore and the Oxwich Point headland. The reserve includes a wide variety of habitats: sandy beach, dunes, salt and freshwater marshes, cliffs, woods and grassland. There are marked footpaths throughout the reserve and board walks give access to the dunes. A path west of the hotel leads through the trees past St Illtyd's Church to steps which climb to the headland and along the coast to Horton. There is an interpretative centre at the car park at Oxwich. At the western end, barnacle and mussel encrusted rocks are found below the cliffs, and low tide reveals pools full of life.

29 Three Cliffs, Parkmill, Glamorgan   OS Ref: SS5488

The ruins of the Pennard Castle stand aloft the river valley which opens out to the eastern corner of this lovely sandy bay, ringed by steep cliffs. A three pointed outcrop of rock curving out from the cliffs on the eastern side gives the bay its name. Wind-blown sand has built a series of burrows at the back of the beach. At low tide the river Pennard Pill completes a wide oxbow meander behind the burrows and then flows across the beach.

Water quality No sewage is discharged in the vicinity of this beach.

Bathing safety It is dangerous to swim at middle tide near the three cliffs due to severe tidal conditions; notices at the entrance to the beach indicate where it is safe to bathe. Voluntary lifeguards from May to September.

Access From Penmaen a lane leads to a steep path down the cliff to the beach. Another path leads from Parkmill. The beach can also be reached from Oxwich Bay along the beach.

Parking Car park at Penmaen, limited spaces at the post office, and a field close by used during summer.

Toilets None.

Food None.

Seaside activities Swimming, diving, surfing, fishing, windsurfing, and canoeing from the beach.

Wildlife and walks Footpaths criss-cross the bracken- and heather-covered headlands, offering good views of the bay and adjacent Oxwich Bay.

30 Nash Point, Marcross, South Glamorgan OS Ref: SS9263

From the headland at Nash Point with its two lighthouses (one now disused) there are good views of the North Devon coast across the Bristol Channel and north-west to Swansea and the Gower. Paths lead down into a deep valley which opens out onto the beach. Impressive layered limestone cliffs, typical of this area of Heritage Coast, extend away in both directions. The sheer walls are very unstable so do not sit too close to them or attempt to climb on them. There is one small area of sand, otherwise the beach is composed of large flat rocks where the cliffs have been eroded backwards. There are numerous rockpools exposed as the tide falls.

Water quality No sewage is discharged in the vicinity of this beach.

Bathing safety Bathing is dangerous because of submerged rocks. Do not climb on the cliffs.

Access There are steep paths from the headland car park to the valley which leads onto the beach.

Parking Parking in private field on headland adjacent to lighthouse.

Toilets None.

Food Car park kiosk sells ice cream.

Seaside activities Fishing.

Wildlife and walks There is a nature trail through the wooded valley behind the beach. A coast path follows the cliffs in both directions.

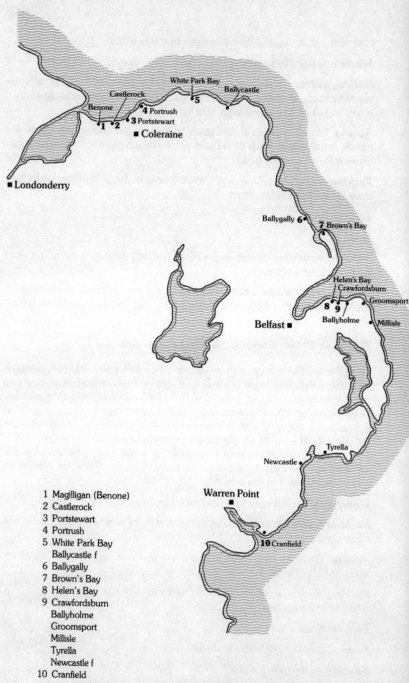

1 Magilligan (Benone)
2 Castlerock
3 Portstewart
4 Portrush
5 White Park Bay
  Ballycastle f
6 Ballygally
7 Brown's Bay
8 Helen's Bay
9 Crawfordsburn
  Ballyholme
  Groomsport
  Millisle
  Tyrella
  Newcastle f
10 Cranfield

f — failed to meet the EC standard for clean bathing water in 1988.
Numbered beaches appear in the following chapter.

Northern Ireland

The coast of Northern Ireland remains largely undiscovered to those outside the province. The most widely heard-of feature in this area must be the Giant's Causeway. It could be classed as one of the natural wonders of the world and consists of huge basalt columns that disappear below the waves like a stairway to the depths. Rich in geology, the coastline is made up of a succession of bays and rugged headlands. There are the strands of County Londonderry with their popular holiday resorts, and the nine glens of County Antrim, each with a little beach nestling at its mouth. There are also the magnificent sea loughs of County Down: Belfast, Strangford and Carlingford, all rich in wildlife.

Beaches monitored by the Northern Ireland Department of the Environment and found not to meet the EC standard for clean bathing water in 1988:
Ballycastle and Newcastle.

1 Benone, Limavady, Co. Londonderry   OS Ref: C7037

From Magilligan Point at the entrance to Lough Foyle, 7 miles (11 km) of firm flat golden sand stretch east to the cliffs at Down Hill. Dunes fringe the wide curving beach, with sand hills covering the peninsula. The eastern end of the beach is backed by 750 feet (225m) cliffs, which are themselves shadowed by a heather-clad land plateau and the Binevenagh Mountains. The new leisure complex provides excellent facilities close to the beach. If you prefer to get away from the sand castles and games, the miles of sand offer solitude with only the sea and sky for company. The 110 yards (100m) of sand virtually disappear at high tide. The beach is cleaned regularly.

Water quality Beach monitored by the DOE and found to meet the EC standard for clean bathing water in 1988. No sewage is discharged in the vicinity of the beach.

Bathing safety Bathing from some areas of the beach is unsafe due to currents; notices indicate where not to bathe. The beach is patrolled by lifeguards from June to September.

Access It is a short walk from the car park onto the beach at Benone.

Parking There is a car park behind dunes with 300 spaces. Car parking is also permitted on the sands but should be avoided on any beach.

Toilets Public toilets at beach and also facilities at the leisure complex.

Food Refreshments are available at the leisure complex.

Seaside Activities Swimming, surfing, windsurfing, sailing and fishing from the beach. Golf course, tennis, pitch and putt available at the leisure complex. A concrete ramp allows access to launch boats.

Wet weather alternatives Benone Tourist Complex.

Wildlife and walks It is claimed that up to 120 different species of shell have been found on Benone beach in one day, and an outdoor field studies recreation centre at Magilligan reflects the fact that the whole area is excellent for those interested in flora and fauna. 140 acres of the sand dune system around the Martello Tower on Magilligan Point form a Nature Reserve and there is restricted access to protect this fragile environment. The coastline is the limit of the North Derry Area of Outstanding Natural Beauty. Inland, the Binevenagh mountains are good for hill walking and afford good views of the coast.

2 Castlerock, Co. Londonderry   OS Ref: C7836

From the Mussenden Temple's windswept cliff-top position there are fabulous views along the coastline. Steep rugged cliffs rise directly from the wide flat sands of Downhill Strand. The beach curves away towards Benone and Magilligan Point, with the hills of Donegal on the horizon. Below the cliffs is the secluded resort of Castlerock. Here a promenade overlooks the sands and gives way to dunes on either side.

Water quality Beach monitored by the DOE and found to meet the EC standard for clean bathing water in 1988. One outfall serving 2,000 people discharges macerated and primary treated sewage at low water mark.

Bathing safety Beware of currents that may affect bathing safety. The beach is patrolled by lifeguards during July and August.

Access Direct from Castlerock promenade.

Parking Parking for 150 cars on the promenade.

Toilets Male and female blocks.

Food Shops and hotels close by.

Seaside activities Swimming, surfing, windsurfing, sailing and fishing.

Wildlife and walks The Mussenden Temple forms part of the Earl Bishop of Derry's estate, which includes the ruined Downhill Castle, Bishop's Gate and 39 acres of landscaped grounds which are now owned by the National Trust. There are woodland and cliff-top walks within the estate which give magnificent views of the extensive sands.

3 The Strand, Portstewart, Co. Londonderry OS Ref: C8338

This is a small quiet resort compared to its near neighbour, Portrush. The town, set around its harbour, is located on a promontory. To the west are 2 miles (3km) of beautiful sandy beach, backed by 185 acres of dunes owned by the National Trust. The flat sands are safe for swimming and good for fishing. There is good cliff scenery extending east towards Portrush, and the North Antrim Coast Path follows the cliff-top. Beach cleaned regularly.

Water quality Beach monitored by the DOE and found to meet the EC standard for clean bathing water in 1988. One outfall serving 5,000 people discharges macerated sewage.

Bathing safety Beware of currents that may affect bathing safety; the beach is patrolled by lifeguards during July and August.

Parking On the beach at low tide, but motor cycles are not permitted.

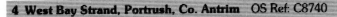

Toilets One male and one female toilet.

Food One confectionery shop at the beach entrance.

Seaside activities Swimming, surfing, windsurfing, sailing, diving and fishing. Two golf courses. Boat trips from the harbour along Causeway Coast.

4 West Bay Strand, Portrush, Co. Antrim OS Ref: C8740

Portrush is the largest seaside holiday centre in Northern Ireland. The Victorian and Edwardian resort is located on rocky Ramore Head and has all the facilities and amusements that might be expected of a traditional holiday town. From its elevated position there are excellent views along the coast to Donegal in the west and Rathlin Island in the east. A low sea wall bounds the soft sands of the west bay which curves gently south from the small harbour. The promenade which runs along the sea wall is on two levels separated by grassy banks. The East or Curran Strand is also backed by a sea wall but this gives way to dunes and a links golf course.

Water quality Beach monitored by DOE and found to meet the EC standard for clean bathing water in 1988. One outfall serving 5,000 people discharges macerated sewage at low water mark.

Bathing safety Beware of currents that may affect bathing safety. The beach is patrolled by lifeguards during July and August.

Access Steps and a ramp from the promenade.

Parking 150–200 spaces at West Strand, 250–300 at East Strand.

Toilets Male and female at each end of West Strand, and on East Strand.

Food Promenade café.

Seaside activities Swimming, surfing, windsurfing, sailing, diving and fishing. Boat trips from the harbour.

Wet weather alternatives 'Water World' alongside the old harbour has a swimming pool complete with jacuzzis. Its facilities include an aquarium and entertainments. Amusements.

Wildlife and walks A section of the rocky shore on the eastern side of Ranmore Head between the Portandoo Harbour and Bath Road is a Nature Reserve noted for its fossil ammonites. Adjacent to the reserve is the Portrush Countryside Centre, an interpretative centre which can provide further information about the reserve and surrounding area. East of Portrush there is superb cliff scenery, including towering limestone cliffs eroded by the ceaseless waves to form arches and caves. The white cliffs are replaced by the brown basalt which forms the famous Giant's Causeway further east. The coastal path follows the cliff-top to the picturesque ruin of Dunluce Castle. Surmounting its rocky headland, it offers superb views along the coastline; (the castle is closed on Sunday mornings and on Mondays during the winter).

5 White Park Bay, Portbradden, Co. Antrim   OS Ref: DO245

Stacks and rocky outcrops stud this magnificent bay owned and managed by the National Trust. The long curve of flat white sand is backed by dunes and circled by white chalk cliffs. On the western shore of the whitewashed houses of Portbradden sit below the cliffs. The village's tiny church, St Gothan's, is the smallest in Ireland, a mere 11 feet by 6 feet (3.3m by 1.8m). Portbradden marks the junction between the chalk cliffs and the brown basalt of the Dunseverick and Causeway coast. The stretch of coast from Gid Point,

the western boundary of White Park Bay, to Benbane Head is the Dunseverick Coast. The dipping rocks and basalt columns are less well defined than
those of the Giant's Causeway beyond Benbane Head. However, the series of
rugged headlands and small indented bays with the cliff-top ruins of Dunseverick Castle and the numerous offshore stacks makes this section of quieter
coastline extremely attractive. The bay is popular with naturalists, for nearly
every type of maritime vegetation can be found along this section of coastline,
including strand line, salt marsh, cliff grassland, maritime scrub and heath.
There is a wide variety of bird and marine life to be seen. Beach cleaned
regularly.

Water quality No sewage is discharged in the vicinity of this beach.

Bathing safety Bathing at the east end of the bay is dangerous because of
strong currents.

Access There is car parking to the east of Templastragh on the A2 and a
minor road to Portbradden on the eastern shore of the bay. There is also a
path from Ballintoy, 1½ miles (2.4km) east of the bay. During July and August
an open topped bus makes the journey between Coleraine and Bushmills with
stops at Portstewart, Portrush, Portballintrae and the Causeway.

Parking Car park near the youth hostel east of Templastragh
and on the cliff-top near Dunseverick Harbour.

Toilets Near car park.

Food In village.

Seaside activities Swimming and fishing.

Wildlife and walks There is a 1 mile (1.6km) nature trail at White Park Bay,
and a leaflet guide is available from the National Trust shop at Giant's
Causeway. The North Antrim Coast Path follows the cliffs west of the bay. It
skirts Dunseverick harbour and castle and continues beyond Benbane Head
to Giant's Causeway. 40,000 basalt columns, formed by cooling lava, create
the unique features of the Causeway. It has been estimated that somewhere in
the region of 500,000 people view the Causeway each year. The main access
point for those not wanting to walk the 5 miles (8km) to Benbane Head from
White Park Bay is at Causeway Head off the B146 north of Bushmills. There is
parking and a National Trust Information Centre. The centre houses an
exhibition of the history, geology, fauna and flora of the area. During the
summer a bus will take visitors from the centre to the top of the Grand
Causeway. To really appreciate this magnificent scenery to the full, a walk to
Benbane Head is recommended. There is a path along the base of the cliffs
passing the Grand Causeway, and other features including the Organ, the
Amphitheatre, the Wishing Well, and Lovers' Leap. The return journey can be
made along the cliff-top. 2½ miles (4km) along the coast path east of White
Park Bay is the Carrick-a-rede rope bridge. The fragile swinging bridge spans a
60 feet (18m) wide and 80 feet (24m) deep ravine which separates Carrick-a-
rede island from the mainland. The bridge is constructed each May by
fishermen to provide access to their salmon fisheries. The walk across and
back is not for the faint hearted! A National Trust car park at Larrybane gives
closer access.

6 Ballygally, Larne, Co. Antrim   OS ref: D3708

A small but good family beach, which is easily accessible. A sea wall edges the sand, separating the beach and road that runs parrallel. Fringed by rocky outcrops, there are lots of shells to be found on this beach.

Water quality No sewage is discharged in the vicinity of this beach.

Bathing safety Safe bathing.

Access The A2 Antrim coast road runs along side of the beach. Access direct from sea wall.

Parking Car park adjacent to the beach.

Toilets At the car park.

Food Restaurant and shop close by.

Seaside activities Swimming, windsurfing, diving and fishing. Golf course.

Wildlife and walks There are pleasant walks in the Carnfunnock Country Park, a mile to the south of the beach.

7 Brown's Bay, Whitehead, Co. Antrim   OS Ref: D4303

Brown's Bay is at the northern end of Island Magee, a long peninsula which bounds Lough Larne. At the northern end of the peninsula two headlands, Barr's Point and Skernaghan Point, frame a deeply indented bay. A mile (800m) crescent of sandy beach with rocky outcrops, containing numerous rock pools, is revealed by the falling tide. The beach is easily accessible and is a good amenity beach, suitable for a family day by the sea. Beach cleaned regularly.

Water quality Beach monitored by the DOE and found to meet the EC standard for clean bathing water in 1988. No sewage is discharged in the vicinity of the beach.

Bathing safety Safe bathing.

Access The B90 circles the northern half of Island Magee and runs parallel with the bay. A sea wall and promenade edge the sand.

Parking Council car park with 124 spaces.

Toilets Public toilets at car park.

Food Nearby shop for confectionery and ice cream.

Seaside activities Swimming, windsurfing, diving and fishing. Golf course.

Wildlife and walks There are local walks on the headlands at either side of the bay but probably the best walking is to be found along the Gobbins – a stretch of cliffs facing the Irish Sea south of Portmuck.

8 Helen's Bay, Bangor, Co Down   OS Ref. J4683

This small sandy beach is sheltered by headlands at either end. From the Horse Rock below Grey Point, the beach stretches to Quarry Point in the east and is backed by a stone promenade and a golf course on the grassland sloping up from the promenade. Grey Point with its disused fort commands an excellent view of Belfast Lough and the Antrim coast. A wooded avenue leads from Grey Point 2½ miles (4km) inland. It was once a private carriageway built by the first Marquess of Dufferin and Ava, after whose mother, Helen Sheridan, the bay is named. Beach cleaned regularly.

Water quality Beach monitored by DOE and found to meet the EC standard for clean bathing water in 1988. One outfall serving 1,600 people discharging sewage through a tidal tank at low water mark.

Bathing safety Safe bathing.

Access Helen's Bay Halt is ½ mile (1km) away and the car park only 50m from the beach.

Parking There is a car park at the west end of the bay.

Toilets Ladies, gents and disabled in the car park.

Food None.

Seaside activities Swimming and golf course.

Wildlife and walks The beach lies on the North Downs Coastal Path. To the east is Crawfordsburn beach and country park. Seals and a variety of sea birds are just some of the wildlife of interest in this area.

9 Crawfordsburn, Bangor, Co. Down   OS Ref. J4783

Crawfordsburn and Helen's Bay are both within very easy reach of Belfast, by road along the A2 and also by train. As a result they can be very popular in summer. The 550 yard (500m) sandy beach at Crawfordsburn is divided in two by the stream that flows from the glen behind the sands. The beach and the glen fall within the Crawfordsburn Country Park. On the right bank of the stream stands the house of the Scottish family who settled here in the 17th century and gave the bay their name. The house is now a hospital and its extensive lawns are a caravan park. For those wishing to escape from the busy part of the beach, Swinerley Bay to the east is more secluded.

Water quality Beach monitored by DOE and found to meet the EC standard for clean bathing water in 1988. One outfall serving 200+ people discharges macerated and secondary treated sewage to the stream flowing across the beach.

Bathing safety Safe bathing.

Access Crawfordsburn Halt is ¾ mile (1.2km) from the beach along the road through the Country Park. The Country Park car park is ¼ mile (400m) from the beach.

Parking Large car park in Country Park.

Toilets Ladies, gents and disabled in the car park.

Food Café.

Seaside activities Swimming, golf course. Orienteering courses held in the country park.

Wildlife and walks The stream from Crawfordsburn village flows through a steep sided valley, wooded with some exotic species. Below the village, it descends to a waterfall and flows under one of the railway viaduct's 80 foot (24m) high arches. Marked footpaths provide circular walks of varying lengths. Information about the park, including its walks and wildlife, is available from the interpretative centre. The beach is part of the North Downs Coastal Path and also forms part of the Ulster Way. It follows the coast from Holywood, passes through the glen to the Clandeboyne Estate and on to Newtonards.

10 Cranfield, Kilkeel, Co. Down   OS Ref: J2611

An Area of Outstanding Natural Beauty adjoining an area of Special Scientific Interest, Cranfield Bay is situated at the entrance to Carlingford Lough. The south-facing sand and shingle beach is backed by dunes and has the magnificent Mourne mountains as a backdrop. The beach stretches from the rocky outcrops at Greencastle Point to the boulders at Cranfield Point. There are good views across the Lough to Ballagan Point and away down the coast beyond Dundalk Bay.

Water quality Beach monitored by the DOE and found to meet the EC standard for clean bathing water in 1988. No sewage is discharged in the vicinity of the beach.

Bathing safety Safe.

Access A new service road leads from Cranfield to the car park, from which there is a short walk across grass to the beach.

Parking Car park with 150 spaces.

Toilets Public conveniences.

Food Hotel, two cafés and three shops.

Seaside activities Swimming, windsurfing, diving, water skiing and fishing. Beach entertainment and band concerts. Golf course.

Wet weather alternatives Analong cornmill and marine park.

Wildlife and walks Mourne mountains are excellent for walking, with the Silent Valley Reserve just north of Kilkeel. A 3,000 million gallon (14,000 million litres) reservoir is set among the peaks and there is some fine parkland on the approaches to the dam.

Index

Join the Fight to Save our Seas

Yes, I want to join the Marine Conservation Society.
Please enrol me as a (tick box)

Annual Member £8 □   Family Member £12 □   Life Member £100 □
(overseas members add £3 a year postage. Institutions may join for £25 a
year)

NAME _____

ADDRESS _____

_____

I enclose a cheque for   Membership fee   £
                         Donation (if you wish) £
                         Total   £

□ Please send me details of how to make my subscription worth nearly £3
more with a Deed of Covenant and how to pay by bankers order

□ Please send me details of "Castles for Clean Beaches"

SEND THIS FORM TO   **Marine Conservation Society**
                         9 Gloucester Road
                         Ross-on-Wye HR9 5BU

Castles for Clean Beaches

The poor health of Britain's beaches has drawn people's attention to the
threats to our shores and seas. The Marine Conservation Society needs as
much support as possible to continue the fight to clean up Britain's beaches
and protect our seas, and you can help by taking part in this campaign.

How You Can Help This summer, let the Marine Conservation Society
benefit from your talents – in construction, design, architecture, planning and
photography!

Build a Castle and enter the great prize draw!
For further details of Castles for Clean
Beaches write to
Marine Conservation Society
9 Gloucester Road
Ross-on-Wye HR9 5BU